BREAKING THE CHAIN ON ABUSE

*"It's not enough to have lived.
We should be determined to live for something. May I suggest that it be creating joy for others, sharing what we have for the betterment of personkind, bringing hope to the lost and love to the lonely."*
— **Leo F. Buscaglia**

BREAKING THE CHAIN ON ABUSE

"Together we can help break the chain on all forms of abuse!"

N J Lutter

BREAKING THE CHAIN ON ABUSE Copyright notice

©Natalie Lutter (N J Lutter) 2018 The 3 E's Series

All rights reserved. No part of this publication may be reproduced, distributed or transmitted in any form or by any means, including photocopying, recording, or other electronic or mechanical methods, without the prior written permission of the publisher, except in the case of brief quotations embodied in critical reviews and certain other non-commercial uses permitted by copyright law. For permission requests, write to the publisher, addressed "Attention: Permissions Coordinator," at the website address below.

Printed in United States

ISBN 978-1-925792-99-7

Disclaimer

Please note well, the information provided in this book is designed to provide helpful and common-sense type information on the subjects discussed. They are insights and experiences from my life experience only. This book is not meant to be used, nor should it be used, to diagnose or treat any medical condition. For diagnosis and/or proper treatment of any medical/emotional of physical problems, it is imperative you consult with a reputable professional physician/therapist. Please be advised that as the reader you are ultimately responsible for your own decisions, actions, and resulting outcomes. The publisher and /or author are not responsible for any damages either emotional, financial or physical that may require medical supervision and are not liable for any damages or negative consequences from any treatment, action, application or preparation, to any person/s reading or following the information in this book. Be it known, that references are provided purely for informational purposes only and do not constitute endorsement of any websites or other sources. Readers should be aware that the websites listed in this book may be subject to change.

BREAKING THE CHAIN ON ABUSE was written to be used in a responsible manner with the supervision of a qualified counsellor and/or healthcare professional.

Ordering Information: - For quantities; special discounts are available on quantity purchases by corporations, associations, and others. *Please Note:* -A percentage of all sales are charitably donated each to assist in the education and prevention of Domestic Violence and Suicide Prevention Australia.

Contact details-
Website address: njlutter.com

Dedication

"This dedication is for many; first and foremost, to my two beautiful children and the rest of our family too, so that we all did not suffer in vain and maybe from our family's experiences other families may be saved."

"I also dedicate BREAKING THE CHAIN ON ABUSE to the many millions of people young and old who have needlessly suffered much abuse, so their plight too was not all in vain, that we may too learn a lesson and be better able to help others."

Table of Contents

Foreword ix
Preface xiii
Acknowledgements xxvii
Introduction 1
Chapter 1 Life As You Know It Now 15
Chapter 2 What Is Abuse? 29
Chapter 3 Types of Abuse 49
Chapter 4 History of Abuse 75
Chapter 5 Who Is Usually the Abuser? 89
Chapter 6 Being Good Role Models 103
Chapter 7 Whether to Have Children 115
Chapter 8 Who Is Abused? 133
Chapter 9 What Keeps Us Locked In? 141
Chapter 10 Taking Things to the Extreme 159
Chapter 11 Child Abuse 165
Chapter 12 Child Sexual Abuse 183
Chapter 13 Spousal Abuse 225
Chapter 14 Self-Abuse (Self-Harm) 229
Chapter 15 Bullying 237
Chapter 16 Cyber Abuse 245
Chapter 17 Preventing Cyber Abuse 251
Chapter 18 Abuse of Elderly, Disabled and Infirmed 261
Chapter 19 Abuse of Our Dearly Departed 273
Chapter 20 Pet/Animal Abuse 275
Chapter 21 Helping One Another 287
Chapter 22 Down So Low 293
Chapter 23 Suicide 295
Chapter 24 Bereavement 315
Chapter 25 Planning A Safe Escape 325
Chapter 26 Protection Orders 335
Chapter 27 Legal Advice 339
Chapter 28 Two-Fold Abuse 343
Chapter 29 Protection For Your Children 349

Chapter 30 A New Life 353
Chapter 31 Workplace Abuse 359
Chapter 32 Emotional Growth and Planning 363
Chapter 33 Self-Reliance 377
Chapter 34 A Relationship Worth Fighting For! 383
Chapter 35 There Is No Greater Love 395
Chapter 36 Forgiveness 397
Epilogue 405
Summary 425
Worldwide Statistics 427
Final Summary 431
Resources 433
References 435
Help Contacts Worldwide 437
Index 447
About the Author 455

Foreword

As an academic and researcher for most of my career, I have been passionate about life-long learning, recognising that we all grow through both formal education and what life shows us. Our experiences shape our outlook on the world and our very philosophy, making us (hopefully) more caring, giving, supportive and thoughtful individuals with high awareness of those around us as we mature into ourselves. Sometimes, of course, the opposite occurs, but that's life! However, few of us go through our life's journey and make a concerted and formal effort to reflect on how our experiences have changed and moulded us, and fewer consolidate what they have learnt into a format which can be shared. What my good friend Natalie Lutter has done, is precisely that: over a considerable period, she has thought about what she has experienced as a survivor of abuse and how, as a survivor, she has coped, changed and emerged as a stronger person. She now kindly shares what she has learnt, with you, as you may have gone through similar challenges and need to understand that you are not alone. She writes with passion, enthusiasm and honesty, providing sound, sensible and supportive advice about coping with abuse.

Natalie also tackles some difficult issues that may be the consequences of experiencing abuse – so the breadth of possible outcomes is clear, and how important it is to take action to avoid serious, undesirable future scenarios. Her final chapters also speak about forgiveness as part of the healing processes, which demonstrates the motivation in her writing to help the reader grow in positive ways.

We all experience abuse at some stage of our lives – within our family, at work, in clubs and societies, and increasingly just on the streets of our cities – and it is important to know that there are mechanisms to handle these situations.

My own experiences, growing up in a dysfunctional family where my mother, sister and myself lived in terror of the frequent drunken, violent outbursts from my father, isolated in outer suburbia with no support and nobody to turn to who would understand our plight. I was always ashamed of our home situation, thinking that our situation was just so different to the 'happy' families surrounding us, which isolated us even more. My very brave mother decided that this had to stop, when I was 17 and in year 12 at school and she was 57, so we did a 'midnight flit', carrying what we could in her old jeep (which I still proudly use), to seek another form of existence. A high-risk strategy for somebody who had been told for almost 20 years that she was worthless and unemployable – naturally, she wasn't allowed to work by my father. We coped, got by, then thrived – as I saw the burden of fear, shame, and lack of self-worth lift from my mother. A few years later, when my father was dying, she took him back – on her terms, in her home – to nurse him until he died (at a relatively young 63). That model of courage, coping and forgiveness is what Natalie's book is all about: I commend her first book to you and hope there will be many more to come.

Professor Margaret L Britz

Former Dean of Science, Engineering and Technology, University of Tasmania, and Assistant Deputy Vice-Chancellor, The University of Melbourne

If I can stop one heart from breaking;

I shall not live in vain;

If I can ease one life the aching,

Or cool one pain,

Or help one fainting robin

Unto his nest again,

I shall not live in vain

- **Emily Dickinson**

Preface

If you're looking for a book written by someone who is 100% percent healed, well you have come to the wrong place 'book'. However, I will tell you this; that this is "one of" the most raw, real and controversial books you'll ever come across. My intent is to endeavour to keep my writing real at all times.

BREAKING THE CHAIN ON ABUSE mirrors my life, and the violence . and hardship. I and my family endured. Some very poor choices were made. My life experience is that of the university of hard knocks! In saying that, I have the deepest most utmost respect for those who studied a university education and graduated. "Professionals" counsellors and doctors who helped me change my life for the better, not discounting the work I continually put in also.

In the writing of BREAKING THE CHAIN ON ABUSE, it has been very cathartic (therapeutically healing) for me and therefore, helpful to others who find themselves in similar situations. Some of it was very difficult to write, as it felt as if I was reliving it. It was 12 years in the making, with the finalising in 2017/18. The path, by which I found in writing this book, was a path that at times was avoided. Simply because it seemed such an overwhelming experience, never really knowing if my books would ever see the light of day. Dragging each foot each step of the way until... I then was diagnosed with breast cancer, which meant some down- time to heal with chemo and radiation. Now nothing but time and what to do with it all; I could no longer ignore these half-done projects. Maybe subconsciously I thought, "I don't want to leave this world without not having written this very important book. It felt almost as if the "Almighty" had given me a project to do and get it done pronto! No excuses now, get this work out there now...

The hardest scariest part for me was in getting my books message out there. I procrastinated a bit because this was such a private part of my life and it took great courage to produce such a book. I was being brutally open and honest and now it is public for all the world to see. Initially, I wondered why I am being so honest and open, however like I have said it was mainly at first a book for my own healing. Knowing once that such private information was out, there would be no bringing it back into the safe confines of my cocoon-*my comfort zone*, so to speak. But, to help others, it had to be released and in doing so, I was released from this ball and chain. Enabling me to also be able to move forward into the next chapter of my life.

On learning to be a writer to get my message out

Ah...no, did not start out as a writer, or considered myself a writer as such. However, I needed to reinvent myself to be one, to facilitate in getting my message out on abuse. Over time having come to appreciate just what it takes to be a proficient writer; it doesn't come without a lot of hard work, effort and a whole lot of frustration. The perfectionist within me would not let this book out until it was right in every way and still I wonder if there is are grammatical errors somewhere…oh well…someone is sure to tell me… Consequently so, this book kept going back to the drawing board until totally satisfied and still it may not be perfect! A university graduate once mentioned how she was not repetitive enough in her thesis and how her lecturers kept saying it was an essential tool needed to drive a point. Oh…, the quest to find that happy medium… I have never been the most eloquent conversationalist. So, hopefully, the important message delivered in Breaking the Chain on Abuse, has been emphasised enough to the reader here. My objective is to obviously stress the vital point driving it home to the reader, and subsequently, only injecting bits of my own experience. However, if I injected more of my experience this book; golly gosh, it would be a thousand pages or more… It is pleasing to hear I am not alone in striving to do my best; this is the bane of most writers. A *maverick* I may be in my writings and that's ok, I am only saying what I perceive. These perceptions are from those of a once abused woman who "has" been there. You may or may not agree with everything I say, but that it the thing, we are all different and have our own mind on things. My job here is not to convert you into any way of thinking, but for you to draw your own conclusions.

However, hopefully, through my efforts, I have finally become not just a writer, but a reasonable one; who can inspire change for the better. Having thoroughly clocked up the mileage and eclipsed the so- called 10 000 hours, they- *"The Powers That Be"*, say that's what it takes to become a proficient writer; I feel somewhat replete. As my parents taught anything worth doing is worth doing properly or not at all. Persistence ., consistency . and determination all of which is hard work, . is what brought me through the writing of this book. Much of my writing is pure common-sense and practical experience from direct and indirect involvement. Though common-sense is a main part of this book, it does still bear consideration.

"Instinctively" I've known what to write…given life experience also. The information I share is what I have gleaned from searching for assistance and personal growth.

On delivering this important message

Yes, I read many helpful self-help books .. I do credit Dr Phil Mc Graw, Robyn Mc Graw and Oprah television programs, to which I am an avid fan. Most importantly, over the years I have done much professional therapy also having attended several domestic violence support . group workshops. The workshop was an eye opener for me and helped me greatly. Apart from Dr Phil McGraw/Robin McGraw and domestic violence support groups, I know of no other strong advocate against abolishing global domestic violence. Their important work has helped many and will continue to help many. Therefore, this vital work they and a multitude of others, should get the recognition it deserves in order to continue helping many more vulnerable people. They have a wonderful strong campaign, "End the Silence on Domestic Violence".

Of course, I do not recommend living the hard life I've lived. Even though it was quite eventful; with learning, living, loving, laughing, crying. There were also far too many times where I only just existed. I'm no expert; *I am simply a life experienced layman who felt and still feels "duty-bound" and "conscience-driven," so to speak to help others.* I simply have practical experience that doesn't come out of a text book. I am not professing to be an expert at all... Seriously, why would I want to be an expert on this! If I can help another, then why not help. Sure, there are some regrets from the difficult life I led. I'd be lying to say otherwise. But I try not to dwell on them, we can't undo the past. One simply "must" move forward.

Mainly, I had suffered many abuses on my journey; simply because of being young, not emotionally or socially mature . enough. Being far too kind-hearted for my own good, naïve and not near wise enough. All this a recipe for the "perfect storm" for any abuser. Wisdom . comes with age and experience, as they say, *"You can't put an old head on young shoulders!"* I was also very meek, timid, and quiet- just didn't know how to ask for what I needed. I do now... some days I holler, just ask my partner! A good piece of advice . *"Learn from my mistakes! I've already paved the way for you."*

Knowing what I now know, I no longer ask "Why?" "Why me?" I say, "Why not!" "Why not me."

The victim mentality is not an easy one to shake off. I felt I had a neon sign, a 'target' on my head that said "Victim," because I inadvertently drew predators to me. But one does not have to continue living as a victim once they make a choice, once they know better. I will though say to you, ***"Do as I say and not as I do!"*** Because it will save you a lot of heartache and hardship.

As a child, I somehow intuitively used coping mechanisms to get myself through some difficult times; it is more than likely what saved me and kept me sane. I was always singing, writing poems, dancing, so outwardly I appeared a reasonably happy child. As a youngster I gratefully had within, the compassion that allowed me to help an older girl with an intellectual disability learn to . read. I adored reading as it was my way to escape; believing it was important to impart this gift that was given to me. Coping mechanisms are an inbuilt mechanism in most of us. However, we need to learn how to activate that coping . mechanism ourselves. As an adult my other coping mechanisms were going to craft classes, singing in the local choir, acting in a play; in particular helping others when possible. Still carrying on as normally as possible, despite our lives being far from normal. In order to cope with trauma, it was important to set a good example for my daughter (who lived with me) to follow. Sadly, my son spent little time with me after my divorce, he lived mainly with his father.

Periodically peppered throughout BREAKING THE CHAIN ON ABUSE, are a few of my own experiences to relate- showing correlations. I am a person who is no different to you; we all have a story. *"We all have our crosses to bear, and at times mine's been just a tad heavier."* In saying that, there are people in much, much, much worse positions than I have ever had to live, and that is exactly how we must view things, so we can move forward. Otherwise self-pity keeps us stuck. Keep in mind it is not a competition abuse is abuse. We should never see our own experiences as being the worst. As there is always someone worse off.

My most difficult experience, particularly the most difficult experience for my son's challenging life, and that of my family, has of course been my son's suicide. Which I firmly believe was a direct result of abuse in various forms ie., domestic violence and bullying. Which is why I'm ever so passionate about helping reduce abuse of any sort, to protect those vulnerable. Hence, BREAKING THE CHAIN ON ABUSE was born. I warn you it is a lengthy book but a most important book. I've written it in such a way so that it is easy to read and absorb.

Please Note Well: - Without meaning to harp, I have most regularly advised the reader to seek Professional assistance throughout. This has been most deliberately done firstly to ensure the victim receives the necessary professional help and secondly to also protect myself. I do not admonish anyone, to do anything they do not wish to do. However, I will provide information, the rest is up to you.

Food for thought: Experiences in life may be difficult. As one must have some sensitivity toward self; it is ok to feel a little sorry for yourself, you are of course only human. But we do not do ourselves any favours when we can protest with self-pity. Even with our emotions, it needs to be everything in moderation, though not to the extreme. When conversing with others instead of talking about you, why not ask someone else how they are? I really had to do some tough soul searching. You will then see that the world is not all about you or me. There is often many in the same boat.

There was a time in my life when I unconsciously or subconsciously, sought out parental figures for approval ., praise . and even sympathy (although one "must" for sanity and their family's sake get their act together). . Later I learnt to seek mentors to learn and grow. As stated before I am not 100% healed, I have insecurities that have taken a lifetime of toll on me and that isn't going to automatically disappear. I still have a distance to go on my journey. Very occasionally, I will still find myself in abusive situations ie., road rage etc and gratefully now having the skills to manage a situation should it turn up in my life as it has done too many times previous. I've gotten a lot better, I'm not cured entirely though. I've come to a place in my life where, if people like me then great; if they don't well nothing can be done about that. Maybe they don't deserve my valuable time and effort! I have had to declutter negativity out of my life, to forge ahead. Proudly I am a "Survivor." However, there are times where I fall back into my old groove. Now hopefully I can be a "Saviour" too. It is my hope that I can inspire those of you that are "Victims" suffering, to become "Survivors" too, or if you are not a "Victim", help you become a "Saviour" and therefore, help someone in need to break free of this vicious cycle. You can lie down and accept that this is your lot in life or do something about it. We all have choices. My motto is *"You can endure and overcome." I am* living proof of this. It is never too late. Some of us are resilient and some of us are not. Some of us don't know how capable we are, until challenged. We can amaze ourselves and inspire others to do the best for themselves too.

"Determination, ambition and persistence in life . is what gets you through and then with that comes strength."

Throughout BREAKING THE CHAIN ON ABUSE; I will share and relate some of my experiences with you.

My life has been a life of dramas and tragedy, something I would not wish on anyone. If you think the television series Dallas had drama, it looked like a walk in the park compared to our lives. Only Dallas was fiction and drama in our life was real. I recently said to my partner after reading books . on the afterlife and reincarnation and if there is really such a thing as choosing a life path well... *"Boy what a hard path chosen; did I think I was Superhuman!"* Then one evening, I cried and begged to God and the angels or into the ether to anyone listening, to change my path to an easier one. I don't fully know whether to believe in God. However, I do believe there is something or someone – (a Supreme Being if you like), out there in the beyond that made each of us. I came to learn what beared true to our lives was; *"What doesn't kill you does make you stronger."*

To someone struggling

If you have a similar story to mine, don't be afraid to tell your story to others, as this may touch some kind heart, and help may come, don't give up. Although in saying that, don't wait forever for someone *to rescue* you, as that may not happen the way you hoped. You need to be proactive . yourself; it is the key to your freedom and true existence. Know also to be careful who you tell your story to; not everyone has a sincere interest in your wellbeing.

Also check the credentials "qualifications" of those who profess to be trained counsellors, this is of utmost importance. Proper skill and training in this area is paramount. Professionals have put in thorough years of specialist training.

I will be the first to admit my life is far from perfect. There are still moments of insecurity, and I am "a work in progress." Still stubbing my toes, every now and then as old habits die hard! Life is still struggle on some levels at times when my heart rules my head, for I am only human. But still there is always so much more to learn. The wonderful thing about learning, is it goes on forever!

Poor choices undoubtedly can be made when we are at our most vulnerable .. Just because you leave an abusive relationship . doesn't mean you are miraculously cured of vulnerability. It doesn't instantly get easy; it takes work and effort.

Treatment is not enough alone ., one must "continually" and "persistently" work on oneself. Only then will you get results; you do whatever it takes; the early morning starts, ercise, journal writing, meditation, visualisation, eft techniques, tapping, hypnosis, improved dietary and lifestyle changes, spirituality and anything else that may help. There will of course be "resistance;" a great deal of the time I found myself failing miserably. But then I'd pick myself up time and again and keep on going. None of us is perfect and I am the first to admit I am far from a perfect mother, daughter, partner, sister- having struggles just like the next person. However, my intentions are good and each day I do my best to improve. Realistically, I was not the first to ever be abused and sadly, I won't be the last. Many women, children, men have suffered for so many different reasons; in the name of culture ., their country and religion, and for so many other diverse reasons and there doesn't even have to be for a reason. It could just be as simple as a matter of being in the wrong place at the wrong time. As I said earlier I made "numerous" mistakes and some big ones too, along the road of life, some of which I am not proud of. There are things I would do very differently if I had to do it over again. I can beat myself up over it and God knows I have done so relentlessly in the past. But why continue doing this as there are enough cruel people who will willingly beat you up over it. So, don't give them the pleasure or the power, as I'm sure there is such a thing as KARMA. Instead vent your frustrations . in a positive way. I chose to turn this negative in my life into a positive and help others, so my life and my family's life was not all in vain. Importantly, so my son did not die in vain. Gratefully, I have learnt much with the assistance of my Psychiatrist, Psychologist and General Practitioner and my loving family and close friends. Mentioned prior, my aim has always been in helping others in need. Hence, this self-help book is essentially a complimentary tool to be used along with therapy. I would like readers to know that I am not a Psychologist or Psychiatrist,

Counsellor or Therapist. It is strongly recommended that you to seek professional . opinion/treatment if relevant to your situation also. If you or someone you know needs help, please seek professional assistance immediately. Procrastination can be our stumbling block, life is too important. In saying that though, I still hold out my hand to you, to help you the best way I know how, as a friend.

As some of the information I give is generalised and since laws differ from state to state, country to country and with laws continually changing over time; keeping it up to date does make it challenging. Hence, the need for you to seek professional . help. As this book is just mainly a guiding light; guiding you to seek help. I know I keep stating this, really it is so important. However, it does not stop you from researching like I have had to do. This can be done by visiting the relevant departments in your area to obtain current information on laws.

Important Note: - In the writing of BREAKING THE CHAIN ON ABUSE I refer to the abuser as "he" and the abused as "her". I realise that this is not always the case. **"Women abuse too, not just men".** "This is done to avoid the use of the clumsy "his/her". So, where I write he you can pertain it to you and see it as "she."

Notes:

Acknowledgements

I wish to express my deep and sincere gratitude to the following people for their assistance. Without

their support . and help BREAKING THE CHAIN ON ABUSE would not have been possible. In no particular order. I would like to thank my Doctors; Psychiatrist Dr Lyndall White, Psychologist Dr Leisa Davina, Dr Laurinda De Wytt, Therapist Joslyn Gardiner. I can't thank them all enough, they have helped transform me into the person I am today; notwithstanding my own work also. Listening, learning, hard work and effort are what reap results.

Doctors/ specialists, the right kind, can be the most caring and compassionate people you may ever meet. Never once did they disbelieve my trials. To not be believed when I felt alone . before was defeating and soul destroying. What a blessing to have found such beautiful souls who have been there just when I needed them. They have given me strength and courage . to carry on just when I felt I had to drop my bundle, due to its sheer weight. My caring and unfailing doctors and therapists helped me through my dismal days and taught me how to empower myself.

I thank from the bottom of my heart and with the deepest most utmost respect my darling daughter and my loving partner who have endured much also, and have been so patient, loving and encouraging. A huge thank you to my beautiful daughter Christy, helping me greatly with understanding the proper formatting and set-up of book writing. Importantly too, I'd like to thank both my much-loved parents for instilling in me strength, fortitude, stamina and endurance. These qualities being my prized possessions ., for without them I would have given up and surely perished. As there were days I just wanted to give up and die. Dying is not an option.

It is important to make mention my role models and idols being Dr Phil McGraw, Reverend T D Jakes, Oprah, Nelson Mandela, Mother Theresa, Brian Tracy, Linda Ronstadt, Ita Buttrose, Dr Wayne Dyer, Deepak Chopra. These are strong men and women that have influenced me greatly and given me much needed information when I have needed it. It has helped mould me into the woman I have become today- a lil bit wiser, one would hope.

Heartfelt thanks and deep appreciation also to my dear friends/mentors both Mary O'Brien Kingman and Joanna Hackett for their unwavering support and wonderful advice. A deep sincere thanks and appreciation also to my dear friend Professor Margaret Britz, who though an extremely busy lady with her students, still so kindly and most generously wrote the foreword for this books message. Margaret also inspired me to do and be all that I can; as she too has chosen to do and has successfully done despite her earlier challenges. I am indebted to this remarkable and brilliant woman. On a recent trip together, I learnt of how she has transformed the lives of her students, we also spoke of my intent on getting my books out there and she encouraged me. This was a real turning point for me. I realised then and there that it was no good just having this vital information sitting dormant in my computer and in manuscripts. Shortly thereafter, working around the clock on getting this vital message out and my books were finally born.

Along the way too, there have been many other women and men too in my community who have graced my life in small or big ways, even by just giving an understanding warm smile. Some have embraced me or have given me much needed advice ., some giving me encouragement, some giving me a pat on the back or a shoulder to cry on when I've needed it. All these sweet women inspired me greatly. I will forever be grateful for these beautiful souls (angels) for being in my life. Two of these 'angels' ladies (old enough to be my mother) also helped me carry groceries to my car when I was receiving cancer treatment. I was in awe, overcome with emotion and gratitude. Sometimes something as simple as a gentle warm smile or a simple kind act can go a long way, they are worth more than gold. Smiles really got me through those dismal days. Heartfelt thanks to my other dear friends, too many to mention here, thank you for believing in me and for your friendship ..

Sharing My Light Bulb Moment

"In my own opinion one of the most important work, is the work of helping the human psyche, for it does and can save lives!"

How so? *Because a sound mind means less irrational . thinking, resulting in less violence . resulting in a world of less wars of the emotional and...physical . kind.* Thus, resulting in less harm .; consequently, resulting in fewer deaths. Of course, this will always be a 'work in progress'. There are no guarantees for a perfect world, however, as long as we recognise the responsibilities . we all have to work in earnest to achieve to a certain degree a better world; not only for ourselves but for our children and the rest of mankind.

Introduction

Abuse is a ball and chain on society. It keeps us in bondage; forever a victim and prisoner to this powerful scourge. So powerful in fact, that it makes our evening news daily. We need to break free and break this chain, so we can live the carefree happy lives we are so deserving of. However, in saying that, we are not helpless we "can" do something about preventing abuse and tightening up on our soft laws. It may mean picketing, crusading or even becoming a politician to effect change. Good on you if you have chosen to do either to help improve the world we live in!

Overall, BREAKING THE CHAIN ON ABUSE covers mainly domestic violence within families. It was written with the aim to raise awareness . and therefore prevention . on abuse. In BREAKING THE CHAIN ON ABUSE, I will also touch on other forms of abuse within society, which is also relevant, as it mirrors domestic violence. You will see the parallels, correlations and similarities between all the different forms of abuse, and how they are all interconnected. It is my belief that all abuse is relative. Abuse can be intertwined with other forms of abuse. So, one can even experience several forms of abuse at any one time, or at some point in their lives.

As a victim we put out a 'scent' a smell so to speak that all types of predators . can pick up on, we become 'targets'. I'll go into this in more detail later. By recognising what is abuse, is the first step

INTRODUCTION

toward preventing it; whether it be physical . or mental. One hit is one too many, one abusive "put down" is one "too many." If you know of someone going through abuse; I implore you to please put this book or better still the sister-book to this **"ABSOLUTELY NO EXCUSE FOR ABUSE!"** version 2 in their hands. It comes complete with an **Action Planner Journal.**

In **BREAKING THE CHAIN ON ABUSE** there is also advice . on what to do if you know someone who is being abused, see in particular, Chapter 1 for **Action Plan** and **Daily Care Routine.**

"ABSOLUTELY NO EXCUSE FOR ABUSE!" also comes with **Action Planner** Journal which is a separate activity guide book to journal in plans, goals and feelings to instigate change.

Abuse is responsible for the damage of many multitudes of fractured, damaged lives. I thought good and hard when compiling this book and what else is equally as important. In **"BREAKING THE CHAIN ON ABUSE,"** you will find some help (coming from my own experiences and through observing others) which is ever-important in this ever-changing fast paced world. How we behave also has a bearing on whether we fall victim to abuse.

"Ethically it was important for me to write a well-rounded book that covered different topics; it is important for people to get a better understanding of prevention . and awareness . of abuse, to alert teachers, nurses, parent's, neighbours alike; that if you see

anything suspicious, act on it. By doing so you 'can' help save a life! Without going on a witch's hunt, if you see regular bruising or strange, odd behaviour and your antennae goes up that something is just not right...Act on that feeling, check it out; seek support/help. We have a responsibility in looking out for each other."

To the woman who feels alone . in her desperation;

"Let me hold your hand and be your friend and help you." In this "BREAKING THE CHAIN ON ABUSE," I will give you practical . hints . of how to set yourself free. You need to know that the step to doing this may seem very hard but is not impossible. We seem to be connected to our abuser through an invisible umbilical cord. Know that you can sever that cord with help.

To the person who helps someone in desperate . need;

I applaud you, for the courage . to help despite the enormity of the situation and the risk to yourself. It is never easy to get out of ones' comfort zone and do something of such magnitude. You are doing a very honourable thing in helping another. You really are making a difference in a life; maybe even saving a life, this is no small feat. Every community needs a hero. A defenceless . life relies on a Good Samaritan. This soul needs the help and action from someone with strength, love ('Agape Love'-love for fellow mankind) compassion ., understanding and kindness.

INTRODUCTION

Undecided on getting involved to help...

People frequently say, *"Oh we don't believe it is up to us to help children who are neglected; it is up to the parents."* Well we can wait forever for the parents to take responsibility. However, we know it isn't going to happen until there are harsh penalties for them to face. Unless this is enforced the likeliness is, the child's situation is only going to worsen. In the first place, the child did not ask to be born into dysfunction and if the parents aren't learning to improve their situation (as the saying goes, "You can't fix stupid"- meaning you can't fix their parents especially if they are stubborn and refuse help but you can certainly try to help the child/children). Why must innocent children suffer; they may not be our family. But these children deserve compassion and assistance. Remember many of these children grow up to be wonderful caring humans with much to offer the world, if given the opportunity.

To loved ones;

Just as my doctors have done for me, why not lend a helping hand to your loved one. Allow them to fall a few times and wholeheartedly be themselves and let them make the mistakes and help them dust themselves off and get back on that horse again. Allow them to ride their horse into their sunset. Through their mistakes they will learn, lovingly be there. Just as good ole Dr Phil says ever so eloquently, *"Be their soft place to fall."*

To the person who sincerely wants change;

Good on you! You can do it! Never give up! May **"BREAKING THE CHAIN ON ABUSE"** inspire positive change and self-discovery.

If you have abuser tendencies;

Sort it out please, your family, your future relationships and you depend on it. Seek medical help/ therapy treatment before taking this baggage into any relationship and burdening another with your abusiveness. Abuse of any kind is inexcusable. Why not do the responsible thing. If you're serious and your drinking problem is the catalyst to abuse, make the effort- seek help. Do whatever it takes and then some. Make a positive step to change with professional help and see how your life improves for the better.

In BREAKING THE CHAIN ON ABUSE, I will cover;

- History of abuse
- What is abuse?
- Is abuse a crime?
- What are the signs of abuse?
- Why it happens?
- Who are the victims?
- Who are the perpetrators of abuse?
- What we can do about it?
- How to break free from abuse

INTRODUCTION

- How to take care of yourself

BREAKING THE CHAIN ON ABUSE was essentially written to help women and children in abusive relationships and for the person who wants to help others or the person who just wants to be enlightened and informed. However, once you have been in an abusive relationship . the lines are often blurred. One who has been in an abusive relationship can often find themselves takers of abuse in all aspects of life. Simply because they know no different and maybe consciously or unconsciously think it's ok to be treated poorly. In this situation one can inadvertently attract abuse.

Abuse knows no boundaries it can affect all races, religions, the rich, the poor, in perfect looking families; it can happen in workplaces, in the school . grounds, hospitals, anywhere. Without meaning to make you paranoid .. Please be aware, abuse can be even in the most unlikely of places by the most unlikely of people. Abuse is really in every fragment of life if one is willing to see. If we are really going to be honest . with ourselves, almost everyone has been abused at some point in their lives of varying degrees. The checkout operator regularly gets verbally abused by the customer; the bank teller held up at gunpoint, road-rage, scary neighbours, the list goes on. With respect "some" of our politicians' abuse and bully each other, not a good example for our children. Therefore, laws don't change "some" of our politicians who are supposed to be looking after us are poor role models they have allowed themselves to become complacent and desensitised about abuse. Politicians need to stay plugged in! In saying this there are of course many good politicians who strive to do all they can. It is important not to tar them all with the same brush.

It is not unheard of to see thug-like behaviour on the football field amongst one player to another. However, our sporting heroes, actors alike need to be aware of the fact, that they could be poor role models for our younger generations. We all have a responsibility to our younger generation whether it be our own children or other children. Children look up to adults. We can desensitise ourselves and turn a blind eye or say and act upon this- that this is inexcusable . and unacceptable. We are not helpless ., there is much society can do. Abusive politicians, nurses, doctors, clergy, scout masters, police, caregivers etc. are in the minority thankfully, most are "not" abusive. Unfortunately, abuse has infiltrated every part of society and hence become a daily part of our world. It is even sadly seen as normal. The world seems to for the most part, become somewhat desensitised to abuse. Violence has become so commonplace; every day somewhere it happens. Not a single day goes by that our evening news doesn't show violence. We have violent computer games, violent movies/ cartoons, news footage, documentaries. One irresponsible television station absurdly and sensationally calling one

INTRODUCTION

documentary series "Serial Killer Sunday," like it's great wholesome family entertainment not to be missed. And we wonder why we have so much violence in the world? Governments, media, television stations, parents, adults. We are all responsible to ensure we have less violence and disrespect in our world. It really is all of our (societies, communities .) responsibility to stop, prevent and/or report . abuse when we know about it and pull together and support . the victims. Whether they be defenceless . children, women, even some men and defenceless animals, nature included. Nature supports mankind, without trees there would be a lack of oxygen, the intricacies of ecology too is all important for our survival. We need to have a good conscience wherever we walk. Sadly, we rape our forests for timber and development all in the name of progress, we poach our wildlife to extinction out of greed and lack of respect, we pollute waterways and forests with our plastic rubbish and chemicals- *abuse is everywhere*. The cracks are more than just beginning to show, our world cannot keep going on the destructive path set by man. Our resources are being stretched to the max, many species of animals extinct. All of it due to *mankind's couldn't give a hoot attitude . .!* It all begins at home and if not there, then at our schools. We can teach our young how to be treated and how to treat others and their environment. We can teach them to be good decent humans and how to be self-sufficient and self-actuating. Ensuring they can know better and can protect themselves from whatever life may throw at them. "Respect" really does begin within the four walls of our homes, where it (respect . or abuse) infiltrates *spills out* into nature and the rest of mankind. It really is that basic. Abuse is a huge problem everywhere. We can no longer ignore this blight on our times- abuse. I am passionate about this and you will see this in the Epilogue.

About getting involved

There is a lot to be said about not getting involved .. Unless we get involved nothing changes. When we don't get involved we are just helping to perpetuate the abuse; simply by not acting. In saying that, there can sometimes be a risk to the saviour of the victim. But nothing is without risk in life; one could get run over by a car when casually crossing the road. In saving a person from drowning, one risks his own life to peril. But that does not stop one from saving a life unless it really does seem futile and the risks outweigh the outcome. Of course, one must avoid harm . to themselves as much as is possible. You need to assess the situation, weigh up risks. Stay plugged in, know what your neighbours are up to without being nosey. If it's abuse, you're not being nosey. How many times have we heard on the news of children being tied up and deprived of food and beaten. Involve the authorities if you must. If we are apathetic and sit on our hands, not taking the initiative to do what is right; what then for the victims of abuse... Weigh up the odds before risking yourself; do not be reckless with you or your family's

INTRODUCTION

lives. Saving a life is important, however, not at the expense of losing then two people. On the flip side, there are also victims who refuse to be saved. Some cannot be helped, no matter how hard you try and you must accept that fact. Rationally, we cannot save the world. But we can each play our role in making our corner of the world a better place, even if for only one person.

Are you reading this book; to help someone or become better informed?

Well done! You have made the first step in helping others by reading this book. Otherwise you may have bought this book just out of interest and that's good too!

Why was this book written in this way?

BREAKING THE CHAIN ON ABUSE is a comprehensive book written on all aspects of abuse known to man. I didn't just make it on one aspect, as all types of abuse in my mind are equally important to cover. Abuse affects the psyche, *the psychological part of our brains*. When reading this book, you will notice the prose in the writing of this book I have deliberately and purposefully written it in first person and third person; allowing it to be easily related by any reader. Therefore, you will often see me switch between the two sometimes in one paragraph. It is widely known and correct that abusers can be either male or female. As it is far from fair to discriminate genders. However, for ease to the reader I have opted to use a generalised approach to call the abuser 'he'. In vain, I have tried not to stereotype a gender too much either way. Please forgive this faux pas, should I mention one gender more than the other; it is not my sincere intention. Now in as much as it irks me to do this, for emphasis; I have most purposefully deferred from the mainstream grammatical correctness. Due to the intenseness of this book, I have most deliberately made some line spacing between sentences to make it easier on the eye for reading. You will notice in a few sections in this BREAKING THE CHAIN ON ABUSE, my underlining, making bold/italics font certain words or phrases highlighting has been most deliberately intended in this way; thereby acting like a red traffic, stop light to draw in the reader's attention and emphasise a point. Since *my experience account has been quite heavy* in this book, you may read some things that don't relate particularly to you; however, it has been my experience. Therefore, you will hopefully get the gist of what I am relating to you- 'the reader'. You will also find in BREAKING THE CHAIN ON ABUSE, that there is a regular use of sayings. I also opted to use this to lighten the mood on the content as it is otherwise a deeply intense book. The use of sayings, "adages", is also regularly utilised in this book for the brain as it helps one absorb and retain vital information said, 'brief and succinctly', just as in a catchy tune of a song. Basically sayings, *adages* are short sentences packed with wise information. Songs play a beneficial role in not just being

INTRODUCTION

entertaining but in telling a story or giving a message; enabling us to get in touch with our feelings and reflect. You will also notice that throughout the book I've shared a couple of poems and a song I've written to help in my own healing. Hopefully it will inspire you to do similar things to help you cope and win this battle we call 'life'. You will see parts in this book where I have become disgruntled with some humans and the frustration of feeling like I have had to redeem myself. Why? Because I am human with feelings. As mentioned this initially was a book I wrote for my own healing, I was going to remove this, but instead have decided to leave it in. Here I share the struggles and frustrations of trying to be a good mum and decent human being.

How to best use BREAKING THE CHAIN ON ABUSE

The following is optional only and only dependant on one's situation. As BREAKING THE CHAIN ON ABUSE is quite intense in parts; it will need to be read in intervals. Since it is food for thought, and to get the most out of this BREAKING THE CHAIN ON ABUSE throughout the book that you can use intermission periods should you wish, you'll see the abbreviation ***STAR 5*** which stands for *"Now if you want to, **S**top, for at least **5** or more minutes, to **T**hink, **A**bsorb and **R**eflect on what you have read;* this is done for the pure intention of enabling digestion, absorption and reflection of information. After the **first chapter** is my **Action Plan with Daily**

Care Routine . (This part of the book is optional, it may or may not be relevant to you). SKIP this section if not relevant to you.

INTRODUCTION

In the following saying I am referring to myself.

"I am strong because I have been weak, I am fearless because I have been scared, I am wise because I have been foolish..."

"A person's most useful asset is not a head full of knowledge, but a heart full of love, an ear ready to listen and a hand willing to help others."

Chapter 1 Life As You Know It Now

The realities of life

The Western world and the system held is still somewhat in the dark ages, there is still much to learn and much change still to happen. The following may be a bitter pill hard to swallow, let alone accept.

However, if I am going to be truthful with you, know this;

- That life is not always fair.
- Unfortunately, bad things "can" and "does" happen to good people.
- Life is unpredictable.
- For the innocent- true justice may never exist.
- Sometimes there are no happy endings.
- Challenges and struggles can be many.
- There are no 100% guarantees in life.
- Crisis does precipitate change and change precipitates crisis.

Should you be in an abusive relationship .?

Coming to a crossroads. By staying in an abusive relationship definitely . makes ones' safety and the safety of dependants' children or pets unpredictable ..

Should you be thinking of leaving . your abuser? Also know that by leaving an abuser, if not done very carefully for you and your children's safety, that this can be an extremely dangerous time for you all. This is especially so if not handled with proper precautions. As you may unintentionally leave yourself and your family open to emotional or physical . attack . that may result in harm . or death.

Life after leaving . can also be unpredictable .. There are some important serious decisions only you can make. You will need to weigh up the pros and cons.

*STAR 5 –Stop, Think, Absorb & Reflect for 5 minutes

Questions and concerns you may need to face are:

- What are the risks in staying?
- What are the risks if leaving .?
- What safeguards need to be in place to ensure yours and your families' safety?

You may find it helps to draw up on a sheet of paper or a page with two columns with a line in the centre to divide the page up and label one column *Advantages* and the other column *Disadvantages*.

Note Well: - If you are in an abusive situation common-sense should tell you to take responsibility and "do not" leave this page or your Action Planner Journal lying around for others to read. If your abuser finds this material, he may dispose of it and abuse/arguments could ensue; putting cease to your efforts. It happened to me. I was going to a support group and my ex found the books and took it back to the support group and he stopped me from ever going back.

"Remember you have the responsibility to yourself and your children to give them the best life you can, this may mean leaving .. Again, this is a decision 'only you', (if you are abused) can make."

Coming to a crossroads in your life

Sometimes we have to reach rock bottom for real change to happen in our lives. Being in denial . is a fear in facing the truth; it takes one out of their comfort zone. If you are considering leaving . an abusive relationship . you will find my Action Plan with my Care Routine . which is there to assist you in a possibly easier departure from abuse.

At times I felt very alone . and uncertain. I only wish I had someone there for me like I want to be there for you. If you are a victim know that you do not have to suffer alone in silence, in thinking you are the only one going through this. I hate to say this but there are a million more like you and me. A book such as this would have helped me greatly, so I write this for you and others. Know though that I am here to be with you through your Action Plan and Care Routine ..

For the person who wants to make change in their lives;

The following Action Plan with Care Routine ., I will say to you after Chapter one, if you feel leaving . is your only option. Because you know it is detrimental . (it risks harm . or death) to the wellbeing of yourself and your children if you continue to stay in an abusive relationship .. If you are not in an abusive relationship, then you can disregard the Action Plan that is at the end of the chapter.

REMEMBER- *I do not know yours or your friend's situation and therefore cannot and will not interfere and tell anyone to leave their partners or spouse.*

To the abused;

If you notice things beginning to escalate ., getting worse and punishments . starting to get out of hand becoming dangerous, this is when you may need to make some decisions. Don't worry about how you will cope financially and emotionally, as there are many professional . people that can help you. However, they won't know unless you approach them. When leaving . do your best not to endanger your family or yourself. Always use common sense, seek the assistance of Support Groups, Police and Professionals (Doctors) also. Never ever feel bad to ask for help. If you can speak to your doctor, I'm sure they would be only too pleased to help you. But you must take that first step yourself. See Action Plan (see next page) to help you, help yourself. Remember there are people who do care ., but as the saying goes "The Lord helps those who help themselves." However, in such a situation do get help. Help is available. Please see the back of book for **Help Contacts.**

Since I first wrote this book between 2006-2018, there has been a fantastic free new mobile/cell phone app for women to use in a domestic violence emergency. It is put out by Robin Mc Graw called "When Georgia Smiled"

See *robinmcgrawrevelation.com www.drphil.com or whengeorgiasmiled.org*

Please also see the "Aspire Initiative" Domestic Violence Education Initiative also put out by Phil and Robin McGraw, it is full of great helpful and sound advice.

***STAR 5**

"Looking after yourself is one of the best gifts you can give to yourself and loved one!"

-N J Lutter

Notes:

Action Plan *(Optional-this is only if things are dire for you and really only you can judge that, not me or anyone else. Be wise and use common sense as best you can)*

You may think you have no friend or few friends;
I am your friend;
So, visualize my hand in yours I am holding your hand;
Now listen, like you've never listened before;
I am talking to you;
I can't stress this enough to you;
Abuse of any kind is wrong;
You "cannot" help this abuser to change;
It is "not" your responsibility or duty to change him;
It is the abuser's responsibility to change;
The abuser "will not" change while you are still there;
Naively believing the abuser promises to change when you have no clear evidence is simply being gullible;
If he has not sought professional . help;
And you both know that's not true, so don't stay in denial .;
Realise this; if your relationship . was meant to be he would have sought help of his own accord;
Accept none of the abusers' excuses .. They don't wash;
Don't make excuses . for the abuser and try to justify their abuse to you or the children;
There is no justification or excuse for abuse;

LIFE AS YOU KNOW IT NOW

A loving partner does not abuse you;

You deserve to be loved and cared for properly and so do your children;

You owe it to your children to give them the proper love and care . without abuse.

You are a good person.

Don't feel ashamed because you couldn't make the relationship . work.

You did not bring this on yourself.

You did not provoke the abuse, don't blame yourself.

Do not get caught up in arguments.

Try not to provoke the abuser as this is not helpful to your situation.

This is "not" your lot in life.

Life has much better to offer you.

You are not as helpless . as you think you are.

You owe it to yourself and loved ones to break free from abuse.

You are responsible to your children and self to protect them by breaking free.

Somehow and someway you must find the courage . to escape this.

Don't suffer this abuse any longer; no one deserves to be treated like this.

Don't be a victim or a statistic.

Every minute you stay you are in danger of possible detrimental . physical . harm . and by far worse emotional scarring.

Be positive and as strong as possible.

Don't let anyone change your resolve, especially if your safety is at stake.

You need to be the adult here and make the decision to leave, don't ask the children to decide and don't tell them about leaving . till the very last moment.

The abuser may seem kind and nice for a while but that won't last forever.

In your heart you know this.

So, what, you have to start again, we all had to, remember you are not alone ..

Many women are going through what you are going through right now and many have left the abuse, you can do it.

There is a whole new world for you out there.

You will even find friends out there to help and care . for you.

So, let them, no one can help you if you stay.

There is no shame in asking for help.

Do not see your life as a failure.

Each hour say this affirmation, "I am deserving of a happy, abuse free life" or "We are deserving of a happy, abuse free life," say it with conviction; feel it, mean it and believe it.

This affirmation will help give you the courage . and strength to leave.

LIFE AS YOU KNOW IT NOW

Each time your abuser puts you down draw on this strength say the affirmation "I am a clever and worthy person".

Even make up an affirmation to suit you, one that is easy to remember.

If money . is a problem, each day whilst your abuser is asleep prepare/pack, save money-you can do this, hide . this money or if possible put it in the bank in your name only.

Do not gamble . or waste your money ., you need every bit of money to leave.

Educate yourself as much as you can on preparing to leave as if a storm is brewing, how you would normally do prior to a cyclone or twister.

What preparation would you make?

What items will you need to take- make a list (put this list in a private spot away from prying . eyes).

What precautions do you need to take?

Abuse can be a brewing storm.

You prepare in case of the worst-case scenario.

Contact the police . or authorities . if you need help that is their job.

If you need to you can speak to them in confidence ..

Just as he thinks cunning so to you- you need to be one step ahead of the abuser.

Don't give him even an inkling of what you are preparing to do, or your plan is gone. ***STAR 5***

BREAKING THE CHAIN ON ABUSE

"Believe in yourself you 'can' do anything!"

-N J Lutter

LIFE AS YOU KNOW IT NOW

Daily Care Routine .:

In the meantime, I want you to look after yourself.

Nurture yourself.

Try to take herbal teas instead of coffee, tea or alcohol. .

Stay away from drugs. .

Pamper yourself with relaxing baths.

Give yourself some 'me time'.

Eat healthy ., nutritious food regularly.

Drink 6-8 glasses of water.

Try and get 6-8 hours of sleep. .

Exercise daily if you can.

Regularly take a multivitamin if you are deficient. See your doctor.

Plant a temporary small garden and tend to it daily-this will give you something to look forward to and relax with.

Play music daily and sing if you can.

Meditate regularly if you can.

Learn to love yourself you are worthy.

Keep saying your positive affirmations. .

If you can get some professional . counselling but keep this confidential (don't let the abuser know what you are doing).

You need to keep yourself mentally and physically strong in order to leave.

When you think you are ready to leave; go through your photos. (Photographs can be saved to iCloud) and mementoes, and important paperwork, ID and items special to your children are important to take. Don't take too much, in case you have trouble transporting it.

Don't worry too much about possessions . they are only material things they "can" be replaced.

You and your loved ones "cannot" be replaced.

A situation may present itself where you have no choice but to escape with only your clothes on your back. But hopefully this won't be so, that you can plan this, so you leave with what you need.

With assistance *"You can do it!"*

I am holding your hand.

I am with you in spirit.

*STAR 5

"May you journey to the core of your soul, coming out of the cocoon and into sky of freedom becoming the beautiful butterfly that you are meant to be!"

- N J Lutter

Notes:

Chapter 2 What Is Abuse?

Is abuse a crime .?

Do not be under any illusions, abuse can be a crime; as there are varying degrees of abuse and although some are seen as subtleties of abuse where there is a grey area. Where the authorities . may not be able to step in until something grave happens. Senseless law but true! One can be charged for physical ., sexual . abuse and neglect. Depending on the severity, the abuser could be charged with a criminal offence.

What constitutes abuse?

The common denominator of all abuse is lack of respect for all; the world and all its inhabitants. Abuse comes in many forms; it is the mistreatment of another person, living things and objects; taking away another person's will. Just as adult victims can be affected for the rest of their lives all types of abuse have an effect on a child as well. A child can end up carrying this with them into adulthood, for the rest of their lives. It is known to some people in relationships as baggage or issues.

A once child victim can end up continuing in playing a victim role as an adult victim or can become a bully, an abuser. As the child that was bullied or even the bully can end up being a bully in adulthood. This is especially so, if the child was not able to work through these issues without the help of professional . counselling and support.

WHAT IS ABUSE?

Back in generations gone by, there was no such thing as going for therapy unless you had a severe mental illness . where one needed committing or serious attention .. Little was known about Domestic Violence due to lack of education and awareness about it, consequently little was done, if ever. Therefore, it was highly understandable that women continued to remain in abusive marriages. Because they did not know better or they felt they deserved it somehow, or incorrectly thought that they in some way provoked it. Also, they may have felt it was their lot in life. It is not unheard of, that for some cultures or religions, it is the expectation by their families to endure many forms of abuse.

Many families continue to remain in denial .. This could quite possibly be part the reason why some marriages seemed to last longer than marriages of today with a lower divorce . rate. Whereas, in this day and age where we have evolved, grown and matured emotionally and socially we now know our rights and that we are deserving of better treatment .. Consequently, in our current era divorce is now more prevalent.

All types of abuse can also have an emotionally crippling and debilitating effect on victims, therefore, making everyday living exceedingly hard. It can also cause some eccentric type behaviour in the abuser which may affect the victim. It can also have a secondary effect on others through marriage . and relationships. Know that you don't have to be hit to be abused. Emotional . abuse is equally damaging to the victim, as it can leave emotional scars that can last a lifetime.

Abuse can be found in all types of relationships, heterosexual, gay, lesbian, transgender .. Abuse knows no boundaries. It can affect the rich, well to do, poor, any race, religion or profession. As hard as it may be to wrap ones' head around, *even people from good family upbringings can be victims or abusers.* Parents may even scratch their heads and think, "*Where did I go wrong?*" It can be that perplexing 'confusing', so stop blaming yourself. In some families, dysfunction may not reign, however, it can still happen. Life is often confusing. Once our children are out of our homes; going to school or work, in a very real sense it feels as if they belong to the world, it is just plain fact, but still we must do all we can to give them as loving and stable home environment as much as is possible.

Some abusive relationships hide . their dysfunction very well, out of shame . and embarrassment . and for the abuser he wants to keep it a well-hidden secret. Because he does not need his so-called reputation . on the line. Many friends, family members may be stunned and have disbelief and even denial . after finding out. When they finally do find out, they may even blame themselves for not noticing sooner. Blame just like denial is negative. One needs to stop blaming themselves or others. Blame is a useless counterproductive . action and doesn't help anyone it only helps keep people stuck.

WHAT IS ABUSE?

Abuse can be motivated through the person under the influence of alcohol . or drugs .. There are also abusers that abuse due to substance abuse, mental health issues, acquired brain injury or PTSD from participating in unwanted acts of violence . such as wars or being involved . with violence. Regardless of the triggers, this does not excuse or condone abuse. Professional help for the abuser can always be sought. I am almost certain the abuser does know and appreciate love; I cannot fully attest to this, as I'm not an expert, I can only speak from my own experience.

The non-abusive parent does not intentionally mean for their child to be sexually, physically or emotionally abused; however, due to their poor choices in partner, and/ or circumstances beyond their control, abuse can inadvertently happen. A lot of the time their hands are tied, or they may not have known, or they may be confused as to what to do. They may often be immobilised by fear, defeat and indecision. However, the non-abusive parent is still abusing their child indirectly by staying in an abusive relationship . or struggling to make changes necessary for their child's sake. **"When you know better you do better."** Instead do not judge them, if anything support . them in good decisions whatever way you can, as they often feel very alone ..

What is not abuse?

- Denying your children from too much unhealthy food throughout the day.

BREAKING THE CHAIN ON ABUSE

- Encouraging your child to eat healthy. .

- Encouraging your child to exercise. .

- Encouraging your child to do their homework ..

- Encouraging your child to get enough sleep. .

- Being strong and firm when you are disciplining . your child is having a tantrum.

- Giving your child second-hand goods ie., clothes/toys/ books when that is all you can afford. .

- Disciplining and refusing to give in and buy a toy should you not be able to afford . it or the child is misbehaving.

- Taking your child to church.

- Giving your child to give appropriate love, praise . and affection. .

- To limit child's television time.

- Monitoring television watching.

- Monitoring healthy . reputable computer internet use.

- Teaching your child manners, courtesy, respect ., patience, love, compassion . and how to share.

- To expect good behaviour.

- To encourage your child to have good work ethic.

- To encourage your child to volunteer and help those less fortunate.

The archaic ages side of abuse-physical ., sexual and emotional .
(Cultural, Religious Beliefs of Parents & Families .)

In some cultures, a whole community can take the side of the abuser and condone and continue abuse on the victim. This can be done by looking down on the victim and "ostracising the victim." This is most painful and extremely unfair. Gossip . does abound in communities . and can cause further hardship . on the victim for the whole of their lifetime. It can be a burdensome weight for a victim to carry, also being in a sense abused by "many" abusers in a closed-minded community.

There are even communities . that condone abuse as it has been happening down through the ages; it is seen as the norm. It has been known that in some non-westernised countries, they still use archaic methods such as stoning individuals with rocks to their very deaths in the 21st century. I read in the news how women were stoned to death for reasons such as infidelity, whilst the man got off scot- free. What?! In the Western world we view this as abuse and never dream of doing such to our women.

In some countries, there is an extremely painful circumcision . of female girls done without anaesthetic. Often these circumcisions become infected where the child can even die. Then there are tribal initiations or the abuse living in certain communes, beheading, child brides as young as 8 years old, child slavery, marriage . arrangements, brainwashing/teaching young lad's suicide . terrorism . tactics, giving children weapons and instructed to kill.

Well...what of abuse in the name of God, Religion . and Culture? To which god are we worshipping? The worlds alarm bells should ring loud and clear! In my mind, all of the above is abuse. The Western World considered long ago that in our countries it is termed as abuse, so why should we not take a dim view if it is brought into our Western World. A question in my mind is; Who is at the helm steering our (world) ship? Parents, Clergy, Teachers, Caregivers, Law Enforcement, Politicians, Our World Leaders, anyone in a caring, control leadership position. We are all responsible in making a difference for the better no matter how small.

Would a loving God commend, command or condone such atrocities? Or is mankind doing this using the guise of religion to misconstrue religious . doctrine to suit one's own selfish agenda? What kind of culture . is this? What about the victims? What about their futures? The dire consequences can likely affect these children into their adult lives. Where does one begin to put an end to it? What do you think? Whilst it is also good to have an opinion, just don't expect everyone to agree with you though.

WHAT IS ABUSE?

A fashion model, writer and humanitarian Waris Dirie (1999) has a compelling and thought-provoking book "Desert Flower" on her sufferings of childhood and female circumcision .. She is the United Nations Women's Rights Activist and has won many awards and is also the United Nations Special Ambassador for the elimination of Female Genital Mutilation. She is doing wonderful humanitarian work through her book and in Africa and she has also launched her own foundation and she now has a project called "The Africa Fund". If one person can do so much, then **just imagine how much "many" people can do...**

Old school culture can have good and bad points

There is an old school . culture . that is alive and well in some countries. In the western world we are only now seeing how very wrong some of the advice . and teachings were to our societies at large. Where some people have been taught to *'Lift your chin up' and 'stand up tall like a man', 'stop crying', 'only sissy's cry', 'pull your socks up', 'don't bother your elders', 'children are to be seen and not heard', 'I'm too busy for this'*. These are unhelpful phrases/sayings that hinder communication ., making one feel unimportant, alone . and a nuisance. Subsequently, the child feels it's better off if they say nothing. They could end up thinking, "What's the point no one will believe me anyway..." Parents then wonder why their children didn't speak up. Children may also feel they have caused the situation themselves, consequently they don't seek help, or they don't know how to seek help.

Gossip . (Legalised Socialised Bullying)

If you have been on the receiving end of gossip (as I have been) . it is insidious and meanspirited; you will see that it can have a very damaging effect on victims. If one knows of gossip going on or hears of it, it is best to steer clear from any gossip. Some people may say there is good gossip and bad gossip. To me, gossip is what it is gossip- don't sugar-coat it. Gossip . is meddlesome and mischievous; and not to mention malice, just another *socially acceptable allowable form of bullying* .. Bullies are predators . that seek out the weak, vulnerable ., soft or their self-esteem may be low. Bullies do this to their victims to elevate their own position. They really are the ones with the problem. Bullying has driven enough troubled souls to suicide .. It should never ever be socially acceptable.

There is a wonderful apt saying, *"Believe nothing of what you hear and only half of what you see,"* it makes a whole lot of sense. I feel this saying, sums up perfectly how people should be when it comes to idle gossip .. Gossip . can be so harmful and hurtful, it can cut so deep. It is bad enough to live through abuse. But the gossip, innuendos and bullying . behaviour of others is soul destroying, all it does- is allow the whole abuse cycle to continue perpetuating. I am a firm believer that gossip is in itself still a form of abuse. Gossip

WHAT IS ABUSE?

mongers are nothing more than glorified bullies, with nothing good to offer, just negativity .- making the already difficult life of the victim even harder to deal with. The tongue can be so sharp, cutting like a knife, so don't go messing around with what you don't know, or you'll have blood on your hands. Gossip can kill or wound, breaking a person's spirit. Therefore, if you hear someone gossiping about another, don't join in their banter. It is nothing short of mean-spirited.

Put yourself in their shoes would you like it if it were done to you? *"No, you would not!"* I'm not religious ., however, the bible says it well, *"Do unto others the way you like to be treated."* and *"Judge not least you be judged."* In other words, never be quick to judge others, you don't know their journey. And one never knows that it could befall them too.

Seriously, who gives one the right to judge another? Walk a mile in their shoes and maybe then you can have a slight inkling into the true situation. Another bible classic is *"Pull the log out of your own eye before pulling the twig out of another's eye."*

My favourite one of all is this *"When you point your finger at someone look at your hand and how many fingers are pointing back at you; three fingers are pointing back at you."* Be constructive not destructive .. If one cannot contribute in a positive way, then one should not contribute at all. *"In other words, if you can't say anything nice don't say anything at all."* Negative contribution is never needed nor is it wanted.

I have a new-found respect for celebrities who have to deal with gossip/paparazzi .. In my own defence; in hindsight, if I had to do it all over again, yes, there are some things in my life I would do differently, but unfortunately there is no undo button. In reality, one should not have to change what they are doing due to gossips, but this is not a perfect world. None of us are perfect however, we need to continue to improve and strive to do our best. When you know better you do better. You do the best with what you know at the time. Ones' intentions do stand for a lot. If you know someone struggling why not offer help and not jump to conclusions. In a world as harsh as this one, that could be refreshment for the soul.

Remembering also of a time when I was stuck on side of the road with a broken-down car how no one stopped to help. Then along came a guy with long hair & tattoos to my rescue. Who was I to judge him, I was just grateful that someone stopped. So, we should never judge a book by its cover. People whinge about the teenagers of today; there are many wonderful young ones who are courteous and helpful. We ought not to look with a critical judgemental eye.

Regarding judging a book by its cover, there were some small-minded people who also judged me harshly as you will see in my following account.

My own learning curve- some hard lessons

During my teenage years, did not go out much socially, never sowed my oats- so to speak, never drank alcohol or dabbled in drugs which is good. From mistakes I made along the way, meeting my husband who was 20 years my senior with me being a naïve 18-year-old, shortly after we married, maybe there was a sort of arrested development on my part...or a serious lapse of judgement... Anyway, we were in a religion that promoted modesty of the highest degree. It was frowned upon to dress in figure hugging clothes, low cleavage tops, and short skirts. Because of having to become a responsible instant mother of seven stepchildren I dressed way too matronly for my age. I was a very good mother to all of the seven children then our own two children shortly thereafter. My eldest stepson was four years younger than me (in many ways I still felt like a child) and the youngest stepchild two years old, it was a crazy mid up situation. In all, there were nine children to look after on my own as my ex-husband was not very cooperative at all, and their mother was not on the scene, due to my ex-husband's actions. Neighbours had warned me later that I was used as a modern-day slave to look after his seven children.

After separating and divorcing my abusive ex-husband I fell in love. I lost weight (not that I was very big), looked trim and felt good; I went from one extreme to another. For a time, I admittedly was a bit self-absorbed with my new found looks and loved going out and dancing on a Friday at night, I did have child minders and did not leave my two children home alone. With my prior marriage I was on a very short leash, rarely able to go out, unless he decided. Then after separating from my ex-husband I believe I made up for lost time. However, despite my making up for lost time, I was still very involved in my children's lives just as many loving parents do for their children; taking my children to counselling, volunteering at school- helping with a learning assistance program in my son's high school, tuckshop duty, P & C secretary, school fundraising, helping at school excursions, helping children read, helping out at girl guides, doing hair/make-up for ballet, sewing ballet costumes, art and drama class, music practise and they were able to go to all school camps and excursions, helping my children with their homework/ assignments, feeding nutritious meals, reading bed-time stories, giving them discipline along with much love, affection, attention and praise. My darling son struggled from infancy, despite good nutrition he was colicky and had other health issues and trauma's. I also had my own health issues but when you have children your issues have to go on the back burner, so I thought. My son Shane had trouble with social maturity yet was very

WHAT IS ABUSE?

academically advanced for his age. Teachers found my son was spaced out daydreaming. Consequently, I had his hearing and eyes checked to ensure he was investigated, and nothing was amiss; found his eyesight wasn't the best so purchased glasses. Found he was ambidextrous (then took him to see an Occupational therapist for regular appointments and we had exercise he needed to do to strengthen his left hand. Shane's Remedial therapist found he had a high IQ, and was too advanced for his class, it was suggested that I substitute his learning with more advanced work as he was bored; so consequently, I ensured he received extra weekly tutoring. I took him to Neurologist; EEG testing showed he had a form of epilepsy and ADHD- so duly ensured he received regular medication, meds had an adverse effect so changed to fish oil tabs. I also took him to regular kinesiology appointments and did exercises daily with him. My son also had a deformed penis and needed an extremely painful Hypospadias operation at the age of seven. I stayed with him in hospital and slept beside his bed and literally nursed him back to recovery to also help free up nurses, who had kids with terminal illnesses. The operation was unavoidable- to correct a constant problem he had with reoccurring urinary tract infections. Because the operation was excruciatingly painful and traumatic for him, he never forgave me for it. He couldn't understand the need for the operation no matter how much I explained it to him. My son also went to regular karate lessons, private swimming tuition, soccer lessons, drama and musical rehearsals with me going to every one of his lessons and rehearsals doing make-up sewing class costumes. My child was bullied throughout all his school years being kicked in the kidney area and face by boys much bigger than him when he was 10 years old. My child was bullied for many different reasons one of them being that I am coloured. Throughout the years I took my child to counselling to deal with the different challenging situations my child was going through. Many times, I went to the school to put a stop to the bullying and stand up for my child. Wrote numerous letters to the Education Department, Local MP and even the Premier to get action, all fell on deaf ears. As he got older I guided him in writing job application letters, showing him how he needed to dress for job interviews. My son was quite a needy child, my daughter also because he received a lot of my attention incorrectly believed that he was my favourite. I explained to her that I did not have favourites and that he was quite needy and that is why at times my focus was taken away from her. I also knew she was stronger, resilient and more independent. It hurt me for her to hear that she had felt that way. It is very important to do ones best to keep a balance. *Please forgive the use of the word "I" as I really do not like to talk about myself, but it is so frustratingly hard to explain and relate without the use of word, "I."*

WHAT IS ABUSE?

There was so much more my son endured that I could write a book on that I won't put here. I had done so much for both my children and even for my stepchildren that no one really knew anything about. All things any loving parent would do...still you will have your critics... It got so, that I found it hard to lift my head high. Even questioning my own worth as a mother and human being, thinking maybe I don't deserve to live; after all what mother has a child that wants to commit suicide...Yet would I judge another person so harshly? Even though you do all you can for your children and doing without yourself, so your children don't miss out on anything you will still have your haters/critics and still too you can lose your child to death or drugs. Life can be cruel as I mentioned earlier. There are I'm sure numerous parents dealing with just the same. Parents and children need to be built up not taken down. Gossip and mean-spiritedness must seriously be stopped; it has led to suicides aplenty. **"Someone somewhere is fighting a battle you know nothing about, so be kind always."**

As always, I did my utmost in everything to keep a balance; knowing I was a very good mother and ensured my children were well-loved and looked after well in my care to the very best of my ability. Yet these small-minded people failed to look any further except into tunnel vision, seeing only what they wanted to see, that is the problem with living in a small community. The irony being that it was these interfering gossips whose children I had voluntarily helped teach reading to at school. Three women actually bailed me up and gave me a mouthful, such soul-destroying stuff; I really had such a hard time with this. The ironic part is these same women had children who broke the law- stealing and running amuck, yet not once did I judge them by gossiping or character assassinating them. Most gratefully, I had other friends in our community who knew my story and my journey and respected me for not jumping in and out of relationships and doing my best to always stay switched on with my children as much as possible.

Nevertheless, I still had the problem of their father my ex, undermining me giving our son large sums of money and I could only give $2 here and there, as I only worked at housecleaning jobs to make ends meet. I couldn't compete with that. I still stuck to my resolve, I was reasonably strict and balanced with my children, they needed to tell me where they were going and what they were doing, and they were made to eat their vegies, do their homework and finish any assignments with my continued help. However, my son preferred to live with his father, who had no rules, my son was also allowed by his father to eat unhealthily much of the time, stay out as late as he wanted, he didn't have to go to school if he didn't want to. Naturally, I could not compete with that, along with all the brainwashing. For a long time, I blamed myself entirely, though I looked at my parenting constantly to see where I could have gone wrong. I'm not perfect, I fumbled and made many mistakes. I now believe that I did the best with what I knew at the time.

Having an unconventional relationship did not help. As being different, being attractive or having a wart on the end of your nose can make you a target of a gossip (bullying). I do though believe that where gossip abounds one does need to be careful to watch everything they do so as not to give fuel to fire 'gossip', as gossip mongers will take anything no matter how innocent and run with it and turn it into something juicy and dirty. It's sad that one must be so careful but that is just a fact of life. People gossip and judge others for many reasons; jealousy, envy, boredom, self-importance and just plain ignorance and nastiness. I wonder would they like the same done to them?

Though one should not have to change what they are doing due to gossips. If I had to do it all over again, yes there are some things I would do differently, I would have dressed more appropriately. Admittedly my dress sense was poor to say the least; a friend once said, *"You have such a flat tummy why don't you get your belly button pierced!"*, next thing that's what I was doing...someone commented that I'd look good in stiletto's next thing I had a pair of 6 inch heels... if someone told me I'd look good with green hair I would have rushed out to get it! Silly girl! Eventually I worked it out on my own. None of us are perfect, however we need to continue to improve and strive to do our best, grow and mature. Again, as Dr Phil Mc Graw says, *"When you know better you do better!"* My doctor also said, *"You did the best with what you knew at the time."* One's intentions do stand for a lot.

What can happen in an escalating abusive situation?

When in an abusive relationship . tensions can heighten, and abuse can quickly spiral out of control, with an expected or unexpected outcome. A death can occur, where a spouse either living with their partner or estranged from their partner ends up maiming . or killing . their partner out of rage, spite or for such situations as claiming life insurance or jealousy and possessiveness. Again, that is why professional . help is important and safely removing yourself from your abuser. You will see me say it over and over, I cannot stress this enough.

Roles in life

Life is like a play with different characters there is "The Villain"- The Abuser, "The Damsel in Distress"- The Victim, "The Knight in Shining Armour"-The Saviour, "The Jester"- Meddler, "The Victorious"- The Survivor.

- If you are the *Victim*, I hope you can become the *Survivor*.
- If you are the *Meddler*, I hope instead you become the *Saviour*.
- If you are the *Abuser*, I hope you become the Survivor.

WHAT IS ABUSE?

In order for the abuser's role to play out he needs a victim

Just like to be "up" you have to be "down", there is no "hot" if there is no "cold." It is really is, as basic as that. However, you don't have to be a victim, you don't have to suffer to experience peace .. Just like if you don't want to live in a cold climate you move to a warmer climate. It may not seem easy, but it isn't unachievable. Make a conscious decision to improve your life and make a change.

Let's not sugar-coat it; a Meddler is an accomplice to an Abuser. I suggest that if you truly are against Abusers, keep away from meddlesome mischief such as gossip .. Leave other people's business well alone ., unless you can do something constructive to help.

What role do we play?

An Abuser, a Meddler, a Saviour or a Survivor?

You don't have to take on that role, you can change it. I hope you aim to be the Survivor or Saviour!

*STAR 5

> "Our prime purpose in this life is to help others,
>
> And if you can't help them, at least don't hurt them."
>
> - Dalai Lama

Chapter 3 Types of Abuse

(various facets of abuse toward spouses, children)

There are many facets to abuse. Later I talk about such things as hoarding. In reality, some of us have hoarded items in varying degrees, I was a lil bit of a hoarder myself, thank goodness I now live more of a minimalist lifestyle! Some of us gamble a bit or we are messy etc, but it is when that gets out of hand when it becomes a problem, none of us are perfect or inherently bad- though some may beg to differ. Some having had difficult childhoods etc; life is not easy, but it is what we do with our lives that matter. As I've said a gazillion times there still is *no excuse for abuse and* as I've said gazillion times before please seek professional therapy. We are all soldiers in this world some call war; we all have our battles or wounds to bear. With addictions, phobias, illnesses but once we acknowledge there is a problem, or we have a problem we can become part of the solution. Solutions are out there, if we are willing to seek help.

Social . Abuse

Social . Abuse is when your abuser does not allow you to have any social time with friends or family. He keeps you isolated and cuts . off your life-line, he never lets you have any alone . time or privacy. When you are not allowed to read self-help books ., magazines or watch self-help programs like Oprah, Dr Phil. He escorts you

TYPES OF ABUSE

everywhere into doctor's room at the surgery (watching what you say), stops you from driving, abuses you if you look sideways at a man, checks up on you even if you are in the toilet, shower or backyard, does not allow you to better yourself educationally or allow you to hold down a proper job.

The abuser may also want to regularly make you pregnant . so you are helpless ., housebound and kept in your place. Because that way you are less likely to flee, with children in tow. If you are fortunate enough to be allowed to have friends- the abuser chooses your friends for you or rids you of your friends or family. Basically, you are a prisoner . in your own home, with none of your own choices. Is this called living or just existing? Or on the flip side you may be forced against your will to have an abortion/s (not social abuse but abuse all the same).

Financial Abuse

The following are examples only. When your abuser controls the money . and does not allow you to have much money and accompanies you to the bank and shopping and gives you very little money to work with so that oftentimes you are scrounging for coins in the sofa just to buy a loaf of bread, then you take on bit jobs just to get enough money for bare essentials. Others having to steal to make it through the week. Large amounts of money . in your account goes mysteriously missing, valuable items go missing. Other relatives, friends' money and valuables go missing. Is he gambling, paying for prostitutes, alcohol, drugs . or hiding it in other accounts? Are they using illegal methods such as theft ., fraud ., embezzlement . in order to illicitly pay and fund for these vices/addictions .? Or are they selfish and controlling? Many pertinent questions to ask oneself...

Infidelity ./Betrayal

When your abuser has sex . with another whenever he feels like it with or without your knowledge. He may tell atrocious lies about you without your knowledge to other loved ones i.e., that you have terminal cancer etc.

Spiritual Abuse

He will not allow you to grow spiritually in a way that improves yourself. He will become enraged should you be assertive .. He may bring you into a strict religious . cult for his own gratification and selfish reasons. He expects you to be subservient (meek, not challenging his decisions).

You may not be able to celebrate special occasions important to you. He may stop you from going to church or social/recreational activities or dictates what and when you can eat, drink, what you wear, read and the music you listen to. You may have few if any rights .. He stops you from emotionally growing or educating yourself. Basically, he is breaking your spirit, turning you into a robot, where you exist with no real life. What gives this person the right to do that to someone who is meant to be their loved equal? Rightly ask yourself, *"If the shoe was on the other foot, would they like that done to them?"*

Emotional . (Verbal) abuse aka Mental/Psychological Abuse

He tells you; you are stupid no one would want you, you are ugly ., you are fat, you are balding, you are frigid ., you are an embarrassment . and swears at you constantly using profanity, calling you swear words and puts you down. He finds fault in everything you do, by saying your cooking and caring is useless, nothing is ever good enough and consequently sets you up to fail. You may be threatened and blackmailed. He may hold your children hostage when you try to leave him, so you can never leave him; for fear of never seeing your children again.

He uses exploitation- using the kids against you. He may use forms of manipulation on you such as guilt . tripping, ridicule ., brainwashing ., *"gaslighting"- demoralising your rationale by manipulating to make you second guess your own actions no matter how rational/sane,* threatening to have you committed.

He may not allow you to make any decisions, loss of free will, he calls all the shots, you no longer can think for yourself, your power is given away to him, you are no longer empowered. He is now controlling, messing with your mind- trying to send you insane, creating ploys and dramas to exhaust and confuse you. Using his guile "cunning", this is all part of his plan, eventually breaking ones' spirit, having you right where he wants you. Pretty soon you cannot think for yourself. You end up believing you can do nothing right. He is the master manipulator, great at being passive aggressive, condescending and patronising- the victim doubts their own mind. Even when you are given freedom to shop alone; you don't think to escape because he has brainwashed you into believing you are helpless, and the situation is hopeless. *It is only when one gets out of denial and strengthens up with courage do they realise they can cut the umbilical cord that binds you to your abuser.*

He may assassinate your character, turn loved ones, even your children and friends away from you 'against you,' trying to muddy your good reputation .. Again, you feel defeated .... Soon you are alone.

Racial . Abuse/ Discrimination

If in a biracial relationship . he tells your child to ask mummy, *"Mummy why are you black?"* and other ridiculing taunts (makes fun of) your heritage with racist . slurs. Sets about to send your child against you where your child says they are embarrassed by you because you are black. He may say things like, "You're my chocolate cookie!" It may at first seem innocent and funny, but it really is insidious and demeaning, another put down. Before long he has even trained your children to put you down also (this is then how children learn to treat their future partners when they have relationships of their own). He may also try to stop you from keeping any of your family's values and culture . from which you may have been brought up with, accustomed to. This is also spiritual abuse; he is taking away your right to be your own person.

Prejudices

The abuser often harbours red-necked attitudes, backward ideas, ignorant and archaic ways and will bully the innocent ., having homophobic attitudes against gay, lesbian and transgender . people, or people of different races, religions or the disabled or poor. He will maliciously attack . the unsuspecting verbally, emotionally and/or physically.

Sexual . Abuse

He takes nude photos when you are unaware- against your will, he hides the video camera and takes videos of you having sex . with him. He then uses it as a tool to blackmail . you with later or for his own perverse pleasure. He forces sex on you against your will- without your consent, in other words rape or forces himself on you especially when you are sick, or he may use sexual acts that are perverse to you. He may use extreme force and physical . abuse, threatening you till you are helpless .. He may force you to have sex with others for his own self- gratification. He may force you to go on diets of salad to maintain your weight for his own gratification and control. Be aware that sexual abuse could also be happening within the home to children.

Physical . Abuse

He hits you either with his fist or an object, throws hot cups of coffee at you, throws food about, punches holes in the wall, burns you with his cigarette, pushes you around and pulls you by the hair, holds a loaded gun to your head, spits in your face, pours his urine on you. Then when you try to ring for help rips the phone out of the wall and tampers with your car by disabling it or by leaving very little fuel in it or he may sell your car, so you can't escape. Later he may give you flowers to apologise and tell you for the hundredth time he won't do it again or he may tell you that you asked for it and you provoked it. He threatens to kill you or your children, your parents or neighbours. He may drive you into oncoming traffic, threatening to kill you and your children with him. He smashes your belongings and any treasured items and tips house upside down after you've tidied it.

The abuser may hurt your pets, kicking the pet, turning the bird cage upside down, or smashing the fish tank, being cruel. He screams and yells at you or your children and even at the neighbours. Drives you to a deserted area and leaves you there in the dark with the children. Threatens and pours fuel around the home to burn down your home or smashes his fist through the wall or your head. There are many ways a person can be abused all of

TYPES OF ABUSE

which are not all written down here as I believe you understand the gist.

The abuser also can take out murder suicide . on his family, so you stay out of fear. I was constantly hiding bullets a regular occurrence or me hiding us in bushes at night to protect ourselves and then sleeping with one eye open every night. Murder-suicide can happen often after leaving . an abusive relationship .. It is now heard of, as it is now becoming more of a regular part of news reports. The abuser can be selfish and not think or care . about anyone least of all his family. Do take all threats seriously and take measures to get help before it is too late. The abuser could very well have mental health problems that need professional . assistance; this is "not" something you can fix at all. Do not kid yourself that you can help him, or that he will change.

Neglect .

Does not allow you and your children to have the basic necessities; whether it be a tidy and sanitary home, lack of food, clothing, medication ., adequate shelter, school . equipment, creating unnecessary hardship . and suffering as if in a third world country. He ensures (makes sure) he gets new clothes and the very best of everything. He takes away the children's pillows or toys. **Please Note:** There are of course situations where families are struggling financially to make ends meet due to poor employment prospects or a family business struggling; whereby parents are having financial hardship paying rent or mortgages and trouble putting food on the table; this of course is a very different understandable situation. This is not abuse, this is hardship, where the government should step in.

Extreme Hoarding (subtle and unintentional form of abuse)

Hoarding may be of items, pets and even rubbish, which plays havoc with the smooth running of a home, even though at one time the home may have been initially tidy. People hoard for various reasons over loss of a loved one- filling their home with things to fill the empty void, or having grown up with little, so things then become a value of sorts. The hoarding can make the home unsanitary ., disorganised and thus uninhabitable. Subsequently, hoarding detrimentally affects the lives of all family members, emotionally and physically. Disharmony, arguments and friction can result as not everyone wants to live like this. Hoarding is usually done gradually over a long period of time, so may not have been viewed as a problem earlier in the piece, it just really creeps up. Hoarding is not done with intentions of harming the family, so one must still have some compassion for the hoarder; however, it still puts the family at grave risk health wise and emotionally (they would naturally feel embarrassed and inadequate to their peers) socially they are unable to bring friends home to visit and may even be bullied by their peers.

Many of us have hoarded in some stage in our lives in varying degrees. Having experienced this with loved ones, I can tell you that, getting cross, shaming, asking and expecting someone to stop their habit and change is simply not going to work. They will need to see specially trained psychologists/ therapists who are qualified to help in this area.

Munchausen By Proxy

I'm not going to go into this particular form of abuse in a big way here as there are many facets to Munchausen By Proxy. Having seen this first hand with two once family members it is extremely disturbing stuff. The abuser continually takes you and the children to the doctors thereby telling you and the doctors that there is something wrong with members of the family even if that is not the case. He wants the doctors to run unnecessary tests and asks doctor for unnecessary medications. Always self-diagnosing the family and constantly telling you there is something wrong with you physically or mentally. This can be very dangerous for the victims involved .. This paranoid . and attention . seeking action is also a mental condition that needs treating. It is seen also as a criminal action when a member of the family is abused in this way.

Addictions .

Addictions . could easily be viewed unintentionally as a form of abuse. Gambling can cause the family to be physically and emotionally neglected, doing without necessities or going into serious debt. Mind-altering drugs . and drunkenness can create disharmony ., dysfunction and in some instances physical . and emotional abuse within families. However, there is nothing wrong with having a little flutter on the pokies or lottery or even a glass or two of alcohol . with your dinner whilst socialising. It is only wrong when it gets out of hand- becomes obsessive and the abuser becomes self-centred and then everyone else starts to suffer due to this. In my mind, I feel it could also be viewed as a slow-paced suicide . to oneself and a disinigration of family, truly a cry for help. Having said this, I have some friends who like more than a couple of drinks they are sound in mind. It comes down to what a person can handle, not everyone that drinks or likes to a flutter to play bingo/pokies is an abuser.

Are your alarm bells ringing?

To be an abuser he may use just a few of these acts mentioned, which still makes him an abuser. If you feel this and the alarm bells ring, listen to them, act on it, intuition is your best guide. Do not stay in denial . hoping it will improve and the abuse will just go away. Always trust your gut instinct.

Something I have come to learn over time and through my own experience and observation is your abuser may not just be your spouse; it could be your workplace ., society, justice system, police

TYPES OF ABUSE

., child welfare, school . teachers, judges, the clergy, doctors, children in the playground even your friends.

Be ever alert, and aware know your rights ., sometimes abuse comes over ever so subtly. You may not see it until it is too late. Sometimes even our abusers don't know that they are our abusers, and some are just in plain denial . or keep promising to change or saying they don't have a problem that you are the problem. This is extremely unfair and whilst this lack of care . attitude . with them remains then the relationship . is doomed to fail. One person cannot pick up the other persons slack; they can't make it work on their own. Unless the other person cooperates it really is just a waste of time. Change begins with you not them; you cannot change anyone.

Then there are some who know very well that what they are doing is very wrong and have absolutely no intention of improving or changing. If something bothers you and they keep on doing it knowing full well of your feelings and value system, they don't act like they care . how you think or feel. It could be someone constantly 'sabotaging' working against you and your value system, you may feel they don't respect . you; they don't appreciate your worth and disregard everything important to you. Where there is zero cooperation there is zero commitment from this person.

Is your relationship . ruled by power, dominance and control and every day is a battle? Do they shut you down as soon as you talk and regularly put you down? They are arrogant . and never believe they do anything wrong, they rarely if ever say they are sorry, especially when they should if they have done wrong. In the meantime, you feel helpless ., defeated ., have invested so much and now feel resentful . and consequently want to give up and why not... They are not playing by the rules; it is not an equal partnership or playing field. Ask yourself will you ever be their equal in their eyes? If the answer is no, then what are you doing? *"It is hard to see how love even gets a 'look in,' in such a relationship."* They keep changing the goal posts. If a person is not willing to emotionally improve and acknowledge their part in the relationship, they will not grow, then this is a futile situation. *"Don't be in denial . (do not kid yourself) any longer. For as long as they believe they are perfect nothing changes, you cannot change them, end of story. "*

Again, you can only change yourself and this is often not enough to save the relationship .. These types of people always believe they are better and above everyone else. They really need to look in the mirror at their attitude . and take a wake-up pill before it's too late and they find their partner is leaving . and has had enough. Unless both parties are committed to change and whilst they don't acknowledge they have a problem then nothing improves. It is just

TYPES OF ABUSE

a vicious never-ending cycle. A most frustrating and exhausting relationship that would feel not worth bothering about. Especially if your partner is not willing to take on board that he or she is not perfect and therefore is not cooperating. I have been there more times than I wished, so I know full well.

If you are 'unappreciated,' taken for granted, why stay with someone who isn't really into you, or invested in your relationship? A relationship . of constant tug of war, is not what any relationship should be going through. Remember the old saying *"There are plenty of fish in the sea."* There are plenty of decent people that would treat you right if given the chance. It takes two to make or break a relationship. Don't be the scapegoat taking all the blame. By always taking the blame you are disrespecting yourself. You can't work alone . on a relationship, it just is not possible.

How much longer are you prepared to keep flogging a dead horse, your relationship .? Nothing's going to change, and you know it. A partnership really? Why keep doing it? You are better than that and deserve some happiness before it's too late. How long can you keep taking the blame? Knowing they have no intention of changing and improving, the relationship is doomed? Your partner may only realise how good he had it after you've gone, by then it's too late. So, lift your head up and do whatever it is you need to do to for you!

Statistics on various forms of abuse

Why are statistics . important?

Statistics are important in many different areas of life. Statistics are a gauge or a yard stick if you like; giving us something to go by for looking at the whole big picture, of how big a problem it really is. However, regarding abuse, it gives us a closer idea of how many people are affected. It really is an eye opener when you see it all in black and white. It is no longer hearsay but fact.

What are the statistics . on different forms of abuse?

According to Family Violence Prevention Fund: -

- Did you know one in every three women worldwide are victims of sexual ., physical ., emotional, and other abuse during their lifetime? If you were to add that up around the world each year it would amount to 1 billion abused women.

According to UN Commission on Human Rights: -

- Sexual abuse statistics . vary between countries and reports but are consistently alarming: Research indicates that up to 36% of girls and 29% of boys have suffered child sexual . abuse; up to 46% girls and 20% boys have experienced

TYPES OF ABUSE

sexual coercion. (*The 57th session of the UN Commission on Human Rights*)

According to the World Health Organisation: -

- There are studies from many countries in all regions of the world that show up to 80 to 98 % of children suffer physical . punishment in their homes, with a third or more experiencing severe punishment resulting from the use of implements. *(World Health Organization (WHO)*

- That worldwide, approximately 40 million children below the age of 15 are subjected to child abuse each year. (*World Health Organization (WHO) 2001*)

- That 150 million girls and 73 million boys under 18 experienced some form of forced sexual . intercourse or violence .. (WHO, 2002)

- It is estimated that 150 million girls and 73 million boys under 18 experienced forced sexual . intercourse or other forms of sexual violence . during 2002. *(WHO, 2004)*

- Suicide is the third leading cause of death in adolescents around the world. (*WHO, 2002*)

According to Save the Children: -

- Approximately a million children worldwide have been imprisoned.

What are the correlations on different forms of abuse?

Abuse can be interconnected or intertwined, with other forms of abuse; so, one can experience several forms of abuse at any one time or at some point in their lives. Because there is such dysfunction within abusive families there is often more going on than meets the eye. Emotional/Psychological . and Physical . abuse can often go hand in hand. Abusers are controlling and often believe it is their right to curse, swear, yell and assault by hitting, bang, bashing, kicking or even murder. The abuser may get so angry that he is going to kick you, and then he is going to kick the dog too and anything else in the way. Nothing and no one is off-limits to them.

Victims can cower in fear and be vulnerable . to all sorts of situations at home, school ., work and the public. They don't believe themselves worthy of any good anywhere they go. They could believe it is their fault things go wrong and readily take on that incorrect tag of blame and become anyone's scapegoat. Without professional . help they will continue to remain victims.

Professional therapists . will try to unravel the entangled ball of abuse that one has. Handling each issue either one by one or all

TYPES OF ABUSE

issues as a whole; depending on the person and the therapists' method and expertise.

Where can physical . and emotional . abuse and neglect . happen?
What I am about to tell you is not so that you become paranoid ., just so that you are aware. Basically, it can happen anywhere even right under your very nose. You could easily be totally oblivious to the happenings.

It can happen (privately or publicly): -
- Within the family home.
- Within foster care. .
- At a relative's home.
- Within sects and cults.
- Within communes.
- In hospitals and institutions.
- In nursing homes.
- At school. .
- Local park
- In the water at the beach.
- In the bushes.
- At church.
- Behind or in the toilet facilities.
- Camping trips
- Caravan/Trailer parks/Mansions

BREAKING THE CHAIN ON ABUSE

- Sleepovers
- Parties
- Cars/vehicles
- Work

To the victim, you have every right to: -

- Be respected.
- Not live in fear.
- Not be manipulated, intimidated or threatened.
- Not be hurt physically and emotionally.
- Not be hit, sworn or spat at.
- Not be put down, demeaned or belittled.
- Not have your children physically or emotionally abused or neglected.
- Not have your children loved and shown appropriate physical . affection. .
- Be loved and shown appropriate physical . affection. .
- Receive adequate medical care. .
- Feel comfortable, at ease, not nervous and on edge, walking on egg shells.
- Have contact with friends.

TYPES OF ABUSE

- Have contact with your family.
- Be able to work.
- Have hobbies, sport or recreation.
- Not have to do all the chores on your own.
- Be able to pamper yourself, doing nice things for yourself- paint your nails, wear make-up.
- Be able to go shopping.
- Have some "me time;" quality time for yourself.
- Be able to go to church or choose not to go to church.
- Be able to drink a glass or two of alcohol, . (provided you are not pregnant . or on any medication . where it is affected by the use of alcohol or it is not your religious belief).
- Have a differing opinion.
- Be able to make executive decisions.
- Not be controlled.
- Not have to answer for everything.
- Not have own personal space.
- Not have to have sexual . relations if one is tired or sick.

- Be able sleep and even sleep . in, provided of course you do not have small children to attend to early or work time to adhere to.

- Have yourself and your children cared about adequately.

- Have your children adequately educated.

- Be able to learn and educate yourself.

- Have adequate food, clothing, shelter and necessities.

- Be able to have some nice affordable items.

- Be able to listen to music and enjoy wholesome entertainment.

- Be able to rest.

- Have a say, be able to make decisions.

- Be able to laugh, be angry or cry.

- Live in peace . and harmony.

What triggers abuse? (Why people abuse)

It can be the way one is brought up being disciplined with abuse, the influence of one's own parents. It can be influences ever so subtle like what we see happening as we grow up on violent . television programs, violent computer games, the people we associate with *gang bully mentality,* one could have an acquired brain injury (known to cause violent outbursts). Other people influenced may have been unfortunate enough to have been around violence . such as war, or the influence of substance abuse (mind altering drugs . or alcohol . or a combination of the both substances which can increase the chances of becoming violent).

With or without substance abuse in their system there is still absolutely no excuse for abuse. Some other triggers may be physical health and/or mental health conditions, stress, work/family or financial pressures or anger issues that need immediate treatment or vital medication .. The person could have a mental illness . that requires medication. This person may not be taking medication regularly or may have themselves totally off medication.

It is vitally important to never mess around with something one knows nothing of. Doctors are qualified to make a diagnosis, instead leave it for the experts to assess the situation and give relevant treatment. With respect ., these professionals . are the ones who spent the many years training and studying their field of specialty, not you nor I.

For the abuser to have an outburst it can be over a variety of things; little or big or even over nothing. They want their meal on time, don't like the meal, their partner is wearing too much make-up or even the opposite-not dressing sexy enough, the children are too noisy, they want more sex, work pressures, financial issues, cult expectations, addictions, mental health issues. None of these are excuses to abuse. But the abuser does not really need a reason to lash out, they just do out of being controlling. Again, there is absolutely no excuse for any abuse.

Avoiding getting into a violent relationship .? (Observe-Signs to look out for)

Once you are in an abusive relationship . it can be very hard to get out of it and if there are children involved ., harder still and you risk jeopardising their lives. Before having children with this person or anyone for that matter, get to know them very well.

What Is grooming?

- The "predator" grooms the victim it is usually done subtlety and over an extended, period of time. Grooming is a calculated, sly conniving method; baiting or luring if you like, to catch their prey. How do they do this? There can be things, that are on, "the too good to be true scale." He opens car doors for you, showers you with flowers and expensive gifts and then changes immediately after he has you. And of course, there are countless genuine honest decent gentlemen who do open doors and shower one with gifts it's knowing to decipher the real from the phoney. But that is just it, the predator masquerades as a decent gentleman. In online dating it is prevalent too where the predator fleeces the unsuspecting of their life savings. Know it for what it is a predatory act- an ability to con the vulnerable of their soul, their savings and whatever else they can get out of them.

Before committing to a relationship . look out for: -

- How he treats others his family and friends.
- Watch out for tendencies of possessiveness, does he keep tabs on you, smothers you- not giving you room to breathe, or your own space?

Questions to ask yourself: -

- Does he isolate you from your family and friends?
- Does he constantly ring you to check up on you on you?
- Does he monopolise . your time (wanting you all to himself)?
- Has he got controlling tendencies and try to make most decisions not really giving you an equal say?
- Is he dominant and takes over a lot, not allowing you to make some of your own decisions- devaluing your opinion?

Food for Thought*: -* (There are sometimes some things far too subtle to see clearly. Save yourself some heartache).

- Does it feel too good to be true?

- What does your gut say? It is usually your first instinct that is right. We all have these senses, we just need to be observant and learn how to use intuition.

The abuse aftermath

I am not a specialist in this field and only speak from my own experience. But **I believe domestic violence, sexual abuse and bullying cause mental health issues and can cause suicide. I also believe those who commit abuse also have mental health issues.** Our children are at risk for their adult future if they are exposed and not removed from abusive situations.

Due to our past experience with abuse. With my daughter we have a quiet understanding that I will only ever step in if she is being used and abused. I also had a quiet yet respectful conversation with my daughters' partner about looking after her well. I believe we need to do all we can to ensure our adult children are well taken care of without us interfering or meddling.

TYPES OF ABUSE

"Non-violence is not a garment to be put on and off at will. Its seat is in the heart and it must be an inseparable part of our being".

-Mahatma Gandhi

Chapter 4 History of Abuse

"What the World Needs Now Is Love Sweet Love" lyrics by Hal David and Burt Bacharach

Abuse in our society .

Abuse can be intergenerational; going down through the ages from generation to generation. From our forefathers to their forefathers on to their forefathers before them and so on. The human and financial cost being in astronomical proportions not to mention the human cost. Unless we break that chain, it will continue to go down the line of generations to come.

Abuse comes in a myriad of forms. There is abuse of the system, abuse of mankind, abuse of nature, abuse of power, abuse of religious doctrine. When we turn on the news it seems it's nothing but bad news. Some of us may have even become desensitised to abuse. It has become a part of everyday life- the norm. It's on televisions, in homes, in society, on computer games even in our school grounds. Abuse is like an epidemic, it rips through countries, causing havoc, upset, maiming . and death to billions, costing billions also.

People incite violence . and hatred against different races simply because of their culture . and dress, many cultures wear their national dress with pride such as the Scottish Kilt, Islam Burqa, Indian Saree, Indian Turbans, Arabic Hijab, Jewish Kippah, German

Lederhosen (Britches), French Beret etc. How very boring if we were all the same. Instead we should be embracing multiculturism and respect . beliefs of others. However, in saying that, sensibility must rein in too, that we will not tolerate and condone ill treatment of women and children such as stoning people to death and circumcision . of young women. Personally, in line with being an advocate of preventing abuse, I do find woman wearing the Hijab somewhat restrictive, that is just my opinion, as you too will have your own opinion. I do understand, that such attire is also worn for climatic conditions. Culturally, many women take great pride in wearing this hijab and if that is their choice then after all who am I, to say what they should or shouldn't wear; this is their right. As long as one does not feel controlled into wearing what they choose not to, there should not be a problem. There is though a women's movement in Islam called "White Wednesdays", they are a group of women who are moving to change old outdated laws. These women want to be able to choose what they want to wear. A friend was commenting that she saw a gentleman with his wife enjoying the beach in singlet and shorts and there was his wife all covered from head to toe in stifling heat. It really did not seem fair to us.

At the end of the day, we really do have to get on the same page as each other. All countries need to live in harmony with each other, showing kindness and goodness to all and above all love, equality and understanding. The song *"What the World Needs Now Is Love*

Sweet Love" written by Hal David and Burt Bacharach resonates with me, it is ever so true. More love, generosity . and compassion . are ever so needed in this world.

The victims of abuse may suffer; poverty, disease, slavery, hunger, homelessness, prostitution, child labour. Then there are the war atrocities like what went on in the holocaust. Such atrocities stem from dictators and systems that run rife with greed ., inciting hate, power and control. Other forms of abuse are road rage, car hijacking, and terrorism . on our planes, where innocent . people are affected. When theft . happens in stores, the rest of society pays the price. Then there are some who abuse the system through theft (embezzlement . and fraud .) social security entitlements and the like; it hits the pockets of us the taxpayers. Taxpayers fall victim too and feel the force of the abuse. People can't afford . their electricity, rent and even groceries. Mortgage payments then go up, now many can't meet their payments, homes are then repossessed, for some even end up homeless.

To illustrate how desensitised our world is becoming; let me give you a prime example of how we feed our children's brains with cartoons of abuse; the caveman with club in hand and dragging his woman by the hair and Sylvester the cat seems always to survive. Hence, the cats have nine lives theory! We all would laugh at this; the world trivialises and down plays abuse. Children then get the wrong view of life that also that Road Runner and Sylvester are immortal, and these are pretty tame cartoons compared to nowadays. Nothing wrong with many cartoons but we do have to supervise and see what messages this sends out. So, you see our society accepts abuse in cartoons and consequently turns a blind eye to the realities that it does exist in real life.

And what of these violent . television programs with murder and mayhem? For some, *"every night"* violence . is allowed to come into one's home. We even invite it in to our homes. *A double standard wouldn't you say!* We allow our children to play violent computer games. Again, we invite violence into our homes.

Abuse is like a raging fire being given the green light taking upon millions in its path worldwide. The fire of abuse needs to be stamped out. Nelson Mandela set a standard for our world. One could stand on their soap box and stand up for human rights . and if it only helps one tiny corner of our world, then that's at least something. If every man and woman stood up for those suffering in various ways, the world would be a far nicer place.

Patterns within families .

Patterns of abuse can also reflect in our everyday lives. If we were abused as children, then we will either copy that abuse onto our children and spouses or partner ourselves up with an abusive partner. Simply because this is all we have ever known. We don't feel worthy or deserving of anything better. We may feel attracted to the strong character of a person and find that you choose a similar person again and again which may not be advantageous to you in the long run. Maybe you do need to choose someone gentle, quiet, sensitive and compassionate. I know what you are saying, *"That sounds like the perfect partner!"* But hey maybe it is time to re-think this.

Regarding children

If a child is physically beaten or continually browbeaten with regular put downs and hurtful words such as *"You are stupid, and you will never amount to anything."* The child can end up believing it and it becomes their reality. Some families have a scapegoat, usually the innocent . child or even the adult. Having someone to become a scapegoat allows for incorrect blame and abuse to be hurled toward the scapegoat child or spouse, where it also allows the abuse to go into denial . to justify abuse. In some families there is a black sheep or scapegoat that just does not fit in and blame is convenient to put on them- the victim.

Remember the victim's self-esteem is already rock bottom, they are vulnerable; . so subsequently they often can make poor choices. Like the child school . yard victim, adults too, attract bullies later in life. It's almost as if the abuser "predator" can sense and smell the fear and vulnerability on the victim "prey ." and targets them as their next victim "spouse".

HISTORY OF ABUSE

It is with that victim that they thrive on violence .. I believe it to be that primal. Windows are the eyes to the soul; when one comes to know a predator, you can literally see a certain look in their eyes, similarly to predatory animals. You wouldn't leave predatory animals such as a lion out on the streets, then one does have to wonder why our courts are so lax to let these predators out on our streets. This is in fact a dangerous situation. Can such people be rehabilitated? Maybe, maybe not...

The abuser is the bully and is in denial . and thinks one more hit or harsh word won't hurt too much or maybe they truly get so angry that they just don't care .. They may not know the life-damaging implications of their actions on the innocent . victim. Or maybe they have never had a good role model to show them how to behave appropriately and hence obviously lack anger management skills. There are so many variables here. *This is not, however, an excuse to abuse another. As most of us do know right from wrong. There is absolutely no excuse; abuse is wrong- nothing condones abuse.*

If in life one finds they feel lonely ., empty and unloved, so the kindness of a stranger can be all that it takes to lure the victim into the predators . (abusers) lair. This could be a child who is outcast from the rest of the herd "family" or a single mother (lonely, doing it hard alone) looking after her child. The predator abuser may stalk an elderly person or disabled person sick or frail, unable to verbalise or tend to themselves or stand up for themselves. Predators look for the weakest link, parents not fully plugged in to all their children. They look for the child or person in a family that they know is easy prey. The vulnerable ., gullible, trusting, naive, innocent . and/or frail; those unable to tend to their own needs are the ones that need protection from predators. Without meaning to fear monger, but bring attention to this serious situation; again, it is so primal, predators sniff out their prey . and then hunt their victim down.

Very important: *"Predators even stalk families that are struggling as their prey, parents beware."* They wait for the right moment and even groom "trick" the unsuspecting. They are a master at what they do.

About sexual . abuse in families (incest) *by relative or with close trusted family friend, clergy, caregiver*

When the abuser forces him on a child, sexual . molestation sometimes with or without sodomy, penetration. He the abuser preys on the weak, young, quiet, innocent . and vulnerable . against their will. Sometimes using brute force, intimidation, threats, guilt . tripping, sometimes subtly and gently coercing a child telling them, *"It is our little secret don't tell anyone, or I will give you a toy later, or you will find it nice,"* or *"I just want to show my love to you"* or finally *"I'll kill your Mum"*- **enough to manipulate any child into**

silence. By calculatingly deceiving the child by saying to the child about it 'feeling nice' puts the *onus* on the child, thus making the child feel responsible, for the child to incorrectly bear the blame and therefore not speak u. In actuality, the abuser uses this form of manipulation to take the heat off themselves and keep victim mute.

A child must always be believed that this is real. Only in rare cases is this made up, but it has been known to happen. Sometimes within families there is much denial . and disbelief by other family members that the perpetrator could do such a thing. The perpetrator (abuser) holds a lot of power over a child towering height, cunning, strength and knowledge.

The child can also feel guilt . and worry that they will break up the family or they may be the cause of upset and distress. The child may have nightmares, become withdrawn, not wanting to go near the perpetrator. A child victim can end up feeling bad and dirty like it was their fault. Sometimes a child may crave for affection ., and may act out by being promiscuous or playing with their genitals or act out by playing with other children in a sexual . way. This should noted as a cry for help not naughtiness.

The child might complain about being sore or itchy, it is possible for them to contract STD's (Sexually Transmitted Diseases). A child could also be drugged by the abuser, so they can use them for their own disgusting . gratification. The child may even wet themselves out of nervousness, their grades may suffer. Sadly, in some cases the child is blamed for making it all up or bringing it on themselves another reason why they don't tell anyone. A child may feel so guilty and dirty that they wash themselves compulsively causing recurrent thrush/ eczema. This obsessive-compulsive disorder of over washing can continue throughout their adult years, along with nightmares, flashbacks, sexual . problems of frigidity or promiscuity. Symptoms are a cry for help.

What to do when a child has been sexually abused

Listen to your child, never berate. Reassure, comfort them that you will ensure that it won't happen again and that it was never their fault. Report incident immediately to police . and children's services. Explain to your child that you will need to take them for a medical examination- stay with them through the process. Counselling . is also most imperative, see a recommended child psychologist, you can obtain a referral from your family doctor.

Child psychologists . can find out a lot of what the child has been through by means of child play or art therapy which allows the child to express themselves in a caring non- threatening manner. Lots of TLC (tender loving care .) will be needed; you may also need to notify the child's teacher. By informing the teacher, the teacher can be sensitive and understanding to what the child has been through and alert and aware of the situation.

Sometimes the parents may not find out till the child has grown into an adult, therefore parents need to stop blaming themselves. Sometimes too a child could be very good at hiding things; believing it is their fault, resulting in them never telling anyone.

The child can't see the point in telling anyone because nothing can be done- they wrongly believe. Parents too can feel helpless . not knowing what to do and like the child be afraid of the outcome. Parents may not want to hear those awful words from their child that they have been molested because this is one of their worst fears, so parents may avoid asking those difficult poignant and painful questions with their child. It can be painful for the parent to hear their child has been molested- *I hear you*. These parents should not be judged, instead they need to be supported.

What can happen later?
Police may interview the child along with the parents then a police . report . made and statement taken. Stay with your child throughout this process as it can be overwhelming for them. The perpetrator may or may not be charged and arrested. Usually corroborating evidence is needed- other witnesses. The perpetrator being very careful making sure there are no witnesses, to make the child appear deceitful.

In some instances, the child is required to testify in court. Such a decision of whether to put the child in court would be daunting for the parent, as the child has been through too much already. If such a situation is incestuous many a family has been known to break up, I so get this- this would not be easy to do. Really what is more important, the break up and admittance of a dysfunctional family? You haven't failed. You've only failed if you don't stand up for your child. Isn't your child important here? Maybe the perpetrator is a loving caring family member and chances are they are, but they still committed a crime against the child; they may be able to get 'help' treatment. But helping the child first is paramount and comes first. You can still show care, concern for the perpetrator, but the child here comes first. The child, "your child is priority." Put yourself in your child's shoes that if you don't attend to this, there will always be a wedge of sorts in your relationship with your child; your child will hold some sort of resentment, holding back- you will sense this in their behaviours. The last thing you want is your child resenting you. The child could easily act out or could end up with emotional problems or mental illness.

Adult victims can join support . groups such as Survivors of Sexual Child Abuse or see a trained psychologist that specialises in this area. Relaxation and meditation CDs can also be help. Lots of TLC and sensitivity is also needed from their partners to help them heal.

HISTORY OF ABUSE

Society .'s perception of women and their roles

There is also the old perception still carried by some; that women do the domestics; and the sole caring of the children, stay home and do their duties, with no say regarding finances and money . doled out to them, tightly reined and budgeted.

There are some women who don't wish to aspire to be anything but mothers and wives, and they are happy doing home duties; taking great pride in homemaking and being house proud and that is just fine if that is what they (the woman) wants. Some women feel content- without the desire to educate themselves through doing courses or training. If this sits fine with the woman, then all is well. However, if one's partner is controlling, and this goes beyond her rights ., will and wishes, then this can easily become abuse. Even if ever so subtle.

Addictive behaviours

Addictions . may be seen as an unintentional form of abuse or as the pinnacle to where abuse starts. Obviously, not the case for every situation. Gambling can cause the family to be physically neglected, doing without necessities or going into debt. Mind-altering drugs . or drunkenness can create disharmony ., dysfunction- in some instances physical ., emotional and/or sexual . abuse within families. Children could copy their parents, carers or role model's addictive behaviours into their own adulthood; ie., obsessive drinking, gambling, drug taking, sexual . addictions ..

Addiction can be financially/ emotionally draining and damaging to the abusers' family.

***Seeking help for addictions* .**

The addicted person may be in denial .-not believing or facing that they have a problem preventing them from seeking help. The abuser/addict may also feel some embarrassment . or fear- wanting to hide . it from others, thinking they have a handle on it or can fix it. Professional help is needed. If you think you have a problem with an addiction you are not alone . help is at hand. There are many support/ therapy . groups that can help such as AA Alcoholic Anonymous, Gamblers Anonymous, Drug Rehabilitation Centres, Sexual addictions ., Eating disorders clinics. Loving support and understanding from their partners is also helpful.

***STAR 5**

"These are the four abuses: desire to succeed in order to make oneself famous; taking credit for the labors of others; refusal to correct one's errors despite advice; refusal to change one's ideas despite warnings."

- **Confucius**

HISTORY OF ABUSE

Notes:

Chapter 5 Who Is Usually the Abuser?

The abuser

There are some instances where victims and bullies were never abused as children. Perpetrators of abuse may be men and/or women but in most instances of abuse it is men. However, in saying that men in general get an unfair bad rap, when women too are capable and more than often the abuser. There can even be both parents as abusers. We really need to keep things in perspective. Although there are some grey areas the statistical fact is, it is predominantly the male gender that is the abuser and also predominantly step parents. In saying that too, more often than not blood biological parents can be abusers too. Even by standing back and knowing what the abuser is doing and knowing abuse is going on and doing nothing about it, one could be thought of in a sense as being indirectly abusive, especially if you have the power to protect the vulnerable or effect change. Though many indirect abusers are really victims also.

Sadly, for some children it can be both parents that are abusers. Abusers can deal out physical ., mental abuse, neglect, threatening behaviour, cruelty, sexual . abuse rape of other adults or molestation of children whether family or not. Abusers are bullies.

Some abusers were abused by their own parents when they were children and it seems to have a firm hold on their being whereby they dole out abuse just as their parents had done to them and then their parents before them. Just because you had a tough childhood abuse-wise doesn't mean you will become the same. Whilst it's true that one may be predisposed (genetically or through learned behaviour) to becoming an abuser, it doesn't have to become ones' reality. You can be in control of your destiny, if you choose to, through seeking professional . help. On the contrary many adult victims, who have been abused as children, don't go on to abuse children. So again, I say there is *"Absolutely No Excuse for Abuse!"* as abusers can seek help to improve their behaviour. Help is out there if the abuser is serious enough in wanting to improve their behaviour. The abuser may or may not be in denial of their own behaviour. Personally, I find it very hard to believe that an abuser is not aware that they have a problem.

What help is available for abusers?

- Specialised therapy with Psychiatrist/Psychologist
- Anger management courses
- Parenting courses to teach how to discipline without conforming to abuse.
- Reading self-help books . along with going to therapy.
- Some abusers deliberately abuse, and some do not. Sure, seek help for the abuser, but primarily seek help for the abused.

Why do abusers get away with abuse?

The abuser can be so charming and plausible and liked by so many, that the victim feels it is pointless reaching out for help. They are good at manipulating; by lying and fooling people with their charm and cunning behaviour. Some abusers can seem or be at different times the loveliest of people. Truthfully no one is all bad. Is it any wonder why many victims are never believed and feel despondent? They have already been victimised and fear being victimised all over again.

Abusers can appear upstanding citizens helping in the community masquerading as volunteers. They can be heavily involved . in the church putting on a front that things are chummy. The abusers could easily be clergy, teachers, doctors, scout leaders, sports coach, youth worker; they can even be relatives of the victim parents, grandparents, aunts, uncles, close friends, baby sitters. Even though we may not want to face that, it can be so hard to wrap ones' brain around. It is a myth to say that it is only a stranger to be careful of, it is usually someone known to the family to be equally aware of. There is no need to go on a witch's hunt, don't get paranoid . here just be aware.

Many family members can be in shock and denial . when they finally do find out and some like to hide . the fact as it is a scandal that the family in their mind can ill afford . to have known by others. So often victims feel trapped, defeated ., alone . and helpless ..

WHO IS USUALLY THE ABUSER?

With the abuser, it may not be cut and dry as psychological and emotional disorders as well as chemical physical . disorders can often play a role. While psychological disorders such as Borderline Personality Disorder, Bi Polar Disorder, Schizophrenia, Postnatal/Postpartum Depression ., ADHD Attention Deficit Hyperactivity Disorder and other types of disorders or other imbalances of a hormonal nature or brain chemical imbalances may play a role in some situations it may not necessarily be the case in every situation. Should a loved one seem to have a disorder, it is up to the professional . to make the diagnosis and treatment required. Treatment must be sought immediately through a General Practitioner (Family Doctor) who will make a written referral for the patient to see a Specialist either a Psychologist or Psychiatrist. Having said this, it is not an excuse for abuse.

In Australia, if cost . is a concern, there is the Medicare system whereby you may only have to pay a minimal gap fee, or you may get back a large proportion of the fee (money .) back. In other countries I am unsure. If you or your loved one lives in another country speak to a doctor you feel comfortable with and state your financial situation and maybe they can do something to help you out in some way with reasonable costings. Often there are free counselling services offered by religious . organisations and such. It is not an impossible situation, obstacles can be overcome there are many caring kind-hearted professional . people that will do all they can if you let them know your situation has some difficulties.

***STAR 5**

Postnatal (aka Postpartum) depression . in mothers
It irks me to have to put this section in this chapter, but we have to be aware that Postnatal depression can play a role in abuse. Naturally, no loving mother wants to abuse their child; this applies to new father's doing it alone without support. Postnatal depression is suffered by many new mothers. I myself suffered it so badly at one point. My screaming baby, my first child, would not stop crying no matter what I did, and this went on for days and months, to the point I was sleep deprived and running on empty. Oftentimes it felt like I was doing it alone, my ex-husband was no help, plus with seven stepchildren- I was stressed to the max. My hormones were probably haywire too and back in the day there was no support either for postnatal depression that I was aware of. I would check regularly that my baby was fed, had a clean diaper, was burped and I rocked, cuddled and comforted nothing worked. I felt for a millisecond like throwing my baby out the window in desperation, if I did that I would have surely gone with him. I was often at the hospital or doctors as I didn't know what was wrong with him. I did get some sleep as the doctor put my child on a barbiturate that would knock him out for days it scared me to see

WHO IS USUALLY THE ABUSER?

my child like this, but the doctor assured me that he would be alright and that he would wean him off the meds. With such enormous stress I can see how some babies can get mistreated 'abused;' it's not right but it is understandable. Mothers have been known to take the life of themselves and/or their baby. Mothers must seek professional treatment and partners and family members must ensure they receive this help for the wellbeing of mother, child and family. Help is available. If you have a young neighbour doing it tough with bub, why not offer some help.

Mothers suffering postnatal depression, you are not alone . in feeling that way, there are many mothers also dealing with depression. Bonding doesn't always happen straight away. It is incorrect to believe all parents fall instantly in love with their babies. The child may have come at a bad time, when finances are already stretched. You could be feeling resentful or scared . with the day to day pressures on you. It is daunting also, having to deal with exhaustion from broken sleep or sleep deprivation ., trying to juggle family and all their many needs/wants and making sound decisions.

Babies don't come with instruction manuals, whilst self-help books are available. Oftentimes during stress remembering information goes. Let alone the mental energy to read self-help books when one is existing on little sleep, depressed and overwhelmed.

The constant crying, not knowing how to settle bub; trying to work out what is wrong with your baby, it can all be stressing. You may be so stressed you literally feel like throwing the baby out with the bath water and who can blame you! You haven't had a moment to yourself, you look a mess, you feel a mess. Naturally you would be feeling depressed. Is it any wonder you feel like this? Trying to be the perfect mother and everything to everyone is hard, if not impossible. You can't be there for everyone. Do you have the support . of your partner, family, friends, or other mothers that understand? You may also have a hormone imbalance? Get it checked with your doctor.

If this is your first child, it's very hard not knowing if you're doing everything right, questioning your role as a mother, such as "Am I a good enough Mother?" Don't be so hard on yourself, ask for help, see your doctor, join a support . group and see if you can get some counselling. Support is so important. Try and meet and talk to other mothers, they will understand what you are going through. You are not going mad or strange. Relating to others is often helpful; one then doesn't feel so alone . or feel abnormal. If you know of someone suffering from post-natal (postpartum) depression lend them a helping hand, it is so needed, be a friend to them or a mentor.

WHO IS USUALLY THE ABUSER?

I once saw a very young lass who looked to be in her teens with two babies on our public transport boat. Both her babies were distressed; she was doing it tough alone and she looked flustered. The poor thing got looks of disdain from other passengers like *"Why can't you shut your kid up."* So, agree it was stressful for all! Having been there myself, I could see she was struggling, so moved seats to sit beside her. She allowed me to play with her other bub; which gave her free hands and then I gently patted the back of the other bub she was holding, and bub soon quietened down, she then learnt how to comfort with gentle back pats, at the time she had her hands full with both bubs crying, sometimes it can be so overwhelming trying to cope and comfort two babies. All this lass needed was kindness not scorn. After seeing this situation another sweet lass who was coping well with her one child moved to where we were seated introduced herself to this lass and encouraged her to join their children's playgroup they also swapped phone numbers. I then quietly went back to my own seat to leave the two young ladies to get acquainted. I never saw this lass again, hopefully, she is doing well. There is much we can do to help our youth. The same kindness has been bestowed on me many times by other kind-hearted mentors, so wherever necessary I pass this on. One example is an elderly lady would wait for me each morning at the bus stop on my way to work and she would help me with my knitting as I was struggling a bit. There is much we can do to help our young.

"Try a little kindness, show a little kindness" **- Performed by Glen Campbell**

Is staying in an abusive relationship, abuse?

A loving parent wouldn't ordinarily allow their child to be abused by a stranger, so then why would a parent stay in an abusive relationship . so the abuse keeps going? Aren't we by our action of staying put, indirectly and unintentionally allowing the cycle of abuse to continue? This then makes us an abuser also.

Though in all fairness, it is not easy to find the courage . or determination . to leave. One can feel powerless. Still one must build up the courage to make a commitment to remove your child/children and yourself from abuse, at least until the situation has been resolved and the abuser has had therapy. The abuser should be the one to be removed if possible.

Abusers do not have the right to: -

- To physically injure, maim or kill their loved ones or anybody else.
- To emotionally abuse their loved ones with shouting, yelling, screaming, taunts, threats, swearing, demeaning behaviour- put downs, belittling.

WHO IS USUALLY THE ABUSER?

- To deny . and neglect loved ones of healthy . food, safe shelter, adequate clothing and education.

- To deny . loved ones of love, care ., attention . and affection ..

- To deny . loved ones from friendship ., socialization, recreation and rest.

- To monopolise . a loved one's time.

- To isolate their loved ones from family and friends

- To be disrespectful . to loved ones.

Foot Note: -

I'm fairly certain in some cases, that the abuser doesn't like to be an abuser. They know what they are doing is wrong-don't doubt that, they feel trapped also. Abusers are also victims unto themselves, however *regardless of this abuse of any kind should "never be condoned," it is unacceptable "on any level," and there is no excuse.* When the abuser seeks help, they need some credit for taking that big step, they need support ., understanding and encouragement also, maybe not so much from the victim, but more so from other family members and friends.

Who can be helped?

Unfortunately, not everyone can be helped. There are numerous reasons one may not be helped. Many go back to their abuser.

Many victims remain in denial and some mentally cannot face up to the fact that maybe their marriage or relationship is not all it should be or they are ashamed or afraid of the abuser, afraid of being alone, afraid of the unknown or maybe they are immobilised and frozen with fear and shock and don't have a clue of what to do where to go and are financially strapped and they feel they don't have a strong support network. Some have strong religious beliefs and feel that it is a sin to leave their marriage. They could lack self-esteem and courage or live in the hope that things will change. Some are headstrong and independent. However, when children or pets are involved and depending on the circumstances one should call authorities or get help. Families often watch on helplessly as daughters and sisters are in abusive relationships, not knowing which way to go and that is more than understandable, it isn't always easy. With my own daughter, she is in a good relationship, however over the years I have said to her that the only time I will ever get involved is if she is being abused. We have that understanding between us. We have kept a good eye out to ensure she is safe, without interfering.

Please Note Well: - Not all of the following signs definitely mean a person is being abused. However, one or more of these signs "could" mean a person is being abused. It is usually more than one sign that a person is being abused, and for each person it could also be different. Do use common sense and try not to assume. It is important to get the facts first before accusing.

Signs of abuse (Can be one or more of the following depending on the situation)

- Unexplained bruises and abrasions. (The victim may explain away bruises by saying that they fell over or hit their head on the door knob. Or they could make excuses for their abuser's behaviour.
- If a child, they may appear unkempt.
- The person may appear nervous, jittery and/ or cower; they could be startled easily by loud noises or raised voices.
- Some behaviour's may be that they are always on the defensive and apologise a lot.
- Confused, have trouble making decisions
- Inability to concentrate.
- Low self esteem
- Underweight due to food deprivation.
- How is the state of the home; Is it extremely messy and/ or putridly dirty? (Although none of this is a sign on its own that abuse is occurring).
- Covering up body with long sleeves, turtle neck tops, make up etc

- Is the person you believe to be abused nervous around certain people; what is their behaviour around certain people?
- How does the alleged abuser behaviour around his family?
- Does something just not sit right with you and you can't put your finger on it, but you feel something is gravely wrong?

Some of my friends were brutally honest and even as much as telling me not to visit them anymore if I could not stop looking at my watch or their clock. Because it hurt them to see me that way, worrying about being out too long and upsetting my husband. It was a bitter pill to swallow to hear this from my friends, but it was the first sign for me that others knew what was going on. At first, I was hurt that they could say such a thing; and saw it as a form of rejection. But later I saw it as an alarm bell and that this was my cue that I needed to get out of the abusive relationship I was in; if we were to have any sort of meaningful happiness. My children and I could be friendless and that really was all we had; friendship that we had for the first real time. It was our solace and breather from an otherwise extremely difficult existence. To this day I thank them for this.

My parents and family did not know how bad the abuse was. I never told, and they never asked. Maybe they didn't ask as they were afraid of the answer and the pain that that answer may bring them? Sometimes there is comfort in not knowing... I also had the

WHO IS USUALLY THE ABUSER?

silly token belief of "I made my bed I should lie in it." I was also quite ashamed and embarrassed of our predicament and blamed myself.

"A man may conquer a million men in battle but he who conquers himself is, indeed the greatest of conquerors!"

-Gautama Buddha

STAR 5 *Please see Help Contacts at back of book.*

"Abuse is an insidious thing; it leaves victims and casualties in its wake."

- N J Lutter

Chapter 6 Being Good Role Models

"Teach the Children Well"- Crosby, Stills and Nash

"Teach our children well so they do not become 'abusers' of the world or 'victims' of the world."

- N J Lutter

What to do to teach our children better?

No one ever said parenting is easy. However, our children really need to be taught about abuse and its effects. This way they will have the life skills in place to help them in their own future relationships. It has been said that the first five formative years are the most important to give our children. It is the best time to train a child, as their minds are like sponges readily absorbing information good and bad. There are also the teen formative years where a child feels no longer a child and not yet an adult. This is a time in their lives where they meet a crossroads and can make either good or bad decisions that could serve them for the rest of their lives.

The responsibilities and obligations on child rearing and guidance-

Fathers giving guidance: -

- Your sons are not to hit a female (or anyone for that matter); no matter how angry they may feel- giving them a moral compass.

- Teaching son/s to regularly talk about their feelings whenever they have any worries, if not to you with someone else they can trust or a counsellor.

- Teaching son/s that it is ok to cry and that this is not a sign of weakness. .

- Teaching and showing by example to his daughter/s what a good male role model should be and what to expect in future partners (boyfriends, husbands).

The last thing a loving father would want is for his daughters to go to the first male (who may be abusive) they see that shows an inkling of interest in them because of whatever lack of attention . they need due to a deficiency of proper fathering, love and attention. Meanwhile predators . lay in wait for their prey .. Don't let your sons or daughters be their next prey. So, it is up to fathers to make sure his relationships with his daughter/s is not deficient of adequate love, care . and attention. Same goes for his son/s. Fathers need to give love, care, attention and guidance .. Otherwise sons grow up without the proper barometer in life which is so essential in these challenging times.

Mothers giving guidance: -

- Teaching her children manners, etiquette and teaching right from wrong- giving them a moral compass.

- Teaching her love, care ., respect . and tolerance of mankind and nature.

- Teaching her children, work ethic, responsibility, reliability, dependability, accountability.

- Teaching her daughters grace, strength and intelligence.

- Teaching her daughters not to settle for second best and not to tolerate any form of abuse or abuse others.

- Teaching and showing by example to her daughter/s what a good female role model should be and what to expect in future partners (boyfriends, husbands).

- Teaching her son/s to respect . women always, not to swear or hit a woman.

- Teaching her son/s to be loving, caring and sensitive to a woman's needs.

- Explaining a woman's needs.

Both parents working together, teamwork: -

- Teaching our children anger management skills and time out- not to abuse anyone or anything.

- Teaching our children to have respect and look after the environment and community.

BEING GOOD ROLE MODELS

- Both parents not arguing and raising voices at each other in front of children. No running down other parent to child and not involving children in adult matters. Parents showing love and affection to one another which in turn sets the example in how children should treat one another. Encourage healthy respectful relationships, friendships and during daily interaction with others always; lead by example.

- Teaching them courtesy, manners and respect . to all.

- To not be stingy with love, praise, attention and affection.

- Teaching our sons and daughters not to take abuse of any kind.

- Teaching their children love, sensitivity, kindness, fairness and most importantly patience.

- Teaching our children not to use physical . or emotional abuse on others; whether it be their peers, siblings and other future relationships.

- Enhancing self-respect and self-esteem in their children.

- Showing loving interactions in their relationship . with their spouse in particular and others.

- Teaching them boundaries and limits.

- Not overindulging children. .

- By setting a good example of proper relationship . conduct.

- Showing respect . of each other's value systems, what each parent considers important.

- Being good role models.

- Reassuring your children that if they are in any trouble that you will always be there for them, should they need you.

- Teaching them life skills- to be self-actuating, proactive . and how to be self-sufficient i.e., how to use a washing machine, change a tyre, cook, clean, budget ., look after their health, sew a hem and button, helping them with their homework and assignments all of these are truly gifts you will have given them.

- Teach your children to not settle for second best in relationships, not to be abused, neglected or unloved. (I have said many times to my daughter, the only time I will ever step in and interfere if her boyfriend or partner abuses and uses her in any way and even then, it will be done in fairness in a socially acceptable adult way).

- Always treating their children with love, kindness, gentleness and respect.

- Keep the lines of communication . open always, as best you can.

BEING GOOD ROLE MODELS

- Lovingly and fairly teaching children to be responsible and accountable for their actions that there are consequences.

- Teaching work ethic, reliability, honesty and integrity.

- To teach their children to compromise; give and take.

- Parents not putting conditions on their love.

- Parents not undermining the other but staying on the same page as a united front. Supporting and backing the other parent in appropriate disciplining.

Such teachings as this enable your child to be equipped with the right survival skills for a world that can be cold and harsh, yet still can be a positive place with positive relationships.

Teaching ourselves: -

- Respecting the boundaries of our adult children, not interfering in their lives where it isn't our place.

- Always being open to communication . with our children.

- Aunts, Uncles, Grandparents, close family friends too can all aim to become good role models, so encourage them to be good role models for your children.

Celebrities, police, sporting heroes: -

Do models, singers, actors, police and sporting idols realise the impact they make on the younger generations? Our youth look up to their idols in honour and reverence. Also, those with the role of authority such as police, teachers, caregivers/ parents need to set the right example in order to expect respect from our youth. Do we use our position of power to maim and abuse? Most parents/ caregivers, police, teachers do not, unfortunately that is not always the case as we see on the news. We all need to realise our roles and actions that they are helping forge the future of our youth. Ones' actions either good or bad can impact on relationships of our younger generations for years to come. *STAR 5

Our communities: -

As members of our communities . we all have a responsibility and obligation to ensure we are all good role models to our younger generation, whether they are our children or not. Without proper example and guidance . it is like letting our children out into the world without proper life skills, then expecting them to behave appropriately. We need to be accountable whether we are parents, teachers, leaders and adults. Some children are not fortunate enough to have loving guidance, so it is only right that adults do what they intuitively know what is right. Particularly in the Western world we have 'nuclear' families without the help of 'extended' families in eras previous.

BEING GOOD ROLE MODELS

Single parents and teen parents: -

Being a parent is the hardest and yet the most fulfilling rewarding job in the world. However, there are young single parents struggling to do it all on their own. They are often criticised left, right and centre for not doing it just right. These young parents need love, care . and support .. They don't need people looking down on them constantly, saying they are bludging off the system. It may be fact in some instances-but not all; we need to be especially careful not to tar everyone with the same brush. Everyone deserves a chance and moral support.

Negative comments are not conducive nor helpful; instead it is negative and counterproductive ., not to mention glaringly judgemental. Some of these young parents do not have the love and support . of family. We really need support networks of grandparents, aunts, uncles, close friends, adopted grandparents, God parents, mentors, community and a system in place to help some of these families to cope emotionally, physically, spiritually and even sometimes financially. Many families need support in this tough fast paced world.

There is a favourite old adage, that says, *"You can feed a man for a day or teach him how to fish and feed him for a lifetime!"* If we can give skills to young ones so they can get on their own feet, this is one of the best things we can do. Despite adversity we can still teach our children to be self-sufficient in the world and how to become decent caring individuals. My children complained to me that I wasn't giving them enough pocket money. I don't believe we should give them money for making their beds, occasionally they received $2 from me for doing chores around the house/yard. As I did not have any more jobs around the house for them to earn pocket money, I decided to teach them how to make money themselves. I took them and one of their friends down to the local store one weekend with squeegee and mop bucket of detergent water, asked permission from store owner and then they washed car windscreen windows for 50c and then the following weekend we sold our homemade pickles down at the local store, they made $40, they were stoked. They realised the satisfaction in earning their own spending money. After that my children learnt that they were easily able and capable of earning pocket money and that I was not the bank. My son then collected and found golf balls and sold guppies, he had quite a little business happening, and my daughter worked at the local restaurant and did odd jobs.

It was important to teach my children to always give their public transport seat to the pregnant, elderly, disabled, it was something my parents taught me to also to respect my elders, pregnant women and the disabled. I heard with pride how for years only my daughter and another lad every morning on their way to school they would both stand up the front of the water bus and give their seats up to older people. Even when I see other people's children taking seats, I kindly encourage (as I'm sure many do) for them to give their seat to the older people and then duly praise them for doing so. These children often smile back feel quite chuffed with themselves. It warms my heart to see. Why judge these children who don't know any better if not taught; the very least we can do is help them rather than criticise. These are all the little moments that fondly stay with you, the times you shared your knowledge on and the special times we shared watching these young ones grow into responsible caring adults.

I want to keep it real here, I also had times when my son run amuck in our community; due to outside influence from his father my ex-husband who told him to misbehave on me, he said as a minor that he our son could get away with a crime and not be charged- he was certainly not a good role model for our son. He also kept my child from me and for the main part had our son live him. With our son running amuck, of course, it brought great embarrassment and shame to me. Not our finest moment in a small community. With gossip-mongers ready to pounce; always on the ready to point the finger and gloat at our situation. But what could I do but continue disciplining my child as best I could; even with all the unhelpful interference from his father. That being said, child rearing for me was not all rainbows and butterflies. I took my son to the police station to face up to the music again. Not my finest hour, but it wasn't about me; it was about my son and teaching him accountability. So, I had to put aside my own embarrassment. My loving partner did the big thing in trying to save me from further embarrassment and took my son to apologise to everyone involved. We then put him to work in the garden and grounded him for punishment. Two minutes later he ran away from home and ran back to his dad's house. Being undermined is not helpful; you need all parents on the same page or it just doesn't work. All we can do is do our very best.

Bringing up children can be a struggle, especially in these hard-economic times, but why should one be made to do it alone .. Help is needed. Young women with babies without their parents need mothering and mentoring same with young men. If you are able and can give a struggling young woman or young man emotional support . and guidance . that is one of the most valuable gifts one can give. *I have a good friend who helped me and took my daughter under her wing, including her in day trips, outings etc. I am ever so grateful to this beautiful friend for taking such an interest in my daughter and being such a wonderful role model. My daughter did not have aunties available to care.*

Abandonment ., abortions ., adoptions ., post-natal depression and abuse of children in some instances can be largely prevented. Strong support networks play a valuable role in society. It can also be most rewarding for not just the recipient but the giver, "volunteers alike". There are I'm sure older mature . women that either have time on their hands or do not have families of their own. *"Why not help a woman in need!"*

Our governments: -

Our governments .; presidents and prime ministers are leaders in our world and of our countries. They are and should be accountable to our younger generation, our youth and need to responsibly lead by example. Laws too need to be fair, common-sense and reasonable, always with thought to our families and children. These children need to be moulded and turned in the right direction. As they too will grow to become the adults who shape the future of generations after them. We can teach them how to knit, sew, do woodwork etc. There are many learning opportunities we can pass on. Please see Epilogue also.

On committed relationships: -

Church counselling before marrying can be very wise. It does not necessarily have to be through a church if you are not religious, but any wise counsel is helpful .. It can give couples a strong foundation for their marriage, relationships . and family life.

"Example is not the main thing in influencing others, it is the only thing."

-Albert Schweitzer

Chapter 7 Whether to Have Children

Being responsible for our decisions

(Please Note: What I have written in my work is not so much what I have done, but what I would have liked to have done as a parent if given the chance). In saying that, I know too, that I was a reasonably good parent despite the hardships. However, we can all strive to be better parents even if we have had a rough start. Don't give up!

We need to ask ourselves some very pertinent questions when thinking about whether to have children or not. Are we having a child for the right reasons and if so, how many can we afford . to have? How many can we cope with? Will we make great parents? It is important to plan and decide well. As once children are brought on the scene, it can be too late. Children can become innocent . bystanders and fall victim to abuse. For instance, what is our tolerance and patience threshold? As children require a lot of love and nurture from both parents. Are we likely to lose our patience easily and say or do something regrettable? Below is a list of questions to ask yourself before deciding to have children.

Should you fall pregnant . by mistake without planning, questions to ask yourself?

- Do I want to keep the baby? If so, will I have a good support . network?

WHETHER TO HAVE CHILDREN

- What is the reason I want to keep the baby?

- Have I got what it takes to rear a child properly?

- Have I adequate housing to raise a child in?

- Can I afford . to have children? Babies need diapers, formula, cribs, high chairs, childcare, school . uniforms and equipment.

- I will need to plan the child's life for the long haul. From diapers to university tuition, a wedding, a car. Can I afford . it later also?

- Am I prepared to make some sacrifices; ready to give up going out with friends, schooling, nice clothes etc?

- Am I too selfish and preoccupied, or too busy and sometimes lazy and therefore likely to neglect or abuse a child?

- Have I the time and energy to give a child the love, care . and attention . they need and deserve?

- Have I got a short fuse and impatient and this could detrimentally cause harm . to a child?

- Am I emotionally plugged in enough to have a child?

- Am I responsible enough? Are we as a couple responsible enough? Will I be a sole parent?

- Am I too young and therefore emotionally immature?
- Am I taking drugs . or drinking, which can affect the child in numerous ways?
- Do I want to adopt the child out?
- Will the child be better off living in another family?
- Do I know all about the adoption process?
- How will I feel if I adopt the child out, what would be the repercussions for myself and the child?
- Do I want an abortion? Research find out about your options in keeping the child, abortion or adoption?
- If I should have an abortion, will I have a good or bad conscience on the decision?
- If the father is involved . what are his feelings and wishes? Will he support . me and the baby?
- Do I need to find work before the baby is due and after I have the baby?
- Do I need to continue schooling during and after pregnancy?
- Who will care . for the child while I work or go to school .?
- Have you seen a doctor for prenatal care .? If I haven't I will need to make an appointment. When can I get an early appointment?

WHETHER TO HAVE CHILDREN

- Would it be a good idea to see a social worker to see what services are available to help?

- Are there parenting . classes?

- Are there prenatal classes? If so, who can I take with me for support .?

- What other support . will we need?

- Should I start a budget . and savings plan?

STAR 5

Questions you need to ask yourself when deciding whether to have a child (whether biological, adopted, foster or stepchildren): -

- What is the real reason I want to have a child? Is it to fill a void? It is unfair to bring a child into the world to fill a job or role.

- Can we financially afford . to have a child?

- Am I responsible enough to have a child?

- Are we responsible enough as a couple to have a child?

- Are we drug or alcohol dependant which could affect our child raising?

- If deciding to have children how many can we cope with?

- Do we have a support . network should we want children?

- If anything happened to us, do we have anyone else we would trust to properly take care . of the children so they don't end up in foster care? Are family members or close friends happy to be put on your will as caregivers should there be a need to, if something were to happen to us?

- Do we have adequate housing?

- Have we as a couple the time and energy to give a child the love, care . and attention . they need and deserve?

- Am I too selfish and preoccupied?

- Do we have the time, are we too busy?

- Sometimes lazy and therefore likely to neglect or abuse a child?

- Are we clean and tidy and can give a child everything they need?

- Do we want a child for the right reasons?

- Could it be an impulse decision?

- Am I committed enough? Are "we" committed enough?

- Is having a child a short time novelty that I may not want for long term?

- Will we be responsible parents?

- Do we know what we are doing?

WHETHER TO HAVE CHILDREN

- Do we know what we are getting into?

- Do we know how to care . for a child properly?

- Do we make a good team? Will we cooperate . with each other?

- Am I certain I want to be a parent?

- Is my partner certain they want to be a parent?

- Do we fight and argue too much? Therefore, have issues we need to clear up before having children?

- Above all are we patient and not have anger issues, therefore placing any future children are at risk of abuse? (If you have anger issues, mental health conditions or emotional baggage it is important to get those addressed adequately by a professional . therapist . before taking on any large commitment).

- Is there a possibility I may have to raise this child alone .?

- Will we have a strong support network?

- Do I/we have health conditions that may impact on child rearing?

STAR 5

If you have decided to have children what types of questions do you need to ask yourselves?

- How many can we afford . to have 1 or 2 children or possibly 4 or 6 or more?
- How many children should we have according to our circumstances?
- What kind of things will we need to consider?
- What debts do we already have?
- Do we have a mortgage . to pay off or credit cards?
- Have we a savings plan and if so, is it enough to start a family?
- Have we a budget .? If not, maybe we need to make one? Write out a weekly budget and savings plan.
- Are we prepared to scrimp and save? There may be sacrifices to be made, such as no more gym membership, give up smoking, no going out Friday night or no extra pint of beer! Where can you trim the fat on your budget .?
- We will need adequate clothing, formula, nutrition, diapers, a crib, a change table, high chair, safety seat and more. Later we will need to afford . school . uniforms, shoes and socks, school tuition, books . and equipment, university tuition, a car, a wedding, our retirement?

WHETHER TO HAVE CHILDREN

- Will our child go to public or private school .?
- Can we afford . private school .? And for how many children?
- If our child struggles with school ., can we afford . tuition?
- Will both of us have to work fulltime?
- Can we pay for childcare every day while we work?
- Do we have to take on a second job?
- Do we have addictions which may affect our child rearing?

*STAR 5

If you are aging . and thinking about having children: -

- Though an older parent to be, will I be agile enough?
- Do I/we have the understanding of the capabilities and patience needed and of what it takes to raise a child well on my own?
- Am I too old to have children? If so, how will this affect children later in life emotionally or physically? Who will look after the children should I pass away suddenly?
- How will the child feel, with an aging . parent? Could they be bullied?
- Do we realise the increase in pressures due to age?

- What other support . will I/we have?
- How will this affect other members of the family?
- Do I/we have health conditions that may impact on child rearing?

STAR 5

If you have a disability . or illness . and thinking about having children: -

- Do I have a serious illness . or disability . that can be passed on to the child?
- Can we afford . to look after a child with a disability . or illness .?
- Do we have the patience to cope with a child with a disability .?
- How will this affect other members of the family?
- Are we prepared to accept a child with a disability . or illness . and get them through crisis after crisis?
- Do we realise the increase in pressures due to disability .?
- Do we have a good support . network behind us if we should have children?
- What other support . is available in the community or with government services?

WHETHER TO HAVE CHILDREN

- I should do some research.
- I need to contact a Social . Worker.

***STAR 5**

If you have decided against having children or more children: -

- We will need birth control? What is available? What are our options?
- Do I need to go on the pill or some other form of contraception .?
- Do we need to go drastic and definitely don't want to have children and therefore should look at having my tubes tied, a hysterectomy or vasectomy? Because it may be too late to undo the action.
- Could we change our minds and want children later?

"You can research on whether you should have children- all the pros and cons."

***STAR 5**

The Realities of Having a Larger Family

What are some reason's people choose to have a large family?

- Some parents who were only children growing up without siblings and often felt lonely and therefore want a different experience to that for their children.

- Some parents may have been used to living in a large family growing up and had a favourable experience and therefore want to continue this trend.

- There are some who do not believe in contraception . due to personal reasons or religious . reasons.

- Many opt for larger families due to the joy of having several children (and I for one totally get that).

- Some want to break world records by having the largest family and see it as a challenge that they believe they are up for.

- Some for religious reasons, want to be fruitful and fill the world; others don't believe in birth control.

- Then there are some who love having babies, because they are cute at that stage, but when the child grows up they feel out of their depth as the child grows.

- Children Hoarders who seem to conceive child after child, with no thought of stopping.

- Some do have more children to receive for more welfare payments, yet they don't realise you can't scrimp on having children.

*STAR 5

Are there disadvantages of having a large family?

- Parents feeling out of their depth "overwhelmed" and not being able to give to all children equally- emotionally, physically and financially.
- One must be able to financially afford . to have a large family as it is expensive.
- One can be spreading themselves so thinly, not having the time and energy needed for each child when there are too many.
- There is the problem that the older children end up having to take over some of the parenting . of the younger children, due to a parent feeling overwhelmed.
- Some parents lack the skill and organisation that is required in having a large family.

*STAR 5

What are the advantages of having a large family?

- One size does not fit all. There are certainly many large families that do it so well, they invest in property to afford . to have large families and seem to be able to handle everything quite adequately emotionally, physically and financially.

- There can be the sense of with large families the wonderful feeling of a large caring and warm family where each child brings love, laughter and happiness into the home.

*STAR 5

What does one need to think about when they decide how many children they should have?

- Having children is for the long haul, one never stops parenting . even after their children leave home.

- With large families there is certainly a drain on the monetary finances.

- Patience and tolerance levels (Large family can be emotionally and physically draining).

- One needs to be motivated and organised and know what can be humanely coped with.

- Having a clean, tidy home.

- Neglect . of emotions; love, affection . and care ., physical . necessities such as adequate nutritious food, adequate shelter, education, clothing and other essentials.

***STAR 5*

Preparing your child with life skills

There should always be much pride in oneself in not going on social security/welfare if one doesn't have to. Can one really feel proud just to keep having children and using welfare to support . their burgeoning, ever-increasing family? Teaching your children good work ethic is important and teaching them not to rely on the welfare system handouts to get by.

Teach your children to be self-sufficient should anything happen to you. You never know what is around the corner, you could become sick, have an accident anything. I taught my son and daughter how to use an iron, washing machine, stove and oven with supervision well before their teens. As loving parents, we have boasting rights, when our children bring us such joy .! My heart swells with love and pride when I talk of my daughter.

To teach our children attitudes of kindness, respect ., caring, sharing and self-sufficiency is one of the best gift's parents can give. I sincerely hope we have done that. My darling girl helps us to look after a young woman with an intellectual disability ., she guides this girl in so many ways and cares for her in our absence, should we travel and stands up for her when ignorant people pick on this lass. Through high school . she always stood up for those being bullied, especially students with disability. Last night she saw an elderly couple receiving bad service at a restaurant she attended with a friend and wrote a letter to management on the poor treatment of the elderly couple. My daughter makes us proud and so can your children. My Daughter would have a fit if she knew I put this in she is so modest. I once felt bad to brag about her, because boasting is not normally seen as a good quality. But when it comes to your children and they make you so proud, loving parents can't hold back their elation. Otherwise what is the point of having children if you can't be proud of them! All loving parents of wonderful children have bragging rights .! Children can bring such love and joy, to boast about your children is one of life's most privileged rewards that parents can have. Our daughter is the apple of our eye; we burst with pride every single day and we love her endlessly. Since writing this passage our girl has now landed her dream job as an Ecologist-Environmental Advisor, moved out of home, bought a car and is doing excellent! We, my partner and I are ever so proud of her as we know the difficult start she had. She is also my inspiration, she shows me anything is possible. I was also very proud of the beautiful decent human my Son was, despite of all his difficulties in this life. I just pray that he is happy and at peace. My deepest saddest regret is the untold suffering my child son endured due to negative people injecting themselves into our lives and his father keeping my child from me emotionally and physically. I only wished I had the opportunity to rear him properly myself without outside influence and interference.

The best any parent can ever do is to give your children the skills in life to survive no matter what comes their way. Educate your children on all the pros and cons of this life and give them all the love and attention . they deserve.

I believe also after having lost my child to death and also having had two miscarriages, you become more tuned into just how precious ones' children are. Never take your children for granted ever. I saw this woman one day at a shopping mall shake her little boy because he was crying and hungry, I felt like shaking her and saying, *"Wake up, I lost my beautiful son. Do you know how fortunate you are?"* One might regularly see children throwing tantrums; the child may be feeling sick, off-colour, hungry, tired or just not like shopping. Why not stop dragging them through shopping malls and maybe sit down with them to an ice-cream. I do know there are little mites who throw tantrums no matter what, that can be challenging. Super Nanny is a great program; I don't have any littlies but still watch it as she makes just so much sense. Why not sit down and watch the program if you do have tantrum problems, it can't hurt.

***STAR 5**

Homosexual parents vs. Heterosexual parents- attitudes, myths or ignorance

There is a red-necked ignorant attitude . where some people believe that children should not be put in families where parents are homosexuals or to deny . the right to homosexual couples to have children. This could be seen as such an out-dated way of thinking.

In our ever-changing world many homosexual people are very good role models and decent respectful people, deserving of respect .. There are many heterosexual parents that are abusive to each other and to their children. It is my belief that homosexual parents can also give a loving and caring environment to a child that needs a home. So, let's not be quick to judge and instead be quick to give all people a fair go, and emotionally support . genuine, caring family relationships for the good of all.

There is an insightful poem . "Children Learn What They Live" By Dorothy Law Nolte, Ph.D .

If you can, look it up on the internet. It is all about being good role models to our children and how 'children live what they learn.' It really does bring it home to you about how much our children need and deserve proper love, care . and discipline. It is so very enlightening; food for thought.

"To support mother and father, to cherish wife and children, and to be engaged in peaceful occupation, this is the greatest blessing."
-Gautama Buddha

***STAR 5**

Notes:

Chapter 8 Who Is Abused?

What type of people are abused and why?

Abuse knows no boundaries, it affects people from all walks of life. Victims can be people of all colour/race, creed, religion, gender, of all socio-economic backgrounds- the wealthy, the poor, and the middle-class. Even professionals . have been known to be abused. Those with self-confidence ., high self-esteem and high intellect can even fall prey . and be a victim, although this may not be the norm.

Victims are predominantly women, children, the elderly, the sick the disabled, the meek and mild, pets as they are often defenceless . making them more vulnerable .. Men too can be victims. However, more often than not it is usually the defenceless, weak, vulnerable, innocent ., trusting, with low self-esteem and the insecure in particular. But you don't have to fall under any of those categories either. In saying that, know that even the well-intentioned good-hearted rescuer can be a victim. Especially when they wrongly believe they can help change a person- the abuser. One can often give their power away to others, allowing others to make all the decisions and not contributing to decision-making, this is not helpful. To be treated properly one must equally interact in decision-making. Only then will they become empowered. We all need to teach people how to treat us. However, in saying this too, this not an excuse to be abused either. *"We can change ourselves, but we cannot change others."*

***STAR 5**

What the victim feels (the victim mentality)

- The victim can end up feeling powerless, helpless . and hopeless.
- They are often pessimistic and can't see any light at the end of the tunnel, feeling alone . in their plight, little do they know there are many other women and children in the same situation.
- They may feel embarrassed.
- They may incorrectly believe the abuse is their own fault.
- They may apologise for everything, even things not of their doing.
- They may not speak up.
- They may think everything is 'always' their fault.
- They may suffer a lot of confusion.
- They may have flashbacks of the abuse.
- They may feel nervous and jumpy at loud sounds, this may go on for many years, even after they have been away from abuse.

What about the loved ones of the victim how do they help, understand and cope?

It is not a helpless . situation at all to help a victim to change. Most victims I'm sure would want to change. It is not a good feeling to have of the prior abuse, and it can spill over into other areas of their lives. It can be most frustrating for the person who wants so badly to change and grow.

A loving partner must be supportive, by showing love, care ., understanding, kindness, sensitivity and above all patience. Sounds like a lot to live up to. But not really when you take into account the fact that this loved one for so many years suffered much abuse and tragedy, and therefore is deficient in TLC (Tender, Loving, Care). So, time to build the TLC up in their system, it is all important. For example, if one is low in a nutrient it affects the whole body. One must then correct this deficiency by taking in the correct nutrition to counteract this, by food or tablets high in the nutrient needed. The deficiency of TLC needs support . and help. Loved ones must be patient. Remember she did not get like that overnight, there is a whole lifetime of abuse for many. They won't know what a normal life is. This is the case for the children of abusive relationships. Ensure you seek adequate counselling for your loved ones.

The victim's self-esteem is affected, and her character is violated in an abusive relationship .. The victim may even *continually apologise* saying "sorry" even if it wasn't her fault; they are super-sensitive and will bend over backwards to please. They feel as if all their rights . have been taken away. Or they may not even know they have rights. The victim may always ask permission from others to do even the simplest things; they worry about offending others. "This is a hard habit to break if one has been living with fear for many years. I liken the experience to a tangled ball of string, that needs untwisting, unravelling and gentle prising apart not only for the therapist . to work through but for the once victim. It takes time and great patience. If you have a loved one who has gone through this, be patient. There may be residual anxiety, see your doctor for advice. Remember the victims' lives were filled with worry and fear. This is a new life they have never had before, so is foreign.

Her abuser told her constantly that she is no good, she may have believed that, so it may have become her reality. The victim even after leaving . the abuser may experience flashbacks stimulated by similar occurrences or reminders, can be very traumatic .. Some may suffer PTSD Post Traumatic Stress Disorder in order for one to be properly diagnosed and appropriate treatment given; one will need to see a professional ., a specialist who deals in depression and mental health issues. The victim may often suffer panic attacks; the victim may blame themselves for everything and anything, even the abuse. A lot of incorrect thought patterns need to be changed too.

*STAR 5

Can you become your own worst enemy?

Learn not to be your own worst enemy a victim of yourself. As is this can carry on into other relationships also. What Dr Phil Mc Graw says is so true, *"You teach people how to treat you."* One must learn to command and also firstly earn respect . from others. A prime example is of my own experience. At times I can be my own worst enemy. Recently we had visitors over and the guests after being invited suggested they bring sweets. I said, *"No don't be silly I have it all in hand."*

Well I forgot to buy custard to go with the dessert and I had no way of getting to the shop as I was in another state in the country also at my in-law's home unable to drive and the nearest shop was some distance away too far to walk. In the end my partner was going out so thankfully I was able to get the custard.

The moral . of the story is if someone offers to bring or do something for you, *graciously learn to accept*. I sensibly should have accepted our guests offer to bring sweets, I would not have had the custard dilemma. On that same day I was cranky at my partner because I felt I did most of the food prep and nice touches; feeling out of my depth, especially after coming out of radiation for cancer. But I try to smile and take it all in my stride, because I don't like to disappoint; being a bit of a people-pleaser. But deep down I was flustered, so my stress levels heightened before our guests arrived. One can be their own worst enemy, there needs to be a balance . in all things. We can put far too much pressure on ourselves to be perfect. After going at it all day trying to make our guests feel hospitable, I felt worn out. I had a feeling of being unappreciated by my partner with all the hard work and effort after radiation. Instead I should have known my limits . and not blamed my partner.

My partner likes to take friends to restaurants and wanted to take the pressure off me, always thinking of cost . and I also wanted the pleasure in make our guests feel welcome and special. Maybe we should have gone out for dinner at a restaurant and the prep and clean up would have been done too. Our lovely guests offered to clear up and help, normally I would say, *"No, sit down and relax, I'll do it."* But this time instead, I graciously accepted, and the clean-up was done in minutes and we gals got to chat in the kitchen. I am learning though some days it seems ever so slow... Being reliable, dependable and easy-going are good qualities to have but can be a hindrance if we are not careful. As others can depend on you so much because you are so capable, never asking for help. No one knows that you are having a difficult time if you don't tell them, or always try to carry the heavy load. Our shoulders, backs, arms and even our very hearts can be stretched to the max, learn to let others help you carry the load.

If people want to share the load with you, let them. A very valuable lesson was learnt. Initially, I had seen it as a weakness . to ask for help. Because of being accessible, reliable, dependable and generous you give the impression right or wrong that you can do anything, that you're capable. Remember your limits ., you are not superhuman. You can't be helped if you think you can do it all. There is no need to be a martyr. I have had to learn to say, *"No!"* – a word very difficult for us 'people pleasers' to vocalise.

My doctor mentioned something very enlightening and important to me that I have an "addiction to giving." I never really looked at it that way and realised, she was right. *"She was so right, that's me!"* Now don't get me wrong I'm not a nutcase, I do have a Psychiatrist and Psychologist of my own volition; sometimes we need some wisdom, assistance and support.

Sometimes we need to take off the mask and let others see we have flaws and weaknesses, for only then will others know we are finding some things tough. For us "long time giving-addicts" it can be difficult, accepting help or taking from others. It can be hard to accept help and it can also be hard to accept gifts and compliments too. If someone compliments me now I try to be gracious and say, *"Thank you"*, rather than saying *"Oh this old dress! Oh really, my hair is a bit frizzy today!"* It's about self-esteem and self-respect that counts. I am still a 'work in progress,' far from perfect. The two things I need to work on is giving a little less of myself, especially when I'm the one needing support, . and to also not try to fix everything all of the time. Learning to say *"No,"* can be hard and realising not everything is our responsibility alone .. We can wrongly take on everything as our responsibility. We can't all save the world, but we can all do it as a united front with other like-minded people. Sometimes we need to delegate, seek the help of others.

"Never worry about numbers, help one person at a time and always start with the person nearest you."

-Mother Theresa

*STAR 5

Chapter 9 What Keeps Us Locked In?

What is Denial .?

Denial . is when we don't believe we have a problem, or if there is a problem it is not too bad, we can fix it ourselves, we don't need help. We keep on believing that things will eventually improve. The victim may think, *"Oh he didn't mean it, he has been in much pain, he has been under so much pressure at work- I should have been more thoughtful ., maybe if I didn't nag so much it wouldn't have happened."* *"Ahh... That's just what the abuser wants you to think!"* The abuser may make excuses . for his abuse such as, *"You keep nagging me, you provoked me or it's your fault."* He may even think incorrectly, that he has a handle on it and that things will be better next time. Denial keeps you stuck it prevents a situation from improving. It stops us from facing the facts as we fear the truth. As we know the truth hurts and can be hard to face. Truth brings one back to reality.

TRIGGER WARNING *(I feel that even as I write that I need to be responsible for the content written should it be upsetting for some to read so feel free to skip if you so wish)*

Why is it so hard to leave?

I felt it important to put this in here, as those who haven't been there do not and will not fully understand just how difficult it is to leave. Often people who notice a friend, acquaintance or a relative in an abusive marriage . say. *"Why doesn't she just leave?"* I myself find myself saying it too at times and I've been there! As I know only too well, having tried to leave many times. I had left and been found and dragged back. I will say this, *"It's not simple to leave, and unless you've been there you don't know. Do you know what it's like trying to leave with children in tow, it isn't easy at all? It's very scary! It's like running from a grizzly bear with dependents in tow! And if you slip you are really in trouble!"* Judging someone in such a situation is far from fair, there are many intricacies one does not fully know.

Leaving is very hard; the victim often feels overwhelmed and does not know where to go or what to do. She may also feel immobilised and frozen by fear and threats. This is further compounded if there are children or even pets involved ., as she may worry how they can possibly leave. Such questions running through the victim's mind could be, *"After all, the children need to have a father, how can I deny . them of this right?"* The victim may feel responsible. Little does she realise; the children would be better off fatherless than having an abusive brute of a father. Denying children of an 'abusive' father/mother is in actual fact protecting them in a situation such as this. When a parent abuses; to me they have forfeited the very right to be a parent.

The abuser has already primed or groomed if you like, the victim with guilt . trips. Other fears may be, *"What if the abuser finds us what will he do to us?"* These are very reasonable, rational and relevant fears. It can all seem far too daunting, which is totally understandable.

So, frustrating, she's still there...

The abuser has groomed the victim into thinking they can do nothing on their own- she is nothing without him. The victim then naturally second guesses and doubts her own abilities. The victim may only see a home and assets all tied up together with her abuser and cannot even foresee how she can retrieve what is rightly hers. The finances look messy to her and impossible for her to start again.

Sometimes the victim may contemplate suicide . because the pain is enormous and hopeless. She cannot see a way out of this situation. The victim may not see the forest for the trees. However, she may not go through with suicide, as she could worry about what will happen to her children under the care . of the abuser.

The victim also may feel insecure and worry about their financial situation; how she can support . her children without any work skills and what about shelter, bills, food, clothes the list goes on. She may not feel capable of doing it on her own, for so long someone else has controlled this.

WHAT KEEPS US LOCKED IN?

Come on leave him!!!

The victim may feel as helpless . as a child. She may still feel some love toward her abuser also, or under an obligation to stay. I believe there is good and bad in everyone, and that can also be true of the Abuser. One of the difficulties is when the victim can also see the good still in the abuser, which just confuses the matter even more. Sometimes the victim can become so confused and have trouble rationalising things clearly, or not trust her own judgment . even if it truly is rational and logical. She may not be empowered and may feel defeated .. I can't say this enough; until one is in the same situation they have no right to make judgement. As it already is hard enough for the victim to leave.

The victim may feel deep love still toward her abuser. Abusers can have some redeeming qualities such as generosity . or other attributes. This can be distorted by the victim as love. She could lose perspective on what real love really is and think she is in a loving relationship . no matter how inappropriate it really is. She could think some love is better than no love.

Another reason people do not seek help is shame ., they are afraid to let others know how it really is. They may feel it is a failing on their part, misplaced guilt . on themselves or they may have such loyalty to their abuser. It may be that they the victim feels that if they should divulge such personal information this is being in a sense unfaithful ., betraying the abuser. Or they fear the repercussions if they do tell and have been blackmailed. Another incorrect notion is the non-abuser can feel they can help change an abuser; they stay in hope of change. Also, the non-abuser which is predominantly the woman, as women are usually smaller in stature and strength than men. So, the scales don't tip in the favour of the non-abuser.

Sometimes we can be locked in through heightened fear and indecision. Some non-abusers are timid, meek and mild, therefore definitely vulnerable . prey .. There may be a language barrier for some from another country, not knowing where to go for help and how to communicate their dire situation. If you are going through any of this don't be hard on yourself for this. Help is available. **Please see Help Contacts at back of this book.**

"Some" so-called religions or for want of a better word "cult", can play a role in the victim staying; as the victim can feel it is her duty to stay in the relationship . or marriage .." She may be conditioned 'brainwashed'. They may feel it is a sin to separate or divorce .. I remember my ex-husband bringing church elders to our home to discipline me into being subservient and submissive; instructing me to give more to my husband sexually and not answering back to his authority. One could say, "Isn't it a sin to put yourself and children in danger by staying?" It really is not that cut and dry, there are some grey areas, so many contributing factors that make the victims decision all the more confusing.

So why don't they leave him????
It can take the victim a long time to work up the courage to leave, get out of denial and brainwashing, have the means to leave and gain back some power.

Personally, I did not want to put in this part of our private lives, however, it is frustrating when others do not understand how very difficult it is to leave safely. We were controlled by many ploys/tactics ie., religion, weapons, isolation, blackmail, threats, lack of funds, shame just to name a few. I can only speak from my own situation (however, I'm sure this happens in far more homes than the public realise). In all honesty, leaving is far from simple. Here are some of my own accounts to give you an idea of the difficulties many women face. There were many threats some may have been bluffs but who is to know what is real and what is not. Especially when he has acted out his threats many times before.

No means for escaping
He disabled my car on several occasions, so I couldn't use it and sold both my cars and then with the one remaining car he insisted that only he drive. You then lose your driving confidence; your main means for escaping gone.

Isolated from help

When my parents phoned to see how we were, he would **blow a postman's whistle as loud as he could down the phone receiver, to stop family from ever calling**. You were **kept isolated from your family**. **Neighbours** were **violently threatened** by him, so there's no help there either. You are **not able to have your own friends**. I try to ring for help, but **he pulls the phone out of the wall and he monitors all phone calls, putting on phone microphones and recording all calls. He may regularly try to buy property in isolated areas, in order to ostracise isolate you from your family and friends.** There must be a God, every time something happened, and the sales kept falling through.

Uses emotional manipulation

With numerous murder suicide threats and holding our children hostage, or threats of killing your parents and family. These reasons keep you from leaving. You are left feeling powerless. I even thought he was more powerful than the police.

Threats of violence

My ex-husband carried a 6' bowie knife with him literally everywhere we went. Often this massive thing was placed in his back pocket and even beside the car driver's seat. I once asked why he needed to carry it in the car, he said it was in case we got into a car accident and he needed to cut the seatbelts to free us. I fantasised with visions of creeping out quietly, but he had the bowie knife also along with his 20" machete positioned right beside his side of the bed every night. In the walk-in robe only, metres from where we slept, and I slept with one eye open, was a bevy of weapons. In the WIR was a revolver, rifles, shotguns, bow and arrow and shanghai and bos of bullets. He later used metal walking sticks to get around with. I happened to upset him and received numerous blows from both walking sticks. I learnt that his 2 constant companion walking sticks were also his weapons. The bruises were many the size of oranges and the pain went deep to the bone, taking months to heal. Wearing tracksuits to cover the bruises until they faded. He was careful not to hit my face, although face hitting still occasionally occurred. He would often practice martial arts and lifted weights, even his arms were weapons with holes punch into the wall and face dislocating my jaw. Even his car was a weapon when he drove up on footpaths to run me over to stop me from leaving or driving us head on into semi-trailer trucks and buses.

"So, each threat/obstacle to deter you from leaving is just another indelible etch marked on the psyche as to why it seems impossible to leave."

My health and the health of my unborn children was compromised. The stress was all too much I lost a child to miscarriage and had two difficult pregnancies with both children born with reasonably serious health issues.

Our abuser one day told me that if he presses in a certain area of the neck, that one firm press can kill. He also said that he has murdered before. It was shortly after his admission, I got the courage up to leave yet again and this time, most gratefully, **"I had help."** We had moved to a new caring small community and I had made some friends. I told them my plans and they helped my children and I safely leave.

**STAR 5*

Why the victim finds it difficult to leave: -

- She has an incorrect thought process to start with.
- Low self-esteem
- She may feel too frightened and scared and immobilised by that fear. He may use weapons to keep her in place.
- She may have children in tow.
- Her religious values may prevent her from leaving.
- Worry of denying . her children the right of their father.
- No support . system.
- No friends or family.

WHAT KEEPS US LOCKED IN?

- Or if she does have friends and family she feels such shame and failure.
- No work skills, poor financial prospects.
- Not enough money..
- No transport.
- Maybe she has left many times only for him to find her each time, so feel helpless and defeated.
- She feels very alone and may not have social skills..
- She may feel confused.
- She feels useless.
- She has zero confidence.
- She may feel uncertain of the future and fear of the unknown.
- The present life is all she knows.
- There may be a language or cultural barrier.
- She may be brainwashed.
- She may feel ashamed.
- She may feel connected to her captor that she doesn't realise she can break free.
- She may still love him.

- She may think she can change him.
- She may still be in denial. .
- She may believe she doesn't deserve better.

***STAR 5**

To make things more confusing, abusers may make excuses . for their behaviour by saying such things as *"You provoked me," "You keep nagging," "You pushed my buttons," "If you hadn't started it," "I never meant to hurt you," "It'll never happen again," "I can't help it," "I'm in pain," "I'm not well and having a bad time of it."* You know none of this is an excuse to be abused. In your mind get yourself out of denial ., by saying *"Well Bucko, guess what we're having a hard time of it too!"* Say this in your mind only (not verbally). Do not provoke an already escalated situation.

Warning- Again, do not however, say this out verbally but think it only, now is not the time though to act all bravado. You are still vulnerable . and he won't take kindly to being challenged. It may only provoke him more and endanger you and your children. So, don't play with fire. But do build up confidence . and get out of denial as this book title says there is, "Absolutely No Excuse for Abuse!"

WHAT KEEPS US LOCKED IN?

What to do in an escalating violent episode?

If you are having trouble escaping a violent . physical . outburst, then you must protect your children and yourself. Do all you can to protect yourself, cover your head and face as best you can to protect it from blows. Never keep any sharp objects such as knives, hammers, as, weapons, guns, bullets in plain-sight, glass bottles can even be broken and turned into weapons. Get rid of acids, fuel, matches, lighters always keep these items out of reach of children and out of the sight of the abuser. If you can lock yourself and your children in the safest part of the house, it may be your bathroom or some room with a lockable door, hide the keys beforehand in a safe place.

Keep a mobile phone on you at all times, you may need to call the police .. Do not let the abuser know you have a mobile phone on you and keep it on silent or vibrate. You may need to privately give your children a prepaid mobile phone for emergency situations such as this and turn their mobile on vibrate also.

Ensure the children are quiet and safe in a room with you or another safe room with a lock, if you can't all be together. Having a lock on your children's doors may be necessary but always keep a key on you for emergencies or in case of a fire.

Document . the abuse, keep a diary . of the abuse when and where and take photos of the evidence of the abuse, you will need this to take to the police to obtain a protection order.

Educate your children on what to do in an emergency and how to call for help, practice with them but not in front of the abuser.

Do not join in his tirade with provocation it will only make things worse for you and your children. Again, you never caused this episode or any other episodes.

Bullies do not like challenging remarks. But the best thing you can do is leave before it even gets to a dangerous level. Because you know it will always get to this eventually and could get much worse.

The consequences of the abuse escalating are dire. It could easily mean that someone will lose their life or resulting in serious injury. Such a situation can leave you and your children scarred for life.

After you have contacted police . and they arrive, *"You must leave with the police right then and there. Take "**all** of your children with you."* This may be your one last chance to leave safely- with the police. Don't worry about your belongings they can be replaced, you and your children cannot. *"You owe it to your children and yourself to be safe. If you have pets take them also if it is practical."*

Caring people may feel locked out and unable to help.

WHAT KEEPS US LOCKED IN?

Even as outside observers of abuse; we may be loved ones, neighbours, teachers. You may often feel helpless to help victims. You put in phone calls to report abuse to authorities, but it seems to fall on deaf ears. Don't give up, that child/children or family need you.

On the news just recently, in Australia alone, 7 women died from domestic violence in the space of just 1 week and on average 1 woman per week dies from domestic violence and 1 man per month dies from domestic violence. How alarming is this, and that is not even speaking of children affected. Children left physically and psychologically damaged/maimed, orphaned or even killed. That is just how dire this domestic violence situation is. This is being my reason for getting this book out. We can no longer ignore it or hope it will go away.

WHAT KEEPS US LOCKED IN?

Victims are often powerless to improve their situations. Keep those phone calls going it may take up to four or more phone calls before someone attends. You can remain anonymous. *STAR 5*

Please see **Help Contacts at back of this book.** For emergency help in Australia on a landline phone dial Emergency 000, on a mobile/cell phone- dial 112, in United States dial 911, in, New Zealand dial 111, United Kingdom 112 or 999 beforehand put it in your phone on speed dial. There is a great list of emergency numbers in all countries worldwide the site is http://www.sccfd.org/travel.html

WHAT KEEPS US LOCKED IN?

"Denial is wilful doubt in the face of overwhelming credible evidence."

Chapter 10 Taking Things to the Extreme

(It is Never a Solution)

It can get better, suicide is n<u>ot</u> a solution

If you are feeling desperate ., defeated ., defenceless ., trapped, and alone ., in unimaginable emotional/physical pain, therefore contemplating suicide .. If I can say this to you, *"Please do not take such drastic and final action, as things will improve. It does get better, help is out there. Promise me and promise your loved ones you will seek help."*

What you feel now, may not be how you feel tomorrow or next week. Things can and will get better. You are important and if you have loved ones, this is so unfair to do this to them. Losing a loved one to suicide . is absolutely devastating . and you never fully recover from the loss. I urge you to seek medical attention . immediately; talk about your feelings, if you have someone to talk to. You may want to have a list of contact numbers of family, friends and your doctor, for times when you feel like this. Make a list prior, before you get to that stage. Talking about our feelings is important, no one can help you if they don't know how you feel.

Whenever I had no one available to talk to, I wrote down my feelings on paper, on my computer or in my journals. Writing really helped keep things in perspective. I know your pain is real, having been there many times before, but this causes other problems for your children and loved ones, please get help or allow others to help you. *"The suffering your loved ones would endure should you decide to take your life would be so unbearable for them .. It is not fair to do that to them and more importantly you so deserve to live and find happier times ahead. I strongly urge you not to 'suicide', not to take your life! You must "immediately" let your loved ones and doctor know how you are feeling!"*

*STAR 5

Murdering or maiming the abuser is n<u>ot</u> a solution

There are instances we see in the news of victims killing . their abuser. This rarely happens but is not unheard of. In this instance, the mind can conjure up so many ideas of how to end the suffering. The mind can rationalise the action no matter how wrong it is. However, if you are thinking of doing this I say in the strongest possible terms, **"STOP!"** This is not worth it; you will spend time in gaol (jail) which is not worth it. Get professional help, involve authorities and professionals. I know only too well of how you must be feeling. It was a guilty feeling I felt more than once. I kept it to myself and worked through it, so I didn't do something I'd later regret. At times I even fantasised; wishing and willing my abuser to die so we would be free and then think how awful of me for even thinking this way- though it is thoroughly understandable but not excusable. Of course, I never did anything to hurt or cause harm. In retrospect, I should have sought help, rather than having those thoughts. Thankfully I never acted upon those feelings; they did not become actions. If you have strong feelings such as this, I urge you to seek help.

There are qualified professionals .; doctors and specialists that can help you. Do not be afraid to broach the matter with your doctor, they can then assist you to obtain the help needed. It is more than understandable and only natural that you may have these feelings in order to escape or stop the abuse. Please know that if you have this feeling this does not mean you are evil or a bad person. But if you follow through with the action of killing . or maiming .. It is only when one acts out the action, that it becomes wrong.

However, should one carry out such actions no matter how desperate ., the law will not look down kindly upon you. Because killing and injuring another with intention to maim or kill is a crime, against the law. As a life is a life, no matter how horrible your abuser was. Instead, I strongly urge you to get help. Your children will be without a parent and this would be most devastating . for the both of you. By maiming or killing you will not have solved the problem at all, if anything you will have made your situation a hundred times worse.

TAKING THINGS TO THE EXTREME

If you are thinking of doing something drastic here are some questions to think about: -

- You will not be able to be with your child/ children. They will most likely end up in foster care ., cared for by strangers. Is this really what you want? So, think good and hard before resorting to such actions.

- Do you want to go to jail/gaol?

- The abuser is not worth spending a life sentence in gaol "jail" over.

- Haven't you already spent a long enough sentence with the abuser? To use violence . against, violence is 'never' a solution.

- Two wrongs do not make a right.

- There is no justification of murdering another unless in the case of protecting yourself, self-defence

- should be the **"only"** reason for murder or maiming ..

- Have you sought help for these feelings?

- If not, why haven't you?

STAR 5

"Unless in extreme cases of self-defence one should never maim or kill another."

Notes:

Chapter 11 Child Abuse

Emotional . Abuse

The abuser may put the child down regularly. The abuser may tell them they are dumb, an idiot and swear abuse at them. They may even tell them things like, *"You don't do anything right," "I don't want to see your ugly face," "You'll never amount to anything," "I don't love you anymore"* or threaten the child with abandonment.

The abuser may think that they are top dog and everyone else is lower than him and less deserving than him. The abuser may in some instances not like or encourage any family member to better themselves educationally. The abuser may even prevent the child from going to school .. He may have a perverse pleasure in watching his child suffer. The abuser may swear at the child; degrade and humiliate them. The abuser may even brainwash them or go out of his way to confuse the child and pit one parent against the other. To hush the child the abuser often grooms the child and tells them if you tell, then this is your fault, such a heavy burden for one so young to carry and an incorrect one at that. The abuser may bring them up to have little respect . for females, vice-versa. Exploitation may be used, using the child against you. The abuser may use manipulation or guilt . tripping to get the child to do what he wants. He may even set the child up for failure, so he can say, *"See I told you, you couldn't do it."*

CHILD ABUSE

The abuser may make the child suffer unnecessary hardship . because he had to as a child. The abuser may teach his child to be violent . to their other siblings, encouraging them to hit each other and bully others at school .. The abuser may not allow the child to have friends. A child is innocent ., defenceless ., vulnerable . and fertile soil for him to mould them into what he wants for his own selfish gain.

I believe that during divorce . or separation, when one parent keeps the child from their other parent, it is also a form of abuse to the child and other parent. By denying his child the right to receive nurturing from that parent, the abuser is punishing the child. Children get caught up in the middle of this vicious selfish game. He mainly wants to abuse the other parent by punishing them. So, the other parent who left due to abuse, is still being abused indirectly; it still keeps the abuse perpetuating.

Physical . Abuse

The abuser may take away their toys and break them in front of them. He may not allow the child to have toys or books. He decides everything for them, taking away their free-will and freedom of choice.

He may hit them with objects, bash and beat them, burn them with his cigarette and throw hot coffee at them. Lock them up in their room without supper. He may hit the child in order to punish or simply because he himself is having a bad day, there doesn't need to be a reason, any rational justification. The abuser may threaten violence . on one child or the rest of family. He may push them out of the car and make them walk many miles home. The abuser may lock them out of the house or deny . his child of the bare necessities. He may turn the child's room upside down after they have cleaned it. The abuser may physically or verbally abuse their spouse in front of their child. There are numerous ways an adult can physically abuse a child. In some rare but still heard of cases, children are restrained with rope/chains and confined to small locked up cages or rooms with little or no food and likely beaten.

Ostracising and Scapegoating

Sometimes in a family there can be a pecking order; and victimisation occurs, where children are all treated better or differently to another child(ren) in the same family. It is often seen in the animal kingdom. It is a very primal thing. You will see in families a member in the family that is different 'the black sheep' in the family. These members never fit in, often they may be quiet and have a victim mentality. They may be regularly left out or deprived of things and regular anger hurled by several family members at them. The smallest or weakest link can be the one that is attacked verbally or physically by family members and ostracised from the rest of the herd 'family' and continually blamed for things they may never have done, because it is convenient to lay the blame on that person. Unfortunately, in the family that is their role to be the scapegoat. That person can be the scapegoat in every abusive situation; they live what they know- it is all they know.

Neglect/Deprivation *.(Deprivation and Overindulgence .-subtle forms of abuse, often overlooked)*

The abuser may not intentionally provide properly for his family or could intentionally out of spite. The child frequently does without. It could be not enough school . equipment or no school uniform provided, no money . for school excursions, resulting in the child end up feeling different to their peers; often ostracised because they miss out and see things are different to other families. They may be deprived of social privileges like school camps, not because of lack but the abuser likes to keep the child feeling socially inept. The child may be limited to having only a scrape of jam on their toast or powdered milk even if there is full cream milk when cost . and availability . is not a problem. There can be a lack of toys, books ., educational . learning aids, food, clothing- not even enough clothes for seasonal weather inclement with warm clothing for cooler weather etc.

The abuser may not look out for the child's well-being emotionally and physically in the sense of not ensuring that the child receive adequate medical assistance when needed. There may be absence of much needed medication and/or treatment .. The child may be left to his own devices at home or locked in the car for long periods of time whilst the parent is out at the local bar, pokies, party etc. The abuser may not care . where the child is or if he is safe and may not care whether the child comes home or who they are with. They may incorrectly think they are safe locked in the car, whilst they go about their business. There may be a total absence of physical . and emotional love, care, affection . and praise .. Negligence could also be lack of loving care and attention that is so vital to the child/children.

Overindulgence .

Over the top overindulgence could be seen as an *unintentional form of abuse.* Most of us, if not all of us are guilty of doing this from time to time to quieten, appease or spoil our child. Our children are not with us forever and in many ways, this is one way in how we show our love. However, . it could be seen in some cases as a form of abuse if taken to the extreme. There is nothing wrong with being generous with ones' child. It is a delicate balance; understanding that there needs to be everything in moderation. The parent may overindulge their child with too much of a good or bad thing.

Bless their hearts- parents that overindulge they are well-intentioned and loving but wrongly believe that what they are doing is right. Most parents would want the best for their child, what loving parent doesn't. We can be over-feeding our child with unhealthy foods which sets them up for failure and obesity for a lifetime. Further causing the child to grow up with serious life-threatening health issues. The child growing up overweight "obese" . sets them up to be bullied by others and it isolates them from physical . play activities and sports. Some parents do this to quieten to keep the child content, but they don't realise the ramifications to the child for their actions. It is done to control or stop tantrums or out of a feeling of guilt not being able to spend time with the child- so a feeling of overcompensating-making it up to the child. I'm sure the child would much prefer their parent's undivided attention than another toy or junk food.

Some parents may overindulge their child with too much television, computer or given expensive material items whatever the child's heart desires. They learn to expect something for nothing and they learn how to use manipulation to get whatever they want whenever they want it. It also teaches the child to become impatient, demanding, possessive. Parents that overindulge can think their children can do no wrong and their children are not held accountable to anything. These well-meaning parents may rescue their child from life's learning curves, so they never really learn from consequences. Constant overindulgence in short teaches children to become selfish, irresponsible and possible moochers later in life with a sense of entitlement, that the world owes them everything and they owe the world nothing. Overindulgence is the early foundations for a user abuser mentality and may even bring about Narcissistic behaviours.

Stopping Overindulgence .

Stopping Overindulgence . is purely common-sense; however, common-sense when in a tough situation sometimes doesn't arise to ones' sensibilities. Whilst not really seen as child abuse as such; it does not do the child any favours. We feel bad for the child and give in. Remove the offending unhealthy foods from the home and replace with healthy . foods and drinks. Being strong, not giving in to tantrums, standing firm on your resolve. Teaching the child to be patient or giving them time-out, can be helpful. Give the child good attention and praise where due . instead, and practice physical . activity with your child. With even something as little as walking the dog to start off with. Reward good behaviour in a healthy way, not necessarily with food or material items. Instead it could be a day at the park or an extra story book at bedtime. Watching a few TV programs of the Super Nanny could be helpful for parents to watch.

Unrealistically High Expectations

The world is a hard-enough place with many pressures and social expectations without us putting unrealistically high expectations on our children. Do we place unrealistic expectations on our children and then find they rebel? Not every lass wants to do ballet and not every lass is academic. Not every young lass wants to marry or have kids. Not every lad is cut out for the football team and not every lad is academic. Maybe your son wants to do ballet, there are many famous male ballet dancers. Not every young man wants to marry or have kids or be famous. Not everyone is a perfect size 8 or has a picture-perfect face. Everyone is different, we have differing value systems; with differing goals and dreams. Just because they are your dreams doesn't mean it is their dreams or desires. There will be less tension when there are fewer unrealistic impractical expectations. The sooner we realise that fact, the sooner the struggle ends, and the child thrive. Love them for their uniqueness. Talent in music, art or academics is not everything; having a healthy, happy, loving, caring child stands for so much more. And so, what…they don't give you grandkids. Would you prefer they have kids to please you and then work out to be poor at parenting and then the grandkids suffer. It happens all the time. The sooner we realise this the easier it will be for all involved. Square pegs don't fit in round holes, why not end this ludicrous tug of war.

Sibling Rivalry (Abuse)

Just as in the biblical story in Genesis, the son Cain killing . his brother Abel. Sibling rivalry does happen in these times. The above is extreme of course, however not unheard of.

It has been said, rightly so, *"Monkey see Monkey do,"* children watch intently at what we do, and their brains are like sponges absorbing information good and bad and their brains have not developed enough to filter out the bad.

The first five years of a child's life are their formative years. During this time, they take in information which helps shape and mould them and their futures. We need to be ever vigilant of our actions, so as not to pass on negative actions. Siblings through their insecurities . will often resort to abusing their sibling due to envy and jealousy . when the parent/s is busy attending to the younger children or new baby. Children need as much equal attention . and praise . from the parent, just as much as being given to the baby. Even relatives and friends can support . you in endeavouring to ensure the older child doesn't feel left out.

Unfortunately, and unintentionally there is usually a pecking order. The older child may have lost his/her bearings about where they belong in the family unit. Are they pushed further down the line? If so, they may try to do all they can to stay in number one position and that is understandable.

They may resort to hitting and abusing their younger, smaller, vulnerable . brother or sister, not because they are evil. But due to needing to vent their frustrations . and insecurities .. To them some attention . is better than no attention whether it be negative or positive attention. The child who is abusing the younger sibling once was the centre of attention and now there is a new kid on the block. Visitors and family members can go up to the new addition of the family bubs and say, *"ooh and ahh"*, and unintentionally forget the child that was there before the new baby. We are all guilty of unintentionally forgetting the older child as we get so wrapped up in the constant care . that a baby requires. With that in mind, we need to make a concerted effort to remember that the older child has needs too. The child bully-sibling abuser in this situation needs to be supervised closely and not be left alone . with the other vulnerable younger weaker child.

Some parents put especially high unrealistic expectations on the older sibling to set a better example for the younger sibling. Parents expecting that they should know better; and that therefore, they should behave accordingly. This can be such a tall order for the older child, as they are still children too, with still so much for them to learn. Such high expectations can make the older sibling resentful . of parents and jealousy . over the younger child. Subsequently, this creates disharmony . within the home.

The older child may also have some anger issues that may or may not be psychological; that may endanger and jeopardise the smaller child's emotional/physical . safety and well-being. For the child psychological help and counselling needs to be sought as soon as possible.

Steps to helping your older child become secure: -

- Talk to your child about the new baby well before it arrives. Let him know when the baby comes, that way the child is prepared.

- Allow the child to be included in all parts of preparation of baby's arrival, letting the child help choose outfits, toys, baby furniture. Also include the child in receiving new items too.

- Do your best to make your child feel secure and reassure him by saying for example, *"We love you very much just as much as the new baby!"* and remind him of how special it was when he first arrived into the world. Take the time to reassure your child and let him know that he still is very special and will always be.

- Explain the process of the baby coming into the home and how you may not be able to spend as much time. Let them know that they will not be forgotten in the process.

- Explain that a new baby can't do anything for herself, and so needs lots of Mummy and Daddy's attention. .

- For example; I read this advice somewhere in some childcare book. I decided to give it a try. Early on in preparation I bought a toy from the baby to give to my child at the time of birth, so there would be less rivalry jealousy .

between child and baby. This little charm worked a treat and my two were very loving and close for almost all of the time they were together.

- Also include them in the caring of the young baby, children love to be helpful.

- Praise your children often.

- Set aside one on one quality time to spend with the older child. Turn off your mobile phone and give the child your undivided attention. .

- Even friends and relatives can do their best to treat children equally. Encourage them to take an interest also in the older sibling. This will certainly go a long way in helping to instil security into the older child. Remember this is your child and your home, your friends and relatives need to respect . the boundaries you give them.

Most Importantly: - "Never ever, ever, **_'ever'_** compare one child over the other!" <u>I cannot stress this enough</u>. It can be most soul-destroying for the child or for the want of a better word, it is breaking the child's spirit. The world can be a harsh enough place, without home dramas too. Children are all unique individuals in their own special way; one is not smarter or better than the other. All children need to be treated as equals always. Each child having their own strengths, .weaknesses, talents and abilities; . whether it be academically, sport orientated, artistic creativity, musically, sensitive, boisterous, beautiful to look at or beautiful in personality are all traits deserving of honour, admiration, praise . and respect .. So, what... that they got 7/10 in their spelling bee or didn't make the football team cut or didn't get a university degree! So what, they aren't as pretty as someone else's child! They are beautiful in their own right! So, what... if they didn't make university, are you that superficial! They may have other talents just as worthy. As long as our children are happy, healthy, decent human beings is what counts. Your children are individuals; appreciate all children for their uniqueness. Comparing and teaching your children to compare; only teaches them to become discontent in life. It teaches them to also be competitive among their siblings and creates sibling rivalry right into their adulthood. There is nothing more disheartening than one child trying in vain to compete with their sibling or live up to unrealistic expectations. Do your utmost best not to have favourites, treat all children equally. When a child acts out, it isn't easy, try not to take the acting out personally or intentionally. Just realise it isn't easy for the child also. Favouritism of children happens in different cultures and down through the ages. For instance, in some cultures a male child is preferred over a female child and vice-versa, extremely sad and so very wrong in my opinion. We can see how the whole female gender inequality came down through from the ages to our present day. Children do take comparisons to heart and can carry this on into their adulthood, which then becomes baggage in future relationships and affects them and their families for a whole lifetime. Which then makes it far harder to remove this baggage later in life. It is far better for parents to be aware and start early in treating their children equally. *"The harsh reality is unless sorted out early these children can grow up to have less self-belief in themselves and end up taking even constructive help harshly."*

When your child is in the care of others (Caregivers are-parents, step-parents, teachers, scout masters, foster parents, relatives, friends, neighbours)

At school ., at childcare centre, at home: -

- Check out the caregiver very carefully, ask for references.
- Talk to other parents to find out about your teacher, without gossiping of course.
- Ensure the caregiver keep you in the loop on everything and any recent underlying health issues.
- Ensure they have recent contact information in case of an emergency.
- Let them the institution know about all allergies and any health issues.

- If your loved one is institutionalised know who is looking after your loved one and visit them regularly. Sometimes pop in unannounced, so you can see how everything is with your loved one when they think you aren't around. This is your right to ensure your loved ones' well-being is being taken care . of appropriately. Be very observant. Check to see if your loved one seems nervous or is behaving differently around certain carers, body language stands for a lot. Does your loved one seem nervous, fidgety, scared, try to yell out? Are there other behavioural problems, or are they off their food or having incontinence problems that weren't there before and is there extreme weight loss or gain?

- Try and give them a good sense of themselves, teach them to always speak up and stand up for themselves. To say no and don't touch me if they can verbalise or show them how to use their hands to push an abuser away or yell out for help. Some of this may or may not be possible due to their age, impediment or impairment.

- Encourage your loved one to communicate . all their concerns or fears with you.

- Be very observant and aware yourself.

- Investigate, snoop if you need; this is all about your loved one. It is your right to keep your loved one safe and it is their right to feel safe also.

Review of some possible tell-tale signs of child abuse *(What to look out for)*

- Collections of bruises ., cuts . and abrasions?
- Circular burns may indication cigarette burns?
- Broken limbs?
- Does the child cringe or seem scared or nervous?
- Unkempt appearance uncombed unruly hair, cold sores, dirty clothing, body odours urine, faecal smell or an unclean smell?
- Does the child soil or wet themselves regularly?
- Nightmares/night terrors?
- Does the older child suck their thumb or other baby behaviour?
- Underweight or overweight .; Does the child appear to be uncared for or deprived not enough ie., food, clothing, school . equipment?
- Is their home and bedroom disorderly?
- On a scale of 1-10 how bad does the house smell each time you visit?
- How does the child seem around certain person/people; are they nervous, scared or angry?

- Do you notice that the caregiver yells, swears and puts down the child?

The child may exhibit all or a few of these signs. Do be sure to have your facts straight before reporting to the police. . As some instances may be innocent ., many innocent people have been hurt through over-zealousness. *STAR 5*

"Children exposed to violence in their family show the same pattern of activity in their brains to soldiers exposed to combat." - The Psyche Mind

Chapter 12 Child Sexual Abuse

What is Sexual Abuse?

This could be sexual fondling, intercourse done to the child and/or the abuser forcing the child to perform a sexual act on them with or without violence, with or without consent. Terms you may be familiar with hearing are molestation, interference, assault, rape and abuse. This can also be done by way of photos or videos and put on the internet or where the Abuser is taunting and coercing a child into engaging in sexual acts.

Wretchedly, child sexual abuse effects are far reaching it. Child sexual abuse can have a ripple effect on ones' life. Infiltrating many parts of a persons' life causing lifelong emotional problems, affecting relationships, and self-esteem issues and sexual problems i.e., frigidity or promiscuity. This baggage so to speak, subsequently inflicts many emotional and physical disorders, depression and even suicide.

It takes great courage for a child to even open-up and speak about what happened to them, so we need to be patient and listen. Statistically in only 1% of cases the so-called perpetrator is wrongly accused. Being believed and understood is so important to the child.

What if my child has already been sexually abused? It's too late to protect them or is it?

Firstly, all is not lost, children can heal with professional help and love. Please do not see them as damaged goods, they can heal with loving care and therapy. Your child may have already been sexually abused. However, there is every likelihood, that it can happen again if safety procedures are not put in place. The last thing you want is for your child to endure another spate of abuse as they are healing. It is very important that you equip your child and yourself with the 3 E's "Equipped, Educated and Empowered." Due to their lack of self-esteem, anxieties, innocence, vulnerability and immaturity they can easily be prey again. Some children are abused multiple times by several different people even in different situations.

Also, we want to ensure our children don't inadvertently put themselves in harm's way when then grow into adults. As we have seen recently regarding our movie stars sexual assault. Sadly, these stars have been slow to seek help. Most compassionately and understandably confusion, fear and shock would certainly have hampered their efforts of seeking help sooner. We need to teach and equip our children early, so they don't grow up damaged or ready to be damaged. See my books **"My Body Is Mine, Not Yours!" (Part 2) and the accompanying "The 3 E's Caregivers and Educators Companion Instructional Guide (Part 1)"**

What is Incest? (Child sexual abuse by a family member) *The elephant in the room everyone is afraid to talk about*

Where a parent, step-parent, sibling or relative aunt, uncle, grandparents sexually molests/assaults or rapes another member of the family, a child. In my opinion molesting and raping are not two different things; both are sexual assaults and equally as damaging to the child. This may be verbal or physical, with or without intercourse, oral sex, forcing the child to sexually fondle (touch) the adult genitals or vice-versa, sex conversation, use of adult sex paraphernalia or pornography, photos or video's taken, sexual verbal harassment and coercion. Sexualising of a child, encouraging a child to dress sexually or to behave in a sexually explicit adult way or dance in a sexually explicit adult way. Some children know no other way and may see this behaviour as a normal way of life; as it is all they have ever known. Do be compassionate and understanding.

Does the family member abuser love the child? When self-gratification and selfishness play such a big role, it's hard to see how love even gets a look in. Maybe in some situations there could be love; the answer could likely be a distorted sense of love. However, the child needs need protection. On forgiveness, this is a very personal thing. Many components come into play here such as; "Is the abuser rehabilitated and truly remorseful? Are they likely to re-offend?" "Will the child be safe?" Whilst forgiving is important not everyone can and that is fine. There is no wrong or right way, it is up to the individual to make their own decision on forgiveness. I might say this though it may be beneficial for healing for a person to forgive as grudges keep people stuck and a perpetual victim. There is good pride in not being anyone's victim. Another way to look at it is with regards to their arrogant unrepentant abuser from the victim's point of view they may choose to **live life well as their best form of revenge.**

I'm almost certain "some" abusers do not want to abuse their child/grandchild, but they need help; the child needs removing from that situation. Some uncles, step-parents may not abuse their own child but other family members children and maybe some children out of a family and not others or they may abuse all of them.

Who is the sexual abuser?

- Often known and trusted by the child and their parents. A child may be sexually abused by a stranger, scoutmaster, teacher (female or male), doctor, family friend, babysitter, step-parent or anybody for that matter often a family member- grandparents, biological parent- mother and/or father, siblings-brothers or sisters, aunts or uncles, cousins, step-siblings. The person can appear very plausible and upstanding and can spin a very believable story.

- Sexual Abusers can be male or female.

- Sexual Abusers are predominantly male.

- Sexual Abusers are predominantly a step-parent.

- Sexual Abusers can often be the biological (blood) parent.

- Sexual Abusers may not abuse their own biological children.

- Sexual Abusers can often also be Domestic Violence Abusers within the family. So that there are several forms of abuse going on at any one time in the family. Where there is sexual abuse, be alert that domestic violence could also be likely happening. There is a relation, correlation between the 2 forms of abuse and vice versa if there is obvious domestic violence be aware there may be also not so obvious sexual abuse. Remember abusers do not have a good moral compass. In their minds, very little is out of bounds to them, crossing the line is nothing to them.

- Any race (country), religion, occupation

- More prevalent within blended step-families, where step-parent is one of the caregivers of the child. (Not implying all step-parents are abusers).

- There may be more than one abuser.

- From all socio-economic backgrounds, rich, poor, well to do.

- From urban (city) and rural (country) areas and suburban areas.

CHILD SEXUAL ABUSE

- Some cults, sects and communes can have abuse issues.

- Can be in what seems an unexpected situation where families appear perfect, no problems.

- The abuser can be a plausible, likeable person or upstanding citizen in the community. Many would have a hard time believing that such a person could abuse a child or children.

- May be a person with high esteemed position in the community i.e., church, PCYC etc

- Some abusers may look (prey) out for careers or recreations where there are children involved. They may become teachers, scout leaders, sports coaches etc. **Please Note Well:** Not all teachers, scout leaders, preachers and sports coaches etc are abusers.

- Some abusers will prey on vulnerable single parents to initiate abuse on the vulnerable child.

- Can be one of the single parents' sexual intimate partners such as a boyfriend, step-parent.

- Sexual Abusers often have been abused themselves.

- Sexual Abusers may regularly exhibit vulgar lewd conversations, though this *may not always be the case*. A rude joke here or there is normal, not my personal choice of a joke. However, if someone is always talking sexually and there are just way too many rude jokes ones' radar should be going off. A balanced person doesn't not need to tell sexual rude type jokes constantly. Remember the old saying "adage", "Your mind is in the gutter!" *Give some real thought to that.* Remember the other old adage, "Where there's smoke there's fire." *I really want you to think here, we need to keep our mind open and aware of what could be going on.* There could be strange occurrences- pick up on these; *have an eagle eye, balance it with the owl's eyes of wisdom.* "Don't get paranoid, just be balanced and keep it all in perspective."

- Sexual Abusers often get off or thrill with the feeling of getting away with their crime.

- Sexual Abusers can have a perverse pleasure in knowing they are hard to stop or catch.

- Sexual Abusers are "predators" they can sense and smell the fear on the victim "prey ." and make them their next target them as their next victim.

- It is with that victim that they thrive .. I believe it to be that primal. Windows are the eyes to the soul, when one comes to know a predator, you can literally see a certain gaze in their eyes, similarly to predatory animals. You wouldn't leave predatory animals such as a lion out on the streets, then one needs to wonder why our courts are so lax so as to let these predators out on our streets. This is in fact a dangerous situation. Can such people be rehabilitated? That is questionable. It all depends on the person; maybe, maybe not?

- The Sexual Abuser can be in denial . and thinks one more assault won't hurt too much or maybe they truly get so angry that they just don't care . or the gratification is just too strong. They may not know the life damaging implications of their actions on the innocent . victim. Or maybe they have never had a good role model to show them how to behave. There are so many variables here. *As most of us do know right from wrong. There is absolutely no excuse for sexual abuse or abuse of any kind; abuse is wrong- nothing condones abuse. These abusers must be held accountable for their crimes.*

Who is at risk?

- Children of any age from infancy to teen years.
- Both genders-male or female.
- Children with or without a disability or mental illness.
- There is an elevated risk and vulnerability of children with disability to be more at risk. Due to disability they may be unable to articulate their abuse to caregivers or authorities

due to age, blindness, hearing, speech impairment, fear, communication problems or mobility issues, etc.

- Children institutionalised. **Please Note Well:** Not all institutions are unsafe and not all are safe.

- Children of single parents who may have to work or do other activities where they have dependent on the support of others (the abuser may be relative of close friend to help in caregiving-giving parents a break or mind child by offering to look after child for short or long periods).

- Children whose parents may have several short-term relationships/sexual intimate partners.

- Can be a known scandal within families where secrecy is used to hide and cover up.

- Anyone who feels alone ., empty and unloved so the kindness of a stranger can be all that it takes to lure the victim into the predators . (abusers) lair. This could be a child who is outcast from the rest of the herd "family" or a single mother (lonely, doing it tough, alone) looking after her child/children, or busy families where both parents are working. *Predators look for the weakest link*, parents not fully plugged in to all their children. They case out the joint (family dynamic)-looking for a way in; they look for the child or person in a family that they know is easy prey.

- *The vulnerable ., gullible, trusting, naive, innocent ., frail, those unable to tend to their own needs are the ones that need protection from predators.* Without meaning to fear-monger but bring attention to this very serious situation. Again, it is so primal; *predators sniff out their prey . and then hunt their victim down.*

Very important: *"Predators stalk families that are struggling as their prey, parents beware."* They wait for the right moment and even groom "trick" the unsuspecting. They are a master at what they do. We ensure are children are sun safe and bike safe with helmet and sunscreen in hand. But have we ensured they are they predator safe?

Why do sexual abusers abuse?

My job 'role if you like,' here is not so much to tell you why it happens but to show you how to be aware. I prefer to leave the nuts and bolts up to the experts. However, for my experienced laymen's gist for what it's worth- this is what I think;

- It is the abusers' modus of operandi- their habit of operating.
- They may have been taught to abuse others.
- For their own sexual gratification.
- It is like an addiction, a drug that they take.

- There may be more than one reason why they do it.
- They are sneaky and sly and know just how to get away with it.
- They get a kick or thrill out of doing it.
- They think little of the victims' feelings.
- Their reasoning is warped- out of kilter.
- The conditions are fertile for them to abuse there is a vulnerable child in their midst.

What Is grooming? *(The following are just a few examples)*

- The sexual abuser "predator" grooms the child and even parents/caregivers it is usually done subtlety and over an extended time. Grooming is a calculated, sly conniving method; baiting or luring if you like, to catch their prey. They'll do whatever it takes to lure their victim.
- Abuser says to the child "This is how I show you my love."
- Abuser saying, "I am your spunky uncle."
- Abuser says, "My favourite girl does favourite things for me"
- Abuser sexualises the child asking them to dance sexy.
- In and of itself love songs can be innocent. Songs such as *"You are my Sunshine"* and *"Love Me Tender"* are quite pure and many parents sing such songs to their child. However, serenading a pre-teen child victim with romantically suggestive/sexually explicit adult love songs is inappropriate. Songs with phrases such as *"Let me lay down*

beside you and come let me love you, let me give my life to you, come love me again." and then **coupled with the other adult abusive actions is nothing short of sneaky and conniving.** *(This was done to me as a child; I was entranced for a very short time- because an adult was showing an interest in me. This non-blood relative {from the extended family} with guitar in hand would sing several inappropriate songs. This was confusing as to context of why these songs were even sung to me. My radar knew that something was amiss; that this was a form of grooming to lure me in along with the rest of the abuse. I did not know how to articulate what was happening to me to receive help.* **There is nothing wrong with singing love songs to your children but when there is other impure intention motive involved then this is very wrong.**

- Buying sexy clothing/lingerie for the child or they may dress in such around the child.
- They may watch porn in front of the child or behave inappropriately and try to make it seem like a normal thing in front of the child.
- Abuser may tell caregiver that they will look after the child over the holidays to give them a break as the child is naughty.

What to do when a child has been sexually abused

- Listen to your child, don't berate them. Reassure them that you will ensure that it won't happen again and in particular that it was never their fault. Report the incident immediately to police . and children's services. Explain to your child that you will need to take them for a medical examination and stay with them through the process. Counselling . is also most important, take them to a recommended child psychologist, you can get a referral from your family doctor.

- A child should always be believed that this is real. Only in rare cases is this made up, but it has been known to happen. Sometimes within families there is much denial . and disbelief by other family members that the perpetrator could even do such a thing. The perpetrator (abuser) holds a lot of power over a child and also towers over a child with height, strength and knowledge.

- The child can also feel guilt . and worry that they will break up the family or they may be the cause of upset and distress. The child may have nightmares or become withdrawn and not want to go near the perpetrator. A child victim can end up feeling bad and dirty like it was their fault.

CHILD SEXUAL ABUSE

- Sometimes a child may crave for affection ., and may act out by being promiscuous or playing with their genitals or act out by playing with other children in a sexual . way. This should be seen as a cry for help.

- Sometimes the child will complain about being sore or itchy, it is possible for them to contract STD's (Sexually Transmitted Diseases). A child could also be drugged by the abuser, so they can use them for their own disgusting . gratification.

- The child may even wet themselves out of nervousness, their grades may suffer. Sadly, in some cases the child is blamed for making it all up or bringing it on themselves another reason why they don't tell anyone. A child may also feel so guilty and dirty that they wash themselves compulsively causing recurrent thrush and eczema. This obsessive-compulsive disorder (OCD) of over-washing can continue throughout their adult years, along with nightmares, flashbacks and sexual . problems of frigidity or promiscuity. All these symptoms are a cry for help.

- If it's happening to one child, it is more than likely happening to other children (siblings, cousins, neighbourhood or school children) also. Do check.

- Do not downplay or discount your child's abuse. It is an abhorrent disgusting thing that has happened to them.

- Child psychologists are professionals and . can find out a lot of what the child has been through by means of child play or painting pictures. This allows for the child to express themselves in a caring non-threatening manner. Lots of TLC (tender loving care .) will be needed; you may also need to notify the child's teacher. By informing the teacher, the teacher can be sensitive and understanding to what the child has been through and can also be alert and aware of the situation.

- Sometimes the parents may not know and not find out till the child has grown into an adult. Therefore, parents need to stop blaming themselves.

- Sometimes too, a child could be very good at hiding things and just end up believing it is their fault; resulting in them never telling anyone.

- The child can't see the point in telling anyone because nothing can be done- so they wrongly believe due to their lack of maturity and limited knowledge (that is why it is important to equip, educate and empower your child). Only now are caregivers and parents gaining an understanding; decades earlier there was little knowledge and even now parents are still struggling to grasp and understand the magnitude of child sexual abuse and all its implications. Therefore, we really need to step away from blame.

- Parents too can feel helpless . and not know what to do and like the child be afraid of the consequences. Parents also don't want to hear those awful words from their child that they have been molested because this is one of their worst fears. Consequently, parents may avoid asking those difficult poignant and painful questions with their child. It can be devastatingly painful for the parent to hear their child has been molested.

It is important that these parents not be judged. Instead they should be supported, they too, are the secondary victims in all this. Naturally, the parent would never have wanted anything like this to happen to their much-loved child/children. Do have some compassion for these parents. However, in saying how painful this is for the parent...Never underestimate what this has done to the child; the primary victim is the child and they need to be made priority in receiving help.

How the victim is affected (I've written this in italics to show the real gravity of child sexual abuse)

The following is not a complete and exhaustive list as each person may have different experiences;

- *They "the victim" feel embarrassment.*
- *They feel guilt.*
- *They feel shame.*
- *They blame themselves.*
- *They feel dirty.*
- *They feel humiliated.*
- *They feel fear.*
- *They feel sadness.*
- *They feel depressed.*
- *They feel distressed.*
- *They feel unloved.*
- *They feel uncared about.*
- *They feel they are being punished.*
- *They feel distrust.*
- *They feel defeated.*
- *They feel betrayed.*
- *They feel confused.*
- *They feel undeserving of good treatment.*
- *They feel alone.*
- *They feel no one will believe them.*
- *They don't like themselves.*
- *They do not feel as good as the next person.*
- *They live with worry and anxiety.*

- They lose a good sense of themselves.
- They may feel a deep hatred of themselves.
- They may punish themselves.
- They may feel suicidal.

Does the abuse change the victim?

- The child may not be as carefree.
- The child may not be as happy and playful.
- The child could become nervous, scared.
- They the child "victim" may behave oddly and be hard to understand.
- They will experience trust issues and may have feeling of defeat.
- They could incorrectly blame themselves.
- Their scholastic performance may suffer.
- Their relationships with family members and friends may suffer.
- They may become unkempt and not care about their bodies, bedrooms or homes. This could be from deep depression, mental illness and/or self-esteem issues/ self-loathing and seem to have a chip on their shoulder.

- *They may feel different from their peers and other family members and therefore isolate themselves by becoming loners, insulated, reserved not feeling good enough.*

- *They could have body issues.*

- *They may have trouble with lack of hygiene or the opposite be sterile OCD clean. That is not to say that everyone that is OCD clean has been sexually abused. It is just that their balance barometer or pendulum will be off kilter and swing dramatically either way. This can be seen in other situations too such as being super clingy or stand offish.*

- *As an adult the victim may have trouble with intimacy and therefore keeping long term relationships.*

- *The child or adult could end up with PTSD or another mental illness.*

- *They may have feelings of fatalism and defeat; just don't care and abuse themselves with drugs, eating disorders, self-harming "cutting" etc.*

- *The victim may become sexually precocious.*

- *The victim may resort to work lines as they mature 'grow' such as prostitution, exotic dancing etc.*

How does it affect families?

- There is carnage of whole families affected ie., Families can be left devastated thereby having fall outs with family members. Fractured broken up families, sometimes for a lifetime.
- Along with the primary victim, families become secondary victims in this too.

What are future ramifications that could affect the adult sexually abused as a child? The horrific reality-the aftermath

The adult may be scarred for life emotionally and even has some physical scars. The emotional scars can be baggage that interferes in the adult having successful intimate relationships (sexual dysfunction) and other peer social adult relationships. There could be frigidity or promiscuity issues that need addressing by a professional and support group.

- Some victims may be diagnosed by professional therapists as having PTSD or other mental health conditions.
- Some victims may become pregnant by their abuser.
- Some victims may contract STD'S sexually transmitted diseases.
- Some victims can self-harm, by way of over-washing, cutting themselves, various types of addictions used for coping

mechanisms- in order to escape emotional pain, especially in times of stress.

- Some may even suicide if the emotional pain becomes overwhelming, helpless and unending and out of their control. Especially if they feel alone without support.

- Some victims may suffer flashbacks, stimulated painful memories.

- Unfortunately for some; they may unwittingly still see their perpetrators- (For example, I still sometimes have seen my abuser in my local shopping centre; I know he knows where I live; he recently moved to the area with which I locally shop. At first it was a bit disconcerting. However, I will not change my shopping route because of this predator. Why should I have to change my shopping habits. I have just chosen to rise above being victimised. I know he's there, but he will not victimise me any longer).

- Some may suffer OCD and other mental or physical behavioural problems. Totally understandable the brain needs some mechanism on how to cope and deal with this traumatic experience. No one comes off unscathed.

- Some victims go on to abuse other children and/or adults.

- Some victims may dabble in destructive or criminal behaviour.

- *Some victims can become sexually promiscuous with others or may do an occupation such as prostitution and similar trades.*

What to do to help a child who has been sexually abused

Children in such situations need an advocate. If you know or suspect a child has been a victim of sexual abuse or if you are unsure whether they have been, all is not lost as there are many good Health Professionals that can help. You cannot and should not do this alone. Take your child to see your family GP General Practitioner or Paediatrician and they will give you a referral to see one of the Specialists or give you advice and information about good Counsellors or Therapists in this field or you may need to obtain for your child a stronger professional approach such as a Psychiatrist or Psychologist.

There may also be support groups for victims and families, your therapist will be able to inform you. Quite often the authorities Police or Family Services may need to be informed so they can intervene to protect and get help for your child and any other children at risk. Though we all know sadly this is not a perfect system it still has flaws.

We can either bury our heads in the sand denying, pretending and hoping it doesn't happen to our loved ones. Or we can realise that our world can be unpredictable and take a realistic approach, whereby we educate, equip and empower our children and ourselves.

Children need to be able to assert their rights when it comes to their well-being; they need to feel that they have permission to stand up for themselves when we aren't close at hand. They need to realise that speaking up for themselves is not being rude or naughty.

As much as we'd like to, we can't always be there to hold their hands every step of the way. Herein, by educating our children we in turn can have peace of mind, knowing we have prepared and equipped our children the best we can for the big world. All caregivers need to arm a child with a voice, that can be listened to and believed.

Abusers do not have the right to: -
- To sexually abuse violate children whether their own children or someone else's in any way shape or form-period.

After reporting to authorities, what can happen later?
- Police may interview the child along with the parents; then an incident . report . made and statement taken. Stay with your child throughout this process as it can be overwhelming and confusing for them. The perpetrator may or may not be charged and arrested. Usually corroborating evidence is needed- other witnesses. The perpetrator is

usually very careful in making sure there are no witnesses, this is done to make the child seem like they are lying being deceitful.

- In some instances, the child is required to testify in court. Such a decision of whether to put the child in court would be daunting for the parent, as the child has been through too much already. If such a situation is incestuous many a family has been known to break up, I so get this- this would not be easy to do. But really what is more important the break up and admittance of a dysfunctional family? You haven't failed. You've only failed if you don't stand up for your child. Isn't your child important here? Maybe the perpetrator is a loving, caring family member and chances are that they are. But they still committed a crime against the child; they may be able to get "help" treatment. But helping the child first is paramount. You can still show care and concern for the perpetrator, but again the child here comes first. The child, "your child is priority here not the offender." Put yourself in your child's shoes that if you don't attend to this, there will always be a wedge of sorts in your relationship with your child. Your child could hold some sort of resentment and hold back- you will sense this in their behaviours. The last thing you want is your child resenting you. Otherwise you could live to regret this.

- Adult victims can join support groups such as Survivors of Sexual Child Abuse or see a trained psychologist that specialises in this area. Relaxation and meditation CDs can also be helpful. Lots of TLC and sensitivity is also needed from their partners to help them heal.

- A professional therapist may do art therapy with the child. With this sort of therapy, the therapist will have the child draw pictures. Pictures often tell a story and can be a subtle non-threatening way of finding out vital information. As children can find it hard to articulate what has happened. Therapists are skilled at drawing out the important information from the child through art therapy.

Where can child sexual abuse happen?

What I am about to tell you is not, so you become paranoid, it is just so that you become aware. Basically, it can happen anywhere. One does not like to think it is possible for it to happen in these places. It can even happen right under your very nose in the same room you're in and you not even notice.

- Within the family home.
- Within foster care.
- Within sects and cults.
- Within communes.

- In institutions.
- In hospitals.
- In nursing homes.
- At school.
- Local park
- In the water at the beach.
- In the bushes.
- Behind or in the toilet facilities.
- Locker rooms
- Camping trips
- Caravan parks
- Sleepovers
- Parties
- Vehicles
- Church
- Or anywhere else for that matter.

When can child sexual abuse happen?

- Whilst parents or caregivers are asleep or awake (otherwise busy).
- When you are at work.
- When you are out running errands.
- Whilst being minded.

- During school hours.

- Right under your very nose-in your own home.

- In a two-storey house whilst you are upstairs, it can even be happening downstairs, in the garden shed, in the back yard, in the swimming pool.

- On picnics, on holidays, in the lake, in the bushes, in the tent, in the car.

- When your back is turned.

- It can happen in moments.

- Caregivers may be drugged so they do not hear their children.

- Children can be drugged, so the abuser can initiate his abuse.

- Children can be working or preoccupied, so the abuser can initiate his abuse.

- It can be ever so subtle-that you may not be aware.

Prevention-Safeguarding your child from sexual abuse

(How to prevent or minimise the chances of child sexual abuse to your child)

CHILD SEXUAL ABUSE

At school, at childcare centre or at home:

- Try not to engage the help of sitters or others you do not know extremely well to look after your child.

- Try to get work for the hours of school hours, so it limits the need for sitters or asking others to mind your child.

- If you require the use of a sitter, ensure it is someone you know very well or someone from a reputable nanny firm.

- Screen, interview all sitters before using their services, ask to see references.

- Ask pertinent "relevant" questions-this is your right and can give so you some peace of mind also.

- You may want to put recording cameras in your home, so you can keep an eye on who comes into your home.

- If a sitter is going to be looking after your child for several hours, ring regularly and ask to speak also to the child. You could have someone you trust drop by unannounced and if it bothers you come home early.

- Know everyone extremely well before they come into your home.

- Do not have too many sexual partners; know them well before bringing them into your home.

- Do not allow people to become overly familiar with your child.

- Make sure you get to know the person, not the other way around the person gets to know your child.

- As much as is possible look after your child yourself, you are the only one you can fully trust.

- Teach your child to not be quick to hug or sit on laps of people hardly known to you. Do they know this person very well?

- Teach your child personal space and their private "out of bounds" areas.

- It does not hurt them to kick, yell and scream to bring attention and ward off abuser/perpetrator. Practise role playing as a preventative measure- in how to empower themselves; using powerful words and actions such as; *"No!" "Don't touch me!" "Leave me alone!"*

- Teach your child about strangers and even about sexual abuse without being too explicit. Teach your children to even be careful of parked vans in inconspicuous places. If they see a suspicious obscure van/SUV for the child to walk across the road away from the van or in the opposite direction and run, yell out if they need to. (Practise role playing as a preventative tool- how to empower themselves with words and actions). Teach them to run to safety of a shop or school and ask someone to contact you. A child could be grabbed quickly and easily and pulled into a van. Parents have to think ahead and teach children to think on their feet. There are tracking watches that you may want to invest in for your child.

- Explain that they do not have to hug, cuddle, kiss or sit on laps or be picked up if they don't want to and that they don't have to be tickled or talk about uncomfortable and private things with their own body. However, in saying that if affection is important in your family and trust is not an issue; a warm hug if that is ok with the child should suffice for affection. Of course, who doesn't like affection and long cuddles, snuggles & kisses. Physical affection should not be stopped if you know and trust this person 100%. Let's not get paranoid, just be sure.

- Give children a good sense of themselves, teach them to always speak up and stand up for themselves. To say no and don't touch me.

- Teach them not to go into cars with anyone other than yourself unless otherwise arranged by you.

- Teach your child to communicate all their concerns or fears with you.

- Be very observant and aware yourself.

- Investigate, snoop if you need; this is all about your child it is your right to keep your child safe. Do all you can to ensure your child's safety.

- Trust your intuition if it doesn't feel right then it's not right.

- Supervise and read to your child an age appropriate "reputable child friendly"- child sexual abuse awareness and prevention book.

- Martial arts or self-defence classes for your child may help them to feel empowered.

- Keep in regular touch with your child's school teacher and group leaders, stay and volunteer if you can. Also inform them if your child is having problems or new situations have occurred. You will also need other people's trustworthy finger on your child's pulse if you can't always be there.

- If your child is institutionalised know who is looking after your child and visit them regularly. Be very observant. Check to see if your child seems nervous or behaving differently.

- Communicate regularly with your child and let them know you will always be open and approachable, should they want to talk or if something is bothering them. Above all never

ever blame the child. Listen carefully to them about their wants, needs and fears.

- Watch for body language between your child and the carers. Do they seem nervous, fidgety, scared, try to yell out? Are there other behavioural problems or are they off their food or having incontinence problems that weren't there before?

Why a child may not let anyone know about abuse happening: -

- The child may be put down, humiliated and ridiculed by their abuser, therefore feels their situation is hopeless and they feel helpless.

- The child simply may not know how to articulate; especially something so foreign to them and hard for them to even understand. How does a child even begin to understand how to explain an adult sexual matter?

- The child may have been threatened or their loved ones threatened by abuser, so the child is afraid to ask for help or alert a caring adult. They may feel they are responsible to protect their loved ones from their abuser. The abuser may use brute force, intimidation, threats, guilt . tripping, sometimes subtly and gently coercing a child telling them, *"It is our little secret don't tell anyone, or I will give you a toy later, or you will find it nice,"* or *"I just want to show my love to you,"* *"I know you like it,"* or finally *"I'll kill your*

Mum"- which is enough to manipulate any child into silence. By calculatingly deceiving the child by saying to the child about it 'feeling nice' puts the *onus* on the child, thus making the child feel responsible, for the child to incorrectly bear the blame. They do this, so the child will not tell. In actuality, the abuser also uses this form of manipulation to take the heat off themselves and not take any responsibility for their actions.

- The child may feel overwhelmed and confused not sure what to do to help themselves.

- The child may feel scared of speaking up should they not be believed or may feel they will be blamed or that somehow, they brought it on themselves. Or they may not want to worry or bother anyone.

- The child may feel you are unapproachable to share their fears with.

- The child may feel too small or vulnerable to stand up for themselves with difficulty to articulate due to age, size, shyness, emotional immaturity or disability.

- The child may feel, "What's the point no one will believe me anyway!"

Signs of sexual abuse in children

It is important to be aware of things such as a child's scholastic performance or their refusal to go to school or anything out of the ordinary i.e., refusal to eat, bed-wetting, tantrums, night terrors etc. The child may suffer insomnia or cannot sleep with the light off. The child may become promiscuous and experiment with themselves or other children. Their self-esteem, self-worth will show signs of suffering, their bedrooms could be in constant couldn't care less disarray and/or their school grades suffering. Remember there is a whole lot going on in that young child's mind, they may be scared or worried or fearing going home or to a place where further abuse ensues.

There may be destructive behaviour where the child lashes out, in other words acts out-misbehaving, breaking things, stealing or rudeness. Acting out is usually a cry for help. Though it is also important not to get too carried away with things either. To allay your concerns, it is always best to see your doctor, who will refer you to the appropriate form of therapy for the child. The child may have misplaced feelings of responsibility, guilt or shame, and even overwhelming feelings of fear, betrayal, distrust (wary), uncertainty and worry. Not forgetting that they may blame themselves along with all these other reasons is such a heavy burden to carry for one so young. Still they have to do well at school and try to keep it all together. These issues may be warnings signs that something might be wrong. Fear and anxiety can be all consuming.

Checklist of possible tell-tale signs of child abuse (What to look out for)

- Bowel or urine incontinence
- The child is scared and nervous around certain people.
- Blood on child's underclothing.
- The child may exhibit immature, nervous, insecure, self-comfort behaviour like thumb-sucking or nervousness-chewing clothing, items. Some thumb-sucking in children is normal, however when a child is doing this and wasn't before you need to investigate.
- The child may seem sexually precocious, talking about sexual matters with a maturity well beyond their years as if someone is coaching or grooming them sexually. The child may play more than usual with their genitals and other children to a certain point this is just normal curiosity, however when it is obsessive that is not normal.
- Child is afraid of the dark and sleeps with light on and sleeps with extra clothing on.
- Night terrors/nightmares
- Tantrums though common if not the usual behaviour need to be investigated.

- The child may touch/rub their genitalia a lot or itch a lot. Investigate.
- The child may speak in sexual adult overtones.
- For the older child- a preteen/teen an unwanted pregnancy or STD Sexually Transmitted Disease caused by the abuser.

What about witnesses?

Are you kidding me witnesses? This is a crime; a criminal will not have witnesses. Occasionally there may be. That's where this gets difficult for the victim; it then becomes his word against hers vice versa. But please don't let that put you off reporting it and getting help. There are rarely witnesses (logic alone should tell you that) to sexual abuse as the predator abuser doesn't want witnesses to their criminal acts. This often makes it hard for the victim to be listened to and believed. In most cases there needs to be "corroborating evidence" witnesses, before the police and necessary authorities can act. That is why some abusers get away with it. The victim also feels alone and defeated, as they don't know of any other witnesses. A child may even make up an imaginary friend they can talk to when they are alone with their fears for comfort and may create a mystical character person or animal which is their knight in shining armour as a coping mechanism to the distress they feel. As a child I did this, this character was formed for a couple of years and then I discovered music.

If there are group situations where there are several siblings, or a group of children being sexually abused, then there are witnesses; corroborating evidence. Even so these victims may feel that there will be bad or grave consequences if they should tell.

The importance of not playing the "Blame Game"

The abuser is totally at fault; it is the vulnerable innocent child and not the parents if they were totally unaware. Parents and caregivers if you have an inkling you must take the necessary steps to find out and report the incident. Ensure your child is safe and get them immediate professional help. One is only to blame if you knowingly do nothing about it.

The loving parent caregiver already feels bad enough it is counter-productive to assign blame. Parents or caregivers should never blame themselves, unless of course they were fully aware and turned a blind eye. But then of course there is denial, many parents or caregivers are afraid to see the truth as it is easier to block out the unthinkable, as to think about it could be unbearably painful. Facing the truth can be hard to face and a bitter pill to swallow. Naturally no loving parent wants to even think about it, but it does happen. Single parents that have multiple partners can unintentionally be bringing in sexual predators into their home and into their child's lives which leaves their vulnerable child open to risk of sexual molestation.

What help is there for adult who suffered child sexual abuse?

One may need to seek the help of professional health experts such as Psychiatrist and/or Psychologist or Counsellor; you may need to see your Family Doctor for a referral. There are also good Social Workers that have all the right contacts and will guide you in the right direction for help. Cost wise, seeing a profession may be covered by Medicare. There are also some that give cost free counselling and advice with some community services such as Lifeline and Crisis Care especially if the crisis happens during the night out of business hours. However, it is best to see a qualified counsellor or therapist as mentioned above. Some health care professionals bulk bill and sometimes you only pay the gap fee. But what is the cost of a life!

If your Psychiatrist wants to try you on medication, never underestimate the good that proper medications can do. Always take the medications as prescribed- in other words, do not abuse your medication. Take it as advised by your doctor or pharmacist. You cannot just go off your medication as this could cause you harmful side-effects. Your doctor can properly and carefully wean you off the medication.

One may also want to join a support group with other victims that can relate and give each other support and friendship. There are also wonderful self-help paperback books or e books, CDS available, go to your local library, bookshop or the internet. You may find some great self-help books that have activities that one can do that can be most helpful with or without the assistance of your therapist.

"I am so sorry this has happened to you, I do understand as I have been there also. However, to help yourself you need to do your utmost not to wallow in self-pity- "Woe is me!" Just as I had to learn and anyone else who does not want to be a victim there is always someone worse off no matter how traumatic your life was or is. It will get better, however only you can do that. You were not the first to suffer and sadly you won't be the last."

Sometimes in life one needs a wake-up call, by working at a homeless shelter or helping at an orphanage, can be very rewarding and can help give one a better perspective on things, as one's problems will likely feel nothing compared to theirs. I'm not meaning to sound harsh. I just get very disconcerted when I do hear people complain and do nothing to change or help their situation. One does need to stop being self-absorbed, instead help others, journal write. You may find watching programs such as Dr Phil, Oprah quite interesting and informative, they are not just for entertainment. There are always things you can do to help yourself. Please don't make any excuses. There are people with horrifically tragic lives that are proactive in their own self-help and have turned their lives around and now they are helping others. Do something positive with your life, no "yes buts". You can do it too! *"It's never too late to have a happy childhood even in your 40's, but the second one is up to you and no one else. That is of course unless you've left it too late."* I can thoroughly recommend a wonderfully helpful book that I read called the "The Courage to Heal" by Ellen Bass and Laura Davis. I also completed the "The Courage to Heal Workbook" by Laura Davis with my Psychiatrist. She is an amazing compassionate caring doctor. Find a good doctor and complete those two books if you can.

Child Sex Slavery/Trafficking

This may or may not be relevant to some. But I believe it still deserves to be documented, though I personally have never experienced such. We mainly hear of this in third world countries, and not so much in domestic situations; but it is alive and well in even western developed countries. Therefore, we need to be aware when it comes to our children. Slavery/trafficking basically is prostitution and paedophilia the selling of sexual acts by the vulnerable, in which the usual victims of this illegal trade are women and children.

Can the abuser be helped?

Your first priority and responsibility are with the child to protect them from further abuse. Also, other children can be protected from future harm.

Some abusers can be rehabilitated, however not all. The best way an abuser can be helped is if you report them to the correct authorities. Don't feel bad if they go to gaol (jail) because what they have done is a crime, don't sugar-coat it, it is a crime. Some abusers are crying out for help and want to be caught so they can be stopped, and many others don't want to be caught or stopped. Abusers can receive help **"if"** they sincerely want help to change. Counselling and therapy can be sought for the Abuser. The Abuser is the responsibility of the justice system, do not take matters into your own hands. Vigilantism is not the answer, leave it to the authorities.

A Balanced Perspective

Know this: -

- There are carers and then there are carers.
- There are parents and there are parents.
- There are clergy and there are clergy.
- There are teachers and there are teachers.
- There are bosses and there are bosses.
- There are religions and there are religions.

    *"I'm sure you get the gist! Know it for what it is a **stark reality**.*

There is good and bad all around, you just need to be observant, educated and aware. Don't get paranoid, cynical and sceptical, just be aware."

On A Final Note: We can either bury our heads in the sand denying, pretending and hoping it doesn't happen to our loved ones. Or we can realise that our world can be unpredictable and take a realistic approach, whereby we educate ourselves and our children. We can lull ourselves into a false sense of security thinking that our children are in the best schools and God is on our side; and of course, who doesn't want to think that! It can happen at any school and God helps those who help themselves. In a nutshell it can happen to anyone. Prevention is the best tool for protection.

"Child abuse casts a shadow the length of a lifetime,"

-Herbert Ward

Chapter 13 Spousal Abuse

(the more commonly known abuses)

See also chapter 3

In Marriages and de facto relationships

As spoken of in chapter 2, there are other types of abuse that can happen in relationships such as marriage ., de-facto or other committed relationships. However here we will speak of the most common forms of abuse. The following are examples of what abuse may be. Your experience may or may not be different.

*STAR 5

Emotional . Abuse

The abuser may tell you that you are ugly ., stupid, never amount to anything, make fun of you, ridicule . you and make an example of you to others, may call you derogatory names. The abuser may say any of the following or more; "you're ugly, losing your hair, you're dying of cancer, you are nothing without him" and laugh at your housekeeping skills. The abuser may stop you from having friends or put you down in front of your family and friends. The abuser may check your every move, smothering you, not allowing you to have your own space. They may constantly ring you, keep tabs in you, and make demands on you. The abuser may put you down or berate you for burning dinner or it not being on time, some of it may be ever so subtle.

Physical . Abuse

The abuser may beat you, kick you, pull your hair, spit in your face, urinate on you, bite you or burn you with cigarettes. Smash holes in walls, throw food about, throw hot coffee at you, threaten you. Hide the car keys so you have no mode of transport at your disposal. Stops you from driving your car. Tie one down constantly having the woman pregnant . child after child, so leaving is difficult. Ensuring she has no other life- no friends, no other outlook on life or aspiring dreams. All she will ever be is his constant caregiver, sex object and his very own personal punching bag.

*STAR 5

Sexual Abuse

The abuser may have sex . or sexual . intercourse with their spouse or partner without their consent, whilst you are well or sick. The abuser may use force to get gratification from you or perform or get you to perform lewd sexual behaviour against your will, convictions or beliefs. You may be forced to have sex with others known to you or strangers. You may be forced into prostitution. He may take videos of you having sex or take photos of you in the nude all without your consent.

Abusers do not have the right to: -

- Physically injure, maim or kill their loved ones or anybody else.

- Emotionally abuse their loved ones with shouting, yelling, screaming, taunts, threats, swearing, demeaning behaviour- put downs, belittling.

- Deny and neglect loved ones of healthy . food, safe shelter, adequate clothing and education

- Deny loved ones of love, care ., attention . and affection ..

- To deny . loved ones from friendship ., socialisation, recreation and rest.

- To monopolise . a loved one's time.

- To isolate their loved ones from family and friends.

- To be disrespectful . to loved ones.

Finally, do abusers love? Well I'm not sure. Only a professional can answer that one. I'd like to think so. The way I see it is that to fully love someone, one must first love themselves. When aggression, abuse and selfishness play a big part, it's hard to see how love even gets a look in. ***Please also see chapter 3.***

SPOUSAL ABUSE

"Sometimes giving someone a second chance is like giving them an extra bullet for their gun, because they missed you the first time."

Chapter 14 Self-Abuse (Self-Harm)

How does a person self-abuse?

- Cuts Themselves for stress relief.

- Over Washing

- Suicidal Tendencies

- Habits & Addictive Behaviours ie., Alcohol Abuse- Alcoholism, Drug Abuse- Addictions . to Hard Drugs and Prescription Drugs, Overeating/Binging

- Eating disorders such as Anorexia, Bulimia

- Sexual Addictions ., Exotic Dancing

- Prostitution

*STAR 5

Self-abusers use their addictions . to escape hardships and emotional pain in life or to comfort them. Self-abusers often feel a release from stress when they are harming themselves. They may not realise there are better coping mechanisms available, however only in receiving professional . help. Self-harm . can also be used to medicate when one feels overwhelming stress, or they feel their lives are out of their control. Drugs and addictive tendencies can take a strong hold. It affects their self-esteem and once on that

SELF-ABUSE (SELF-HARM)

vicious cycle it is hard if not impossible for them to become rehabilitated on their own without professional assistance.

Self-abuse is like a two-edged sword the victim is also the abuser the harm . they inflict on their own-self can lead to physical . and psychological harm even death. Once the person feels hopeless and depressed, thinking there is no way out of their situation it can quickly escalate . into them feeling suicide . is their only option. They could feel that will free them from the bondages of great emotional pain and suffering.

Obvious forms of self- abuse

Personally, I have pondered at different forms of self-abuse, but thankfully I never even dabbled in it. Instinctively I knew this would be a tremendous mistake even though at the same time, it would seem the only answer for release of pain and escape.

Once you open up the Pandora's Box or can of worms, if you like; shutting the lid would be so hard. Not to mention the devastation you would leave to your loved ones. I believe when one succumbs to these habits, addictions ., it would be so hard to break and so selfish to give in to it. However, I totally understand how one could give in to it also.

*STAR 5

Subtle forms of self-abuse (the not so obvious or well-known forms of abuse)

Then there are the subtle forms of abuse that just creep up on you when you least expect, where one needs to be ever mindful of, like taking a bite out of a cream bun. My guilty pleasure, comfort eating was to have a cappuccino coffee that came with a free donut from the local café near my work place nearly every morning and then it snowballed to with every cup of tea I had to have biscuits and so on. One must rein themselves in. Or one can be hard on themselves calling themselves idiots or stupid, that also is self-violence of one's own soul; we need to learn to rid ourselves of negative self-talk and negative thoughts of ourselves. We are often our own harshest critic. And instead learn to love ourselves; when we love ourselves, we can love others wholeheartedly. It is not easy we probably all have been like that to varying degrees. If you have lived with a lifetime of this; it is not going to automatically improve out of sight, it will take some time. The struggle is real, but at least now I am aware and distract myself from negative thoughts and on being hard on myself.

In order to help oneself read self-help books ., see your doctor, get counselling, rehab if you need to, and let loved ones and friends help you. You are only human, no one is perfect, and there are many others in the same situation who can relate to you. Wouldn't you do the same for a loved one or friend? I'm sure, you would!

SELF-ABUSE (SELF-HARM)

Don't try and do it alone ., ask for help, or accept the help when it's given to you. Every day is a new day; emotional pain can be temporary, recognise it and do something about it before it takes hold. If it has taken hold it is still not too late, but you must act in a timely manner.

How can self-abuse- affect others?

Self-Abuse can affect relationships with others, mainly family members also ones' friendships. Families . can be abused verbally and physically. Some abusers steal from family to afford . their addiction which in turn causes financial and relationship . hardship . and disrespect with families. Also, the abuser/victim becomes self-absorbed, thinking mainly of their addictions ., finding it difficult to focus on anything else. It can change a person's demeanour making relationships difficult. Addictions and mental illness . often go hand in hand with Domestic Violence and Sexual Abuse.

*STAR 5

How can you help yourself from an addiction?

If you suffer from addiction, you must get yourself out of denial .. Being in denial will only bring you down and stop you from helping yourself. Sometimes one needs to hit rock-bottom before one realises the extent of the problem. You cannot heal yourself alone .. You must get professional . help. Speak to your family doctor or local hospital, they will turn you in the right direction or you may get a referral to see a professional therapist . or rehabilitation centre.

No one can help you if you are not committed to change. It will require willpower on your part, you need to stay committed.

Realistically, you will need to remove yourself from people that will keep you down, such as drug pushers or other drug addicted friends. *"As they say birds of a feather flock together!"* This may mean leaving . town, leaving behind all your old haunts, leaving your old friends behind. You must do whatever it takes if you are serious about changing.

Well it is up to you, it is not anyone else's fault or responsibility but your own. Change cannot happen until you face these facts and get out of denial.

How can you help someone in this situation?

Self-Abusers need to be supervised and watched carefully and steps taken to seek help for the self-harmer. It is important not to enable the addict when they ask for money . for food or essentials, don't kid yourself the money will go on funding for more drugs ., alcohol . or others' addictions .. Do not be an enabler; giving money to the addict for supposed food or bills, instead the money will go on the addiction, so it really is not helping the addiction. They may be lying about what they need the money for and you may never see the

SELF-ABUSE (SELF-HARM)

money again. Instead you would be better off giving tough love, sometimes you may find you need to be cruel to be kind.

Remember rock-bottom is what the addict may have to reach before change can happen. If you know of someone in this position, you can assist them to seek help. You cannot help them on your own, there are professional . counsellors/therapists . and rehabilitation to help them to get back on their feet. Even with help sometimes a situation can be beyond hope depending on the person.

***STAR 5**

Abusers do not have the right to: -

- To harm . themselves.

- To allow their self-abuse to emotionally or physically impede detrimentally and negatively on their loved ones.

- To emotionally abuse their loved ones with shouting, yelling, screaming, taunts, threats, swearing, demeaning behaviour- put downs, belittling.

- To deny . and neglect loved ones of healthy . food, safe shelter, adequate clothing and education.

- To deny . loved ones of love, care ., attention . and affection.

  .

- To deny . loved ones from friendship ., socialisation, recreation and rest.

- To monopolise . a loved one's time.

- To isolate their loved ones from family and friends.

- To check out emotionally or physically.

- To be disrespectful . to loved ones.

*STAR 5

SELF-ABUSE (SELF-HARM)

She got quieter

Her night got longer

Her blades got bigger

Her sleeves got longer

Her meals became smaller

She became skinnier

Her music became loud

And no one noticed...

Chapter 15 Bullying

School yard bullying

Bullying may start out ever so subtly, but if not stopped will escalate . out of proportion and what's more can be deadly or emotionally debilitating, scarring your child for life. Why do bullies do this? For one thing; their own self-esteem is more than likely lacking and needs boosting. The only way they know how is to be parasitic and feed off the weaker. It is that primal, you will even see it in the animal world, there is a pecking order. The bully also may be bullied at home or as mentioned earlier may have been a victim in the past of school . yard bullying . themselves. They may also be jealous of the victim and the only way for them to handle this is to bully them. The other reason they do this, is school is no longer stimulating for them and this is the way they get off- they do it for kicks and to get laughs receiving bravado from their fellow bullies who egg them on further. In "some" situations their home life may be very difficult, and they may be victimised in an abusive home. They may have also been the bullied. I was a bully for all of two minutes. I had been severely bullied as I am coloured and was even sexually assaulted by two of these bullies at school to the extent that I wanted to die and contemplated suicide as a real option, but it's not an option; the bullies were not going to win. Growing tired of being the bullied and wondering 'fantasising,' what it would be like to be the bully...was it easier...was it a form of self-preservation of sorts, to take on the role of bullying... to keep oneself from being bullied? So, I followed my friend, who was bullying a guy and regretted it immediately. I felt lousy and was most remorseful, shortly after we started it, I soon stopped. Only for a small while, I felt false confidence and a bit of a high- an exhilaration of sorts, when I was the bully, but at what cost to the victim...Then this year I was invited to a school reunion and I know the four main culprit bullies will be at the reunion. I would have loved to have gone to see my other friends, but I will not put myself through the worry of the bullies showing up. Also, I can't remember much of schooling due to my constant fear. An anxiety and awkwardness I don't wish to put myself through; at least now as an adult I can choose what I won't and will not put myself through.

Targets for bullies

The school . yard bully targets the weak, quiet, vulnerable ., the pretty, the not so pretty, overweight ., skinny, socially immature, low self-esteem, slow learner, or the disabled in some way or a child that looks different, or a child's religion, race. Victims are not responsible for the bullying and should not have to change to protect themselves. Though nowadays even the perfect looking person can be the target of the bully. The bully will often gather together his own gang. Bullies were often victims themselves that were bullied, this is often the case.

A cry for help for victim as well as the bully

Whilst it is ever so important to get the victim help, it is important to get help for the bully also. Who knows what their home life is like? Education for all is key. It's important to keep an open mind and not thrash out on the bully.

Who is to blame?

If parents are aware their child is a bully and do not take the necessary steps to discipline their child and to prevent from future abuse they are to blame more so than even their child. The same goes for the school system that has children under their charge, they are accountable and liable if they know and do nothing to stop or protect and prevent bullying of any child in their "duty of care." It is the education department that has a responsibility to ensure your child is safe in their care. It is frightening to think we entrust our children into what should be considered a safe-zone only to find they are anything but. Some parents too can be in denial . and believe their child can do no wrong; that they are perfect little angels. Then there are some parents with such red-necked attitudes with radical discriminatory viewpoints that encourage such vicious abuse. These parents may be charged and maybe even have their children removed from their care .. The child may also be put into a detention centre. The media and society in general can inadvertently nurture and encourage bullying of anything or anyone that does not fit the norm. What are our children doing with their computer games and what are they watching on television and what about their social media influence? Facebook, Twitter, Snapchat and other social media sites are arenas where children can be relentlessly bullied even to their deaths.

Parents of bullies

Parents of bullies need to get themselves out of denial .. Naturally no parent likes to know their child is a bully, it could be quite shocking and challenging for the parent to accept. As they may be great parents that never taught such things to their child. Children can learn this behaviour from their peers. No child is a complete angel 24/7. Being in denial over it is unhelpful to all, even to the bullies. The parents of bullies need to put themselves in the shoes of the victim or the victim's parents. The bully's parents need to realise that they can be charged for their child/children's behaviour, they too need to take some responsibility along with their child- the bully. Bullying is serious it's dangerous and damaging in just so many ways. Bullying can cause serious physical . and emotional harm .. It can lead the victim to take their own life. With the victim feeling they need to resort to suicide . to get away from the bullying . and emotional pain they are in.

Street bullying and thug behaviour

Thugs who abuse others to harm . or kill can act alone . or with a gang (group of people). A very dear friend of mine lost her son this way. This innocent . lad was bashed to death by a stranger over a pair of joggers whilst he was in the city on a night on the town. It was so evil and needless. My friend will never be the same again, her loss is inconsolable. Just recently on the news another lad lost his life, he was king hit from behind by a stranger, he was innocent and in the wrong place at the wrong time. For his family his life is final- lost forever... they too will never be the same... Wrong place at the wrong time just doesn't cut it. Laws need to get tougher, the sentencing does not fit the crime. Their children forever taken from them. Naturally for these families they may feel bitter and hardened, who could blame them. Really, where can one go without having to looking over one's shoulder? I don't wish to scare you just make you aware, nowhere is completely guaranteed safe. One must keep their wits about them, take precautions. By educating our children the best we can on how to protect themselves. This could also be by way of giving them self-defence lessons with a reputable martial arts club. Until laws get tougher bullying . will continue to happen.

Abusers do not have the right to: -

- Physically injure, maim or kill anyone.
- Emotionally abuse anyone with shouting, yelling, screaming, taunts, name calling, threats, swearing, demeaning behaviour-put downs, belittling.

BULLYING

Victims have the right to: -

- Seek medical assistance.

- Seek assistance from the authorities . ie., Police, Judicial system, Department of Family Services etc.

- To be treated with justly, with respect, proper assistance and protection from the Police and Judicial System.

Signs of a child being bullied

- Bowel or urine incontinence-wetting/soiling
- Eating disorders-Loss of appetite or overeating
- The child is scared, nervous, is withdrawn and retreats to their bedroom and no longer wants to play with others.
- The child does not want to go to school/truants, does not want to go to certain places. .
- The child may exhibit immature, insecure behaviour like thumb-sucking- a pacifying comfort and sometimes nervous behaviour, chewing clothing- a nervous behaviour. Some thumb-sucking in children is normal, however, when a child is doing this and wasn't before- investigate.
- The child has lost interest in activities they once enjoyed.
- Nightmares/terrors
- Insomnia- Child is afraid of the dark and sleeps with light on.
- A child's behaviour around certain people; are they nervous, afraid or exhibit anger/tantrums-if not usual, investigate.

Where can bullying happen

- At school, at work, at home, social settings, online media, anywhere.

Some may think building up a resistance in our children; teaching them how to be resilient is the way to go. Whilst I believe it may help, not all children are able to be resilient. Some children are born tender, gentle souls. Mainly we need to educate against bullying and reduce bullying and its effects.

BULLYING

Notes:

Chapter 16 Cyber Abuse

(Cyber Bullying, Cyber Stalking, Sexting, Paedophilia aka Pedophilia)

Technology playing a role in abuse

Abuse now comes in so many forms. Cyber Abuse is becoming more prevalent now with other modes of communication . readily available to our generation through modern technology such as mobile phones, internet. We now find (predators .) abusers use these modes 'tools' as they are readily available in order to prey . on their victims to bully, stalk or use paedophile behaviour and at the same time hide . their identities so as not to get caught.

Social . Networking sites such as Facebook, Twitter, Snapchat, Myspace, WhatsApp and Instagram are public arenas accessible and easily utilised for the Bully or Stalker "Predator" if you like; to use for his selfish sordid ulterior motives. These sites are areas where many people congregate and use on a regular basis hourly, daily, a big part of many people's lives.

What is cyber bullying . and why must it be taken seriously?

Is where a person uses the internet either through public emails or social networking sites, public forums, chat rooms, blogs and even texts on mobile phones. This is done to troll, bully with harassment ., humiliation, degradation and torture to another person, the victim. To make an example of them to a whole host of people or even to torment the person on their own. This is done either through embarrassing the victim with degrading, demeaning photos, videos, verbal incrimination- such as slander, character assassination, name-calling.

Hence, this leaves the victim helpless . in a hopeless situation. Taunts such as this make the victim's life torturous and unbearable .; where they can't face a day without feeling humiliated beyond their control. It affects the victim's everyday life where they lose interests in activities they once enjoyed and loom into deep depression. Some can feel stupid, embarrassed and gullible; afraid to tell others of their dilemma. It is so serious that the victim is violated, and many have felt alone . and in so much despair, they do not see a positive outcome or a way out. Consequently, they commit suicide . just to make the excruciating emotional pain and torture end.

Recently, I even noticed it myself as an adult going to an online support group to do some networking for my work. So, beware adults too, the bullies can even be on these sites.

*STAR 5

Who is the cyber bully?
Cyber Bully is usually known by the victim. The bully may be a fellow school . student, work colleague, community members or the like. There can also be more than one bully who eggs on other bullies.

What is cyber stalking?

Cyber Stalking is where a person the stalker 'predator', uses the internet to voyeur on another person-the victim's life for their own selfish gratification. In a stalking situation it is mainly found to be done by a possessive ex-boyfriend, ex-girlfriend, ex-spouse who cannot accept the end of a relationship . and in order to still control that relationship they will scare, threaten, control and intimidate their victim at all cost .. Stalkers can resort to murder. Stalkers can also be strangers with an unhealthy obsession with the victim needing to infiltrate the victim's life. The victim's every move is followed, where the victim's privacy is violated.

The stalker accesses the internet to get personal details about the victims, such as their address, phone number, thereby enabling the stalker to make direct contact with the victim. Further putting them in risk of danger-harm . or death.

*STAR 5

Cyber Paedophilia (Paedophilia aka Pedophilia)

Cyber Paedophilia is where the paedophile has indirect access to children/teens via the internet, using chat rooms, emailing and webcams. They deceive a child into thinking they are close to their age. Adults masquerading as children or young teens; therefore, hiding their true identity.

The paedophile is a predator that seeks out their 'prey,' .vulnerable ., innocent ., victims-a child that is lonely and in need of attention .. The child may or may not be looking for a friend; someone who cares to listen to them. The innocent child may also have low self-esteem all these attributes of the child are like flashing neon signs to the predator. With that the predator may lure the victim with praise ., kind words and encourage the victim to reach out to them. The predator may try to befriend the unsuspecting victim and groom them. They could ask the victim to undress and show their naked self on webcams and they may offer to meet with your child somewhere and abduct the child. This is a real possibility that law enforcement regularly have to deal with.

The predator, a paedophile can also act like a young boyfriend to entice the teen and often it works. They will later ask to meet the victim (child) at a place away from the victim's home where the victim is then open to danger- abduction ., rape or murder.

Signs of a child/teen is involved . in cyber sex .

- The child/teen retreats to their bedroom and no longer interacts with rest of family.
- The child/teen may become secretive.
- The child/teen seems to have lost interest in their usual friends.

- The child/teen may seem sexually precocious, talking about sexual . matters with a maturity well beyond their years as if someone is coaching or grooming them sexually.
- The child/teen may dress more provocatively
- The child/teen acts out, if not the usual behaviour needs to be investigated.

*STAR 5

What is sexting?

Sexting is the act of sending and receiving information of a sexually explicit nature. This can be by way of photos and videos of a sexually explicit nature via mobile phone which can then be posted onto the internet by paedophiles; where it can be sold to other paedophiles or put on pornographic sites with the chance of going viral or for their own selfish devices. Children and teenagers are vulnerable . and can be involved . in this if they have use of mobile phones. *With one push of a button once information is "out there" forever in cyber space, never to be retrieved.*

*STAR 5

Abusers do not have the right to: -

- To physically injure, maim or kill anyone.
- To sexually abuse in any form any person.
- To abduct or hold hostage any person.

- To emotionally abuse any person with shouting, yelling, screaming, taunts, threats, swearing, demeaning behaviour- put downs, belittling.

"Suicide is one of many serious side effects of bullying."

Chapter 17 Preventing Cyber Abuse

There are things you can do to stop and prevent cyber abuse

On social networking sites such as Facebook, Twitter, and Myspace there are privacy settings you can use to block undesirable people and intimidating behaviour. See Esafety.gov.au for advice to help keep your child safe.

One can also report . of inappropriate behaviour to the network site to get action. Ensure your child/children never give out private phone numbers or mobile phone numbers, residential address, passwords, place of work or school . or any identifying information about them. Teach them to be very selective of who they choose as friends on these forum sites. Many parents wisely choose for their children not to have Social media access to Facebook, Twitter etc.

*STAR 5
Educating your child about cyber abuse

Cyber friends may not be who they appear to be and can often be very deceitful cunning individuals. These predators . who are usually paedophiles are imposters and could be 'catfish' and masquerade as a 16 years old, handsome skateboarder and in fact could be a 65 year old overweight . male who sends her fictitious pictures not of himself but of some other young person- *it is important that we point this fact out to our children.* This crime has been done time and again, with dangerous results, losing one's own life. These predators will use every trick in the book. They will try and befriend a trusting child, who is bored or lonely. He will groom them, tell them they are pretty or clever, pretend to listen to them and care . about them when they are feeling down, giving the child the undivided attention . they so crave.

***STAR 5**

What to be wary of on the internet: -

- The predator may want to become a Facebook or Twitter friend and give you a cool photo of someone else not them.

- Ensure your child knows to come to you whenever she is feeling down. You as a parent need to be kind and approachable and never too busy to listen to your child's concerns.

- Really does your child need to have access to social media such as Facebook? Encourage other forms of wholesome entertainment, recreation or hobbies. The internet is not the be all. Go hiking, do some gardening, drawing, bake cookies there are so many better interests you can share with your child. The main thing is to get them through this delicate time safely.

- Ensure your child knows not to give out private information such as where they live or where they go to school ., their age and anything that may trail to your child a possible victim. These predators . seek out this information and could easily find your child and abduct, abuse and likely kill. Sounds a scary story but is ever so true. Of course, we don't want to talk about the unthinkable.

- Ensure you have a parental lockout system for your computer.

- Ensure your child's computer is not in her bedroom or tucked in the spare room.

- Regularly check what your child is doing while on the computer.

- Have a good relationship . with your child so they don't have to turn to a predator for praise and affection.

- A predator can detect a child that has deficiencies of love, care . and attention. .

- Know all your child's friends and keep the lines of communication . with your child open at all times.

- Do not allow use of webcam without your supervision or maybe better still don't get one...

Important: After speaking to your child ensure she has a good understanding of cyber abuse and have your child paraphrase back to you, so you are sure your child is not confused by the information and comprehends.

Webcams

Webcams though innocent . to most, are a sly tool that paedophiles use to exploit, violate their victims-usually children/teens. The paedophile can then use the images at their disposal to do as they wish to put on the internet on pornographic sites or sold to other paedophiles. It is best not to have a webcam on a child's computer. To have caring parental control and peace . of mind it would be better to not have the computer in a child's room. Instead keeping the computer in the lounge or family room where a parent can easily monitor the child's usage and content on the computer.

For some peace of mind, since we are not able to supervise . 24/7; there is also parental control lock out system software programs for computers available. These programs are designed to lock out undesirable content on computers such as pornographic sites from children. Educating your child about the pros and cons of internet usage and stranger danger is also important and the best form of prevention .. By doing having all these safety nets in place, the opportunity for your child to be violated is significantly reduced. Please see Esafety.gov.au

Television/Android/ Cell Phone Screen Time

Who babysits your child? We are all guilty of this. Monitor how much television your child watches and what they are watching. Try and keep the television out of the child's bedroom. Social media is something to be wary of; ie., violent addictive computer games. Even the innocent non-violent games one needs to be careful of as strangers,' "predators" can still easily get to your child through the online chat features whilst they play their computer games. It is such a shame our children can't be allowed to grow up carefree without all these worries. But it is best to be educated, equipped and empowered safeguarding them from predators.

What to do if cyber abuse is affecting you or your child
Cyber Abuse is an offence; laws differ from state to state and country to country. If you have the internet you may find information that may help; also visit your local police . station and make a statement with them. They will take all your details.

Keep all evidence of abuse by saving to your computer or mobile all texts, phone messages, emails, photos, video footage that show trails .. This evidence can be helpful in catching these criminals.

How do you know if your child is being bullied either at school . or on the internet?
Is your child tired, disinterested in things that once interested them, is teary, clingy, easily upset and listless, off their food or appears to be comfort eating? Not doing as well in their studies, their grades are slipping. Your child comes home cranky, introverted, bed wetting or withdrawn and hides in their room. Is your child crying or going through tantrums? Your child doesn't want to go to their

friend's birthday party, not a usual occurrence. These could well be signs, alarm bells that all is not well with your child. Now is the time to sit down and talk to them.

Just the two of you sit down quietly in a conducive non-threatening setting; calmly over a milkshake or go for a nice drive together and talk about it. Sometimes children are afraid to speak up against their bully either because the bully has threatened them, they don't want to look like dobbers. Or it may be that no one will believe them anyway, they feel they will get the blame, or they feel pessimistic that nothing will change for the better. Seek professional help.

It doesn't hurt for you to talk to their closest friends with the permission of their parents of course, or School Teachers, School Principal in confidence; . do some of your own investigation. Also see the School Guidance Counsellor, Chaplain or Social Worker who is obligated to support . your child. Or go and

 help out on sports day to observe from afar just what is going on in the school . playground.

One of the biggest tell-tale signs of schoolyard bullying . is when your child complains of being too sick to go to school . or point-blank refuses to go or truants (also known as wagging or running away from school). Due to the social media age school yard bullying can also be linked to cyber bullying. It is important to get your school or day care . centre to provide emotional support . for both your child and yourself. Some counselling for your child and yourself is in order. See your family doctor who can refer you to a qualified therapist ..

Where a child is physically bullied and has scrapes and bruises . it is important for you to document this with your family doctor and authorities . such as police. . By taking the necessary photographs of the injuries and time, date and place where assault occurred. This can be quite a traumatic . experience for both child and parent. Emotional bullying is equally as bad as physical bullying if not more so in the sense that the scars can last a lifetime. Parents can feel helpless . and blame themselves.

*STAR 5

What to do if your child is being bullied

Firstly, make the school . principal, teachers aware of the bullying . within the school so that precautionary measures can be put in place not just for the welfare of your child, but others like them. Counselling . may help your child; all schools usually have a guidance . officer, chaplain, social worker or counsellor.

Talk to your child and reassure them that you will do your best to protect them, keep them informed. Try becoming more involved . in the school ., canteen, volunteer classroom help, playground assistant. Remember bullies too are victims of themselves and who knows what is happening at home.

Enlist the help of teachers and principals most of them do have your child's best interest at heart. The school . and the education department also have a responsibility of "duty of care" . to your child. Failing that, try enrolling your child in another school for a fresh start- it may help. Then finally if all else fails home-schooling can be a very good option.

Sometimes children just can't socially adapt to the larger school . environment and just may never fit in. Home schooling can bring parents and the child closer together-learning together can be fun. All in all, some children have been known to suffer separation anxiety from their parents. If you feel the option of home-schooling could create socialisation problems, in that your child will be without friends you can put them in a swimming, karate or art class; where they can express themselves and make friends at the same time. Social . interaction is very important. In the meantime, help build up their confidence . with praise . and lots of TLC (tender loving care .). On a final note, know that the bullied can also become the bully.

*STAR 5

BREAKING THE CHAIN ON ABUSE

Optional reading; Here is one of my healing projects, which I am sure you will be able to draw from.

What I Deserve (You Are Important Too!)

I deserve to be happy.

I deserve to be treated with dignity and respect. .

I deserve to treat myself with respect. .

I deserve to be treated with kindness.

I deserve to live without fear.

I deserve to be loved.

I deserve to be liked by myself.

I deserve to feel secure.

I deserve to feel safe.

I deserve good treatment from others.

I deserve good treatment from myself.

I deserve the necessities in life.

I deserve good health & fitness.

I deserve nice things.

I deserve better days, weeks, months & years.

I deserve to no longer suffer.

I deserve to be "the me" that I need to be for me.

I deserve not to be hard on myself.

I deserve not to feel unnecessary emotional/ physical . pain.

I deserve to not have feelings of unworthiness.

I deserve to have adequate comfortable sleep. .

I deserve to feel complete.

I deserve not to feel guilt . and shame. .

I deserve not to feel praise . myself.

PREVENTING CYBER ABUSE

I deserve to have loving family & friends.

I deserve to be able to have goals.

I deserve to live the life I want and need.

**STAR 5*

Chapter 18 Abuse of Elderly, Disabled and Infirmed

Who are vulnerable .?

Earlier we spoke of women and children, but abuse can affect others of all walks of life. Let's have a look at who else can be affected and how. People such as homeless youths, those with a disability . physical . or intellectual, those with a mental illness, the elderly who are sick and frail or those suffering from senility or foreigners unable to speak the countries language fluently or have a clear understanding of language; therefore the inability to communicate . well can be taken advantage of by unscrupulous individuals such as abusers 'predators ..' This can be done by some family members, so-called friends, carers or strangers.

*STAR 5

What types of abuse can occur?

- Theft of money . in their residence.

- Mooching of money, resources, not paying their own way, expecting free lodging of victim. This could be done by family members or friends. (With elder abuse and mooching; I often wonder if it is in fact a direct result from having over-indulged adult children when they were younger and not teaching them to be responsible for their actions. Consequently, it gives the 'adult child' a feeling of entitlement and they deflect their responsibility and blame others), not accepting any accountability for their actions.

- Theft of valuables; jewellery, blank cheques.
- Theft of money . in their bank accounts.
- Are there work men/women taking advantage and overcharging for their services.
- Fraud- forgery
- Constantly borrowing money and never paying back their loans.
- Expecting to be bailed out of all his/her financial problems.
- Physical . abuse- hitting/ harming, punishment, cruelty, even murder of elders/parents, disabled and infirmed/sick.
- Emotional . abuse-name calling, swearing, put downs, threats
- Sexual abuse- molestation, rape
- Alienation- alienating, stopping the victim from having contact with friends and family. Or alienating victim by refusing contact by not visiting elderly.
- Neglect .- Deprived of food, proper health care ., hygiene and necessities.
- There could also be a lack of adequate care. .

- Subtle things like holding interaction hostage i.e., stingy with time and affection-withholding love, kindness and care.

- Trampling over feelings; constantly forgetting birthdays and important dates held important to the elder.

Safeguarding your loved one (How to prevent or minimise the chances of abuse to your loved one)

At home: -

- Try not to engage the help of sitters or others you do not know extremely well to look after your loved one.

- If you do have to get work, limit the hours enough so you can still adequately care . for them without having to get outside assistance that is if you are not burnt out.

- Watch for body language between your loved one and the carers, do they seem nervous, fidgety, cringe, scared, try to yell out. Are there other behavioural problems or are they off their food or having incontinence problems that weren't there before.

- Check out the carer very carefully, ask to see references or recommendations.

- If you have to use a carer, ensure it is someone you know very well or someone from a reputable firm and ask all the pertinent questions and for references.

ABUSE OF ELDERLY, DISABLED AND INFIRMED

- Screen all carers before using their services.

- You may want to put recording cameras in your home, so you can keep an eye on who comes into your home.

- If a carer is going to be looking after your loved one for several hours, ring regularly and ask to speak also to your loved one, have someone you trust drop by unannounced and if it bothers you come home early.

- Know everyone extremely well before they come into your home or look after your loved one. Look at their employment references. Check them out if concerned or for your own peace of mind.

- With regards to your children; do not have too many sexual . partners. Know them well before bringing them into your home. As you could be putting your loved one in harm's way.

- Do not allow people to become overly familiar with your loved one.

- Communicate regularly with your loved one and let them know you will always be open and approachable, should they want to talk or if something is bothering them. Listen carefully to them about their wants, needs and fears.

- Try and give them a good sense of themselves, teach them to always speak up and stand up for themselves. To say, **"No"** and **"Don't touch me,"** if they can verbalise or show them how to use their hands to push an abuser away or yell out for help. Some of this may or may not be possible due to their age, speech impediment or physical impairment.

- As much as is possible look after your loved one yourself, you are the only one you can fully trust. This may not be possible if they have high dependency needs. Or you may need respite care . for your loved one. If you are feeling burnt out. Don't feel bad to check out what is available you need a break also. You also don't want to run the risk or yelling or smacking your loved one because you are highly stressed and exhausted. Ask for help. You don't need to be a martyr.

- Talk to your loved one about strangers and even their carers; make sure they too feel comfortable. Explain that they do not have to hug, cuddle and kiss others if they don't want to.

*STAR 5

In an institution: -
(Hospitals, Detention Centres, Gaols, Nursing Homes etc) Most Westernised facilities are quite well regulated, so abuse is not

common although it is not unheard of either; it is always best to take precautions.

Try and give your loved one a good sense of themselves; teach them to always speak up and stand up for themselves if possible...

- Encourage your loved one to communicate . all their concerns or fears with you.
- Be very observant and aware yourself.
- Investigate, snoop if you have to, this is all about your loved one. It is your right to keep your loved one safe and their right to be safe.
- Ask to see their bank accounts and receipts of expenditure.
- Ask about their diet, any behavioural or health problems.
- Trust your intuition if it doesn't feel right then it's not right.
- Keep in regular touch with your loved ones' carers, stay and supervise . if you can.
- Ensure they keep you in the loop on everything and any recent underlying health issues.
- Ensure they have recent contact information in case of an emergency.
- Let them the institution know about all allergies and any health issues.

- If your loved one is institutionalised, know who is looking after your loved one and visit them regularly. Sometimes pop in unannounced, so you can see how everything is with your loved one when they think you aren't around. This is your right to ensure your loved ones' well-being is being taken care . of appropriately. Be very observant. Check to see if your loved one seems nervous or behaving differently around certain carers body language stands for a lot. Does your loved one seem nervous, fidgety, scared, try to yell out? Are there other behavioural problems or are they off their food or having incontinence problems that weren't there before and is there extreme weight loss or gain.

- Communicate regularly with your loved one and let them know you will always be open and approachable, should they want to talk or if something is bothering them. Listen carefully to them about their wants, needs and fears.

- Talk to your loved one about strangers and even their carers. Ensure they too feel comfortable. Explain that they do not have to hug, cuddle and kiss others if they don't want to.

- Visit your loved one regularly. There are some sad cases where loved ones with disability . or are aged are left in nursing homes and institutionalised and they are left and forgotten. No one visits, rings them, brings flowers, rubs their back, gives them affection ., they are left to live a lonely existence to eventually in time die alone .. They may have senility or lost some brain function, but do understand more than you realise?

"Please don't let this be your loved one feeling lonely and unloved."

*STAR 5

Rescuing (helping) those in need

I once witnessed the abuse of a disabled young man, who was neglected. The action of his carer or should I say the non-action of his carer could easily have caused him harm . or even death. This young man was not able to speak, fend or even defend himself. I as an able-bodied person and secondary carer to him was able to speak up in his defence. This young mans' so called "duty of care ." was gravely in question. I made a formal complaint against a carer; the complaint did not make me popular. I wasn't out for popularity vote, my main concern was the danger this young man was in. I wrestled with myself over it internally but knew my conscience would not allow me to overlook what was important, which was his future care. All I could think of was what if he was my child?

On another occasion one of the carers was spending their clients' money . freely and extravagantly not on themselves but on the client without thought to budgeting money for this person's future in their care .. I lodged a complaint. If I had to do it over again, there is no doubt in my mind that I would.

***STAR 5**

Rescuing (helping) others can sometimes feel in vain

Sometimes we can delude ourselves into thinking we can help everyone in need, how I wish that were true. Sometimes people really don't want help and sometimes the "system" too can let us down badly. In the end we know in our hearts we did the best we could that is all one can do.

On another occasion an acquaintance abused her young son physically and emotionally, I reported the abuse, nothing was done but at least I had a clear conscience knowing I took my responsibility as a caring citizen seriously. I followed up with the report ., but was unfortunately not given any relieving information about the child's situation. Some years later we ended up caring for this homeless young man, sadly the abuse he received earlier on in his life was so deeply entrenched that everything we did as a family to help him made no difference. Just because you rescue a person it doesn't always mean a happy ending. People can't be helped if they can't help themselves. Despite this what if this was my child; I would like to think that whoever I entrusted with my child is looking after his safety and well-being.

We looked after another homeless young man in trouble; alas nothing could be done to help him, as he didn't want to help himself. I hear now he is helping himself, which warms my heart.

To this very day, I struggle with the thought of how I am able to help another's son but yet not my own son, but not from lack of giving it my best with what I knew at the time. A good friend lovingly fostered my child for the interim period when my son was troubled and confused, which I was ever so grateful and indebted to her and her family for. We became good friends for many years and keep in touch when we can.

Not being able to help one of my own- my son is a sadness that will haunt me forever. We had an orphaned young lad come and stay with us who suffered from epilepsy. When I sat on the floor and held this lad in my arms while he had an epileptic seizure, so he wouldn't get hurt. Poignantly, all I could think of was how much I wished this was instead my own son in my arms taking away his emotional pain when he needed me the most. Feeling such sorrow and heartbreak for both boys this motherless child of someone else's in my arms and to know my own child I could not comfort in his own time of grief- a most wretched thing. Thankfully this young lad is doing ok.

Rescuing- sometimes there are happy endings

A dear friend of ours passed away from terminal cancer. As she was about to go, she held hands with my partner and made us promise to look after her 19-year-old intellectually disabled daughter. She had the fear that most loving mothers have; she needed to know her disabled child would be cared for in her absence-passing .. This friend also left her home to her daughter and wanted her to live in it as independently as she could with some support ..

It was a hard road for my partner, my daughter and I along with this young lady, we all had a lot to learn and we had way too much going on in our own lives let alone try to help someone else. Throughout the time helping her we had our own crisis' happening one tragedy after another, so we weren't always able to help this young lady in the fullest way, but we did what we could when we could and that is all anyone can ever do. We lost my son, my mum, my mother-in-law, father-in-law, my father's numerous health scares then I was assaulted at work and then battled cancer three times all a bit much really... Yet this young lass had to weather these storms with us, she watched as we had to put our lives together time and again. My partner is her financial guardian and has been a wonderful support. Well this young lady, has gone from leaps and bounds not without her own difficulties. She holds down two jobs and goes to work every day with a smile on her face. She also volunteers once a week, she goes for her regular piano lessons each week for playing a musical instrument and she joined a dance group and regularly goes dancing. Financially she is doing very well and wants for nothing financially, plus her health is good. She is an absolute joy; we have watched her blossom and grow into a lovely young lady.

We live in a small community, where everyone knows this young lady and we all look out for each other; I like to think "we all as a **community family**" all played a part in helping her to blossom and grow. It can be very rewarding helping others and watching them succeed and grow. That is why support . networks are very helpful to have in place for these young people.

I have wonderful friends and acquaintances who either foster children or pets. It really is so heart-warming to see such goodness in the world. Millions do such good throughout the world and we have to continue to nurture and encourage such goodness.

**STAR 5*

"Helping one person may not change the whole world but will change the world for one person."

Chapter 19 Abuse of Our Dearly Departed

Desecration of gravestones and disrespect of our loved ones passed

It is hard enough to lose our loved ones to death, grief can be all encompassing. When our dearly departed's headstones, war memorials, ashes which are held sacred to us, are abused in any way it can stimulate the pain of loss.

Desecration of graves in cemeteries is a form of abuse and tampering with human remains is a violation also. So too is the way one speaks of a loved one or friend where they are unable to defend themselves or stand up for themselves. A loved one's ashes were brought home and a distant family member spoke to the container of our loved one's ashes, in our opinion in a disgraceful, derogatory and not to mention disrespectful . manner. As it is widely known, *"One should not speak ill of the dead."* We calmly and quietly put the ashes in a better position where it would not be so prominent to ever be violated again in anyway. There was no point in arguing the point or bringing it up, enough hurt was there from our loss, we didn't need to cause conflict . on top. It is not what our loved ones would want. As we know everyone has different value systems, not everyone is sentimental, that is in not in any way to condone abuse or desecration of a loved ones' memory. Another person mentioned it was only a joke, my partner and I though took it seriously.

Then there are others who are sensitive and in saying that never underestimate how important their loved one's remains, or memory is to them. We need to be respectful of others' feelings and beliefs. We don't have to feel the same, but we need to keep some dignity and honour about the situation at hand.

After losing my child to abduction to his abusive father and then losing my child to death; my ex-husband tried to steal his ashes unbelievably cruel...it was the last straw. Too many losses over our child, his ashes were literally all we had left but a few treasures of Shane's. Most gratefully my partner was able to put a stop to this. I considered putting his ashes out to sea, where Shane loved to be, but to this very day I have trouble parting with his ashes.

Sometimes ashes and photos may be all a loved one has of their loved one. Let us always be mindful and think of other's feelings just in case we say something that could hurt. I'm not saying walk on egg shells. We need to be ever careful to respect . our dearly departed- those cherished as we would like the same done of us too. One just needs to be tactful before speaking. I would like to think that when it is my time that I am thought of well. Just some food for thought.

*STAR 5

Chapter 20 Pet/Animal Abuse

Nurture Nature

Abuse happens when we have a lack of respect and it is happening throughout our world. I contemplated as to whether I should put in something about pets and animals. I believe pets/animals are defenceless . and deserved a mention here as many are abused and they deserve protection and defending. Unfortunately, every second of the day a pet is being abused. Unthinkable crimes have been done to mans so-called best friend. Many of us have pets that we consider to be part of our family. As with having our children, with pets also is a commitment and responsibility too that we should never take lightly. When we bring home a pet they depend on us to feed and water them and give them the best care . possible. To many our pets are our children.

If we should buy a kitten or puppy, we need to realise that they do grow up to be cats or dogs and their life span is many years, so unless we are committed to go the long haul then maybe we shouldn't get one. I also don't believe in giving pets as presents. I bought my parents a cockatiel parrot as a gift many years ago, it parroted words well and instead of easing stress levels it increased them. Consequently, the poor thing had to be rehomed. So, we can't always know or think we are doing the right thing for others always. My parents had a love of birds that talked Cockatoos and

PET/ANIMAL ABUSE

Budgies; I didn't know their preference was that specific. I'm happy to say the cockatiel was found a loving home.

This is nothing against children, but they can be too immature and irresponsible to take care . of the pet adequately and you may find you do all the work. Remember cute little puppies and kittens grow up to be dogs and cats not quite as cute as before and their life span can be many years. So, unless you're in it for the long haul think before you buy. If you really can adequately afford . to look after a pet. Consider purchasing one from the RSPCA or ASPCA, as you are giving an orphaned discarded pet a loving home.

If one can't maintain the upkeep of a pet or can't afford . to pay the vet bills, then one should simply not keep a pet. Don't be guilty of animal abuse and neglect, do not buy one if you cannot ensure the pet is well cared for. If one finds it difficult to care . for the pets you already have in your care, do not abandon and discard it by dumping in the street or down drains. This is a despicable and cruel thing to do and is irresponsible. The correct and responsible thing to do is to give it to someone who will appreciate and look after it or contact the RSPCA or ASPCA.

***STAR 5**

BREAKING THE CHAIN ON ABUSE

Abuse of animals can be: -

- Animal/Pets deprived of fresh food and clean water, either through neglect or punishment.
- Lack of adequate shelter, housing- no room for exercise. .
- Animal deprived of proper health care . when sick or injured.
- Animals physically beaten
- Animals abandoned . by their owners due to them moving home or other reasons.
- Animals threatened or emotional abuse through threatening behaviour.
- Animals permanently chained up on a very short leash.
- Animals kept alone . in car with inadequate ventilation (Windows not opened enough) on a hot day. I try not to take our dog in the car, because I have the fear that I may forget and leave our beautiful girl in the car.
- Animal hoarding, too many animals kept in small confined living quarters against local council regulations, thus causing unsanitary . living conditions which may lead to sickness, disease and consequently death.
- Dogs used in dog fighting or cocks used in cock fighting, causing injury or death.

PET/ANIMAL ABUSE

- Cruelty to animals.

- Polluting our waterways with our rubbish is abuse to our marine life.

- Destruction of animal habitats on land and water. Our trees provide shelter for our wildlife and oxygen for all living things.

- Animals neglected, not clean and infested with fleas/mites.

- Exploitation of vulnerable defenceless animals- smuggling, poaching, over-profiting and the taboo topic avoided in talking about and exposing it literally as a crime; dare I say the horrendous obscene act of bestiality. Sadly, in some parts of the world bestiality is legal. All abuse should turn our stomachs, and this is equally ever so wrong. We jump up and down about children being sexually abused, what about our pets and innocent animals that are being sexually abused for porn, they are defenceless too? Is it still going on? I don't watch porn, so I wouldn't know. But unfortunately, it is still heard of occasionally. I doubt paedophiles stop at children; much is hushed up. It amazes me that nothing here gets done to incriminate these criminals that do these horrific acts.

To prevent abuse to animals: -

- Ensure they have adequate clean fresh water.

- Ensure they have adequate nutritious food.
- Ensure they have room to move and not chained up for extended long periods of time.
- Ensure they have a safe fenced yard.
- Ensure their home is clean and sanitary.
- Ensure your pet receives adequate veterinary care . and regular medication . if relevant.
- Ensure you don't lock your pets in hot cars.
- Ensure you never hit or yell abuse at them.

When veterinary care . is needed: -

(Some of this may seem like common sense but there are times when one can be uncertain especially during a crisis)

- If your animal has a venomous tick on them.
- Have been bitten by a snake or spider.
- If wounds are bad and not healing.
- Do not try stitching up a wound unless you are experienced or qualified or giving the animal herbal remedies.
- Do not give the animal human medication ., human medication can kill animals.
- For nutritional advice . and help

PET/ANIMAL ABUSE

- For regular vaccinations
- For anxiety
- For arthritis injections
- Your animal may have an illness . that needs necessary veterinary treatment.
- If the animal is listless and lying down too much.
- Animal is limping.
- Animal is frothing from the mouth.
- Animal seems very dehydrated.
- Animal can't eat or drink.
- Animal is drinking an extreme amount of water.
- Animal is losing weight rapidly.
- Animal has gained extreme amounts of weight.
- The animal is injured.
- Do not try to do your own veterinary care . especially if it is serious.

Where can animal abuse happen?
- At pet shops
- Pet mills
- Animal shows/ Zoo's

- Circus
- Home
- Businesses
- Farms
- In a hot car.
- In an abandoned . home.
- Or if the pet's elderly owner had died, therefore it is at risk of harm . or death due to no food, water or medical attention . etc.

If you know of any abuse and neglect inflicted upon an animal, you need to take that information to the authorities . immediately. Should you hear a dog howling or crying, don't tune out, tune in and act on your instincts.

Questions you need to ask yourself before getting a pet: -

- Can I afford . to keep pets?
- Could we afford . the veterinary bills, food and essentials such as medication .?
- Are the children old enough and responsible enough to help care . for the pet?
- Would all family members be committed in caring for a pet?
- Is my yard adequately fenced in already?

PET/ANIMAL ABUSE

- Do I have adequate housing kennel, cage, aviary?
- Can we have more than one pet and if so how many?
- Will the other pets get on with the pet?
- Will the place I'm renting allow me to have a pet?
- Do I work all day, which means the pet could get bored, anxious and lonely and therefore bark all day or be destructive .?
- Have I the time and energy to regularly walk/exercise ., play and give the pet adequate attention .?
- What about when I go on holidays, have I anyone to mind my pet?
- Am I too selfish and preoccupied, or too busy or too forgetful and sometimes lazy and therefore likely to neglect the pet?
- Could it be an impulse buy, buying a pet?
- Am I committed enough? Is having a pet a short time novelty that I may not want for long term? Remember cats and dogs can live up an excess of fifteen years and cockatoos eighty years therefore they can outlive you.
- Am I responsible?
- Will I be a responsible pet owner?

- Do I know what I'm doing?

- Do I know how to care . for pets properly?

- Am I patient and do I have anger management problems or emotional/mental health issues or an illness ., that could therefore put future pets at risk of abuse? (If you have anger issues or emotional baggage it is important to get those addressed adequately by a professional . therapist . before taking on any large commitment). *You need to own whatever truth there is.*

If you have decided to get a pet: -

- Do your research on the pet and its requirements by either surfing the internet for reputable sites, go to the library or buy a book on specific pet care. .

- Write yourself out a checklist of items you will need before getting a pet. Your list may include food and water dishes, worming treatments, nutritious foods, brushes, pet shampoos, leashes, tanks, kennels, muzzles, heaters, water conditioners. Ensure you have a fenced yard if you decide to get a dog and have an enclosure if you decide to get a cat or keep it indoors at night, so your cat does not attack and make extinct our . native fauna.

- You may decide to have pet insurance or could have a savings account specifically for veterinary treatments.

- You may need to arrange pet care . whilst you go on holidays, so research everything.

- Does your living situation change regularly and therefore there is no stability for pet's future?

If you have a pet and can no longer keep it: -

- Ensure your pet either goes to a loving family or take your pet to the RSPCA.

- You must do the right thing by your pet, do not dump, abandon your pet.

What of rescuing an animal in need?

I once was a person to act first and learn the consequences later. One morning I decided to go down to our local shop and came across an abandoned . dog that was literally skin and bones. The pharmacist assistant said children were throwing rocks at it. The poor thing looked hungry and scared. I couldn't bear to leave her behind to be further abused. So, I put the dog in my car and took it home thinking that a good feed and some TLC might put her right. Well... my family thought I was bonkers, in fact our family dog thought I was bonkers. In fact, in hindsight, I think I was bonkers! Lol

This poor dog was an American Pit Bull which I didn't know at the time was illegal, I fed and patted her. She was happy we took her in, but she was too far gone, still she ate. I would have loved to keep her and give her the home she so deserved. Even in her emaciated condition she was very possessive and protective of me. Our dog wanted to play with her, but she was far too weak. He even noticed she couldn't play and just stared at her pitifully.

"Out of the mouths of babes!" My daughter who I swear has at times far more common-sense than her mother, said, *"Mum are you out of your doggone mind, she could have any disease and could give it to our dog and what's more she's illegal, she an American Pit Bull, what if she was vicious?"* She was right, alright! We ended up taking the dog to the local vet, who had no choice but to euthanise her and here I was thinking I was helping her. I know I could be that crazy cat or dog lady! Ha-ha! So, I can ill afford to let my heart rule my head!

As a child I often rescued animals and later also was wildlife carer, so thought nothing of rescuing this poor dog. I could most easily be an animal hoarder! Good intentions are not nearly enough, sensibility must reign. We need to think with our heads and not just our hearts. *As mentioned earlier if you should come across an abused or neglected animal report . it immediately to the authorities ..*

The moral . of this story, is if in doubt call the experts.

PET/ANIMAL ABUSE

Abusers do not have the right to: -

- Physically injure, maim or kill pets or animals
- Emotionally abuse pets and animals with shouting, yelling, screaming, taunts, threats, swearing, degrading behaviour.
- Deny and neglect pet or animals of healthy . food, clean water, safe shelter and medical attention. .
- Dump/ abandon their pets for any reason.
- Deny pets of adequate care ., attention . and affection.

Animals have a right to: -

- Be fed healthy . adequate food on a daily basis.
- Be given fresh clean water on daily.
- Not being physically or mentally abused.
- Be given adequate shelter/housing.
- Be given appropriate medical attention. .
- Be given adequate care ., attention ., kindness and affection.

"The greatness of a nation and its moral progress can be judged by the way its animals are treated."

-Mahatma Gandhi

Chapter 21 Helping One Another

Saving a life from abuse

On the news we hear of horrific acts of violence . by neglect and abuse towards children by their own parents, step parents and/ or foster parents. Unfortunately, it is not unheard of to shockingly hear on the evening news of children locked in cupboards or basements or chained and fed mouldy bread, children deprived of food, not able to toilet or shower, play, see daylight and/ or beaten, sexually abused. This too also goes for countries around the world that have appalling conditions of neglect and abuse in their orphanages.

It is my belief that if we are aware of abuse we have a moral . obligation to report . it. We must do all we can to stop this inexcusable . abuse; otherwise we are guilty of being aware of it and doing nothing about it. If you suspect or know of such atrocities you "must immediately" report it to the authorities .- police ., child protection.

***"The only thing necessary for the triumph of evil is that good men should do nothing!"* -Edmund Burke**

HELPING ONE ANOTHER

Regarding abuse signs to look out for: -

If you are a teacher

With students be alert for signs of abuse and neglect with your students such as unkempt appearance-dirty clothing, poor hygiene standards, bruises/welts ., behaviours of timidness or aggressiveness bullying . others, fatigue, or incontinence (wetting/soiling) *neglect-* they never have enough school . equipment, too many absent school attendance days, no packed nutritious lunch. Watch out for anything out of character, the interaction between parent and child (does the child appear overly afraid of the parent)?

If you are a classmate, work colleague, health care . worker

If you see bruises ., or the victim opens up to you listen and report . it to a teacher or a boss and ensure they follow up and report it to the authorities ..

If you are a neighbour, friend, concerned citizen or relative

If you see anything of a suspicious . nature you "must" report . it immediately a child's or children's life could depend on it. *You can report this anonymously, so your private details are kept confidential.*

Hence, if you happen to see or hear or even suspect bullying . or physical ., sexual . or emotional abuse or neglect to a child, the disabled, the elderly, work colleague or fellow man whether it be a stranger or someone you know, or a pet. I encourage you to immediately report . it to the necessary authorities ..

If you fear repercussions to you or your family, as said prior; you are well within your rights . to make an anonymous complaint and not give your name. Yours and your family's safety is important too. Where the complaint goes to after this is no longer your responsibility but the responsibility of the authorities . you advised. We oftentimes don't have power over the end result. However, we can feel clear of conscience that we did the right thing, that you did your best to help. Though in saying this, let me be very clear here, you need to be very clear and concise about what you saw or heard. You do not want to make a fabricated complaint on an innocent . person and run the risk of ruining theirs and their family's lives. Not to mention wasting vital resources police . time and money .. The economy can ill afford . it; simply said, vexatious claims waste tax payer's money and valuable time. With vexatious claims and complaints or over-zealousness, time can be taken away, "valuable time" that can be used in *factual dire situations.* Without humour, as the adage by Senator John Macarthur says. *"If it looks like a duck, quacks like a duck, then it probably is a duck."* So, trust your own instincts, your gut feeling or intuition if you like. If you should need to make a complaint be careful to analyse your claims first. Always using common-sense as the "key". In some situations, people are afraid to get involved .. Our society does hold some apathy where it is far easier for some people to turn a blind eye to crime. It is easier to pretend it isn't happening or pass the buck, someone else will handle it. With that in mind, if we were the victim, wouldn't we want someone to come to our aid? Abuse under any circumstances should never be tolerated.

This next section is slightly off the beaten track. Yet I'm sure you'll see the relevance; in that everything we do plays a big role in improving life for all.

As fellow citizens how can we better life for others?
Helping others can be rewarding. There are so many problems in this world where volunteers are much needed. Don't be afraid to get out of your comfort zone as long as it is safe and go on crusades for what you believe in. What talents do you have that can help others? Why not use it? Whether it be political lobbying for change of laws, standing up for injustice, volunteering your time for a good cause ie., helping at the school . by teaching children to read, teaching art, working in a soup kitchen for the homeless, being part of a hospital auxiliary volunteer team. Volunteers play a very important role in society. Where would we be without our valuable selfless volunteers! Why not become a volunteer? There are so many areas all around our world that need your help, your help is valuable. *What's more, it can be rewarding for you too!* ***STAR 5**

"The best way to find yourself is to lose yourself in the service of others." -Mahatma Gandhi

Notes:

Chapter 22 Down So Low

"I'm not cavin in, let another round begin, live to win!"- Paul Stanley

Depression . leading to suicide

To some family and friends, who don't often deal with depression, when their loved one gets a bit blue or down, it can be perceived as, *"Oh they'll get over it. They are just having a bad day or going through a bad trot."* They can be wrong on both counts. It is when their loved one doesn't come out of depression and it lasts longer than a day here or there, they just don't seem to bounce back like before. This is when medical treatment needs to be sought as soon as possible. It becomes an emergency. Thinking one is helping them saying such things as *"Snap out of it or keep your chin up!"* are not helpful sensitive things to say to the sufferer. Some victims often are good at hiding their pain, so as not to bother anyone or they regard it as a sign of weakness .. They could be worrying about, what will others think, or they may incorrectly think, *"Nobody cares anyway."* or *"Nothing can be done."* or *"I'm a failure, no one will miss me, the world is better off without me."*

Loved ones can be "totally oblivious" to the fact that their loved one or friend is close to suicide .. Remorsefully, "some" don't realize till it's too late. There can be a hereditary component involved .. However, this may not be the case, there can be many contributing factors or no clear reason.

I myself suffered with suicidal thoughts, which thankfully I never acted on. Deep inside me I knew this would be wrong to put my children through. Although through my marriage . my ex-husband threatened suicide . numerous times. It was debatable as to whether it was a real threat or a form of manipulation. However, with what my child was going through and had gone through, I can only imagine the torment he must have felt.

In hindsight, I saw the signs but all too late. I was also so scared to hear the word "suicide", so I think maybe subconsciously I avoided hearing and believing it. I was more than likely in "denial .". Denial . is not good because it stops one from getting help. I also believe that when you do not know anyone who has suicided; it makes it all the vague 'unclear'. It does not become a reality in your mind. However, I don't ever remember it being a conscious real concern, as I always thought I was vigilant and on top of it. I used to think this happens to other people. Please see **Help Contacts page at back of this book.**

> *"Never be complacent, heaven forbid, it could sadly happen to anyone."*

*STAR 5

Chapter 23 Suicide

(The Final Blow-Abuse of Self)

There may be contributing factors, not just one reason but a culmination of different factors.

The victims of suicide . are far too many to mention, it is not just the person who suicided who is the victim but family and friends who deal with their loss and the whole aftermath. Suicide knows no boundaries it affects young and old, rich and poor, people of any race even the famous or the even the bubbly happy person you thought you knew. According to the World Health Organisation 2018, Suicide is one of the leading causes of death globally and globally one person every 40 seconds commits suicide; such staggering stuff.

***STAR 5**

Suicide signs to look out for (with your friend, partner, boyfriend, child, parent, work colleague, school . friend): -

- Depression . that last longer than a few days.
- Being fascinated and absorbed about death ie., movies, books. .
- Giving away their prized possessions.

SUICIDE

- Tying up loose ends, attending to paperwork, putting their affairs in order.

- Erratic mood changes for no apparent concise reason.

- Sudden elation after a long bout of depression. Because it could mean that have resigned their self to the fact of going through with suicide . that soon their pain will be over.

- Speaking about suicide ., a fascination for disturbing dark songs about suicide and hate, writing poetry or notes about it. Even not talking about it, odd behaviour not sharing their worries. On the extreme end on the pendulum.

- Saying goodbye to loved ones.

- No longer interested in pleasurable activities.

- Sleeping too much or opposite sleep . deprivation.

- Unkempt messy appearance, not properly looking after self-hygiene wise, home may also be in disarray, also not eating or overeating.

- Seems angry at the world, God and even self.

- Previous or current acts of reckless behaviour (not caring about own safety/health), self-harm ., suicide . attempts- **the previous attempts they may have survived but the next time they may not.**

- Hermit like behaviour, withdrawing from friends and family.
- Saying odd and strange things, that does not make sense.
- They have been ridiculed.
- Saying such negative phrases for example, "I'm better off dead!" "No one will miss me," "The world is better off without me!" "No one cares!" "Nothing's going right!" "I'm so stupid!" "You can find someone better than me!" "I'm so tired!" "I can't do this anymore!" "I hope you feel bad!" "I wish I was never born!"

There are many good books and support . groups too that can help. For help and advice . please see the References section and the **Help Contacts** section at the back of this book.

*STAR 5

What are some triggers of suicide: -

- Financial problems due to loss of job, gambling, addictions . or poor investment choices.
- Addictions that have given them a sense of hopelessness, never being able to get off the vicious treadmill.
- Feelings of guilt ., feel they have let people down.
- Making big or small mistakes.

SUICIDE

- It may be an impulsive or compulsive behaviour that needs serious attention.

- Done something so awful in their own eyes where they feel they cannot be redeemed or forgiven.

- Poor self-worth/self-hate

- Feeling a failure.

- Being egged on to go through with suicide. .

- Angry and fighting either physically or verbally or both with loved ones, bullies, the system.

- Distorted thinking, irrational . thoughts.

- Loss of loved ones, breaking up with partner, isolation or estrangement from others.

- They have recently been through a traumatic . situation.

- Unbearable emotional pain

- Physical . pain

- Lack of sleep.

- Low self-esteem-feel ugly ., stupid, useless, unworthy

- Feeling alone. .

- Feeling unloved and unwanted; like no one cares (I had a hard time understanding this, how my son could feel unloved and unwanted. As I would have died in his place in a millisecond). Even though loved ones/friends do care- they the victim may have distorted thinking and feel unloved despite it being the opposite.

- Everything going wrong; can't seem to get a break.
- Constant overwhelming sadness.
- Overwhelming anger and frustration
- Being bullied, abused sexually, physically, emotionally, can't see a way out of an abusive situation or relationship. .
- Shame and undue attention . and focus being on them via media from television, paparazzi . or social media such as Twitter or Facebook where one is open to being mercilessly bullied beyond relief. Being humiliated/ridiculed.
- Embarrassed beyond belief over a situation, feeling ashamed.
- Overwhelming everyday pressures
- Pressure to succeed.
- Nothing left to lose.
- Seeing no way out of problem, no solution in sight.
- Things magnified-not kept in perspective and blown out of proportion.

SUICIDE

- Feeling sensitive, overly emotional and teary.

- Feeling hopeless, nothing to look forward to.

- Nutritional deficiency missing out on vital vitamins and minerals that the brain needs to function properly causing chemical imbalance and consequently incorrect thought process.

- Not taking vital mental illness . medication and not going to therapy.

- Not eating properly and regularly- is not so much a trigger, but a sign of instability and lack of nutrition vital for healthy brain function. .

- May have a mental health disorder and/or phobia, depression that needs professional . treatment.

- Sometimes there is a hereditary component, some family history either biological or learnt behaviour.

- Feeling inadequate.

- Feeling disconnected from life and everyone.

- Seems to have a death wish, never speaks of the future and has no aspirations to look for work, drive a car, have a partner or family, or grow spiritually and emotionally.

- Lack of self-belief.

- Is overly tender and sensitive can't bear to see anyone or anything in pain, wears their heart on their sleeve.

- Looking for something else not of this world.

- As a child saw a future not on this planet, but of another future beyond. No sense of belonging to anything or anyone on this earth.

- Wants to be in control of their own destiny as to whether they live or die and of how they die and when they die. So they commit it their way, in their time.

- Never fitting in with humans in a family, social setting, schooling, workplace. .

- Has more of an affinity with nature, animals in particular than of people.

- Lack of social maturity and social skills.

- Different logic to the majority.

- Incorrect belief on life and self.

- Troubled childhood.

- Troubled relationships.

- Haunted feelings of doom and gloom.

- Addictions . taken hold, feelings of no hope.

SUICIDE

- Believe suicide . is their fate or absolve them of guilt . or a sacrifice to God.

- Unfairness of life.

- Belief in God or no belief in God.

- Different expectations of what they believe the world should be. They can't cope in this world, never fit in with everyone else; feel different as if of another world.

- Brainwashing . of others, sects, partners, guru's, unusual religious . beliefs.

- Living in a constant troubling relationship ., don't know what to do anymore.

- Contribution of many things occurring, being overwhelmed.

- Addiction they are having trouble beating.

- Longstanding or terminal illness ., no longer wanting to endure unbearable . physical . and emotional pain and suffering.

- Scared and afraid

- Emotionally Spent-Tired of fighting, feeling defeated ., given up; they cannot see a way out or an end to their problem, dilemma.

- There can be a feeling of exhilaration and even recklessness for the suicidal victim as they may see that their problem will soon go and that they will be free from pain and anguish.

- Sometimes there is no clear motive for the action taken.

*STAR 5

In my own opinion I believe that addictions . and self-abuse such as alcoholism, drug addiction and anorexia are in a sense a form of suicide . a slow way to kill oneself and their spirit- a way to escape emotional and/or physical . pain. I believe these problems to be a cry for help.

*STAR 5

Please Note: - As every situation is different some victims may relate to some or all of the above. Kindness and understanding is what is needed and immediate professional . help sought. You may have to ring the police . and a mental health clinic for help.

Saving a life from suicide

Suicide is an extremely serious matter, it is an emergency, as once one makes the decision to end his or her life it is **"FINAL!"** It cannot be undone. One should never taunt another with saying such things as *"Go ahead and do it!"* or *"I never loved you!"* this is "not" helpful because the troubled person will more than likely go ahead with it. It is important that we never play around with someone else's mind. Instead take them to the doctors; seek 'professional treatment' if you can, attend the consultation with them if they want. *If they have attempted suicide or speaking of it; you must stay with them until medical assistance arrives, don't leave them alone ..* Try to keep yourself and the other person calm. Never ever make judgment . on the person; you really don't know all they are going through. Importantly, never discount or dismiss what they are feeling, even if it may be irrational . or distorted thinking. Leave it up to the experts to make the diagnosis.

Try to only say soothing and kind things to the victim. Give them reassurance of hope that you do care . and can get them help. Help them to feel good about themselves as hard as it may seem; people going through this need building up not bringing down. They need to know this is only a temporary feeling that will go away with professional . help, time and possibly medication.

Suicide should always be treated as an emergency situation
Suicide can sometimes be a manipulative action, there is no way to fully knowing. Never underestimate the situation, always treat suicide . seriously as real. To the real sufferer it is a cry for help. I stayed in a troubled abusive marriage . for many years as my then husband would always use suicide as a tool to make me stay and it worked time and again. One of the main reasons I stayed because I would feel dreadful and responsible if I left and he suicided. Most heartbreaking is when my child went to live with his father my ex-

husband after our divorce, my ex-husband also said to my child that if things get tough for my child to end his life. Even from the age of nine my child did not want to live and even from his babyhood to childhood was quite traumatic. I sought professional help for him regularly throughout his whole childhood. Suicide was my biggest fear.

In hindsight, I should have left this marriage much earlier. Although I had tried numerous times to leave only for him to find us. The saddest irony is in the end, it was my son who was the one who ended up suiciding. So, you can see how domestic violence can have a troubling effect on children. Do not delude yourself from thinking that abuse doesn't have a bad effect on children; that they are resilient, as not all children are. Some adults are damaged souls from the epidemic proportions of domestic violence.

The rest of the family members never really ever get over suicide .. Suicide leaves an emotional mark on the brain of loved ones left behind that cannot be rubbed away no matter how hard you try, it is most devastating .. To loved ones left behind; especially for the parent/caregiver the mind succumbs to the guilt . of constant "what if's", the record plays over constantly in one's mind. One can become a prisoner . of their own mind.

It can be confusing to work out whether suicide . is a real threat or a manipulative action. Nevertheless, suicide should *"always,"* be seen as a real threat. Because I was vigilant, I thought it could never happen to my child, my family and I, how wrong I was. *Anything is possible*, even the thing you fear the most. Without meaning to be fear-mongering; _especially_ the thing you fear most.

To Summarise: - Factors causing abuse, depression, suicide .- loss of job, difficulty finding work, financial debts difficulty paying bills, rent, mortgage . and making ends meet due to lack of funds, sometimes there can be psychological factors, death of family member, hardships. Something can always be done if sought early enough and with support ..

*STAR 5

To those left behind after a loved one has suicided

Personally, speaking from a mother's experience and this experience I would not wish on anyone. For a loving mother it is the worst thing to ever happen to her much-loved child. You could take away my arms and legs and it still would not be as bad as losing one's child.

A parent never ever gets over the loss of their child/children; I was and still am inconsolable. Every single day I ache for my child. I'm not a mess. However, there is such a hole in my heart- a huge void that no one else can fill. I just wanted to hold my son and rock him in my arms like when he was little. I miss my beautiful son dreadfully as our whole family does. I was overcome with grief for my daughter too who lost her very best friend, her much-loved brother, they were so close. I feel a part of us all died that day. I feel I lost my beautiful daughter that day too, she was forever changed. I mourned also my precious girl who suffered such a great loss as well and had to grow up too quickly from that traumatic experience. In a sense, the experience I feel hardened *us, "our family"* somewhat, maybe- hardened isn't exactly the word. We became more introspective of ourselves and the world. We see the world in a whole different way, we are changed forever. I always worried about my daughter's emotional health from before, after and for the future. I know she is strong but for years I worried.

When my son died, I even feared losing my daughter to death, she is my one and only child. It even got to the point where when my daughter had a cold I would ring emergency help. My mind conjured up that she could have meningococcal virus, the flu. I was so over-vigilant, though in time I did try not to be over-protective. I had to continually rein myself in; as I didn't want to stifle her life. Our family was affected badly. At that time, I hardened toward the world somewhat and in our immediate family we all insulated ourselves by keeping distant from each other; because our own pain was too much to bear to be able to help the other. My precious daughter needed me, but I was in too much pain to really be present for her; for that I will always feel great sadness.

SUICIDE

Suicide is a wretched thing. The guilt . one feels as a parent, can be all-consuming. I was consumed with the worst guilt ever, as I vowed and promised my child the day he was born that I would always protect him from any harm .. I felt I let my child down in the worst way. I think I will hold that guilt forever. I have sought much professional . help for this, it has helped.

One thing that bothers me is when I hear people flippantly say, *"I wish I was dead." "Get lost"* or *"Go kill yourself."* While such people say such thoughtless insensitive stuff maybe in frustration or out of anger, there is someone, somewhere in the world; in fact, there are millions that are struggling, just to stay alive. If their thought processes are not right, such an insensitive thing said could be the thing that pushes them over the edge. We need to spare a thought for those who struggle daily with thoughts of suicide- of dying.

Optional reading: *Sharing with you 'my novel of a poem' . I warn you it's a long one... I wrote it when I lost my son and was angry at the world. Anger is one of the stages of grief.*

Sweet Heavens' Gate

The evening brings on my fears
On my pillow I cry so many tears
Help us please I cried for years
Who to turn to, where to go
I just don't know

BREAKING THE CHAIN ON ABUSE

Does evil prey .
Entrust your child to us they say
Sitting in their shadows with bureaucratic perks
In the shadows the pusher and the pedophile lurks

Son of my heart I love you so
Don't be alone . son
Come on home

The evening brings on my fears
On my pillow I cry so many tears
Help us please I cried for years
Who to turn to, where to go
The father hated the mother so
The father's rage ready to blow
Shuddering from roar of thunder and lightning
Oh so frightening

Son of my heart where did you go
Don't be alone . son
Come on home
The evening brings on my fears
On my pillow I cry so many tears
Help us please I cried for years
Who to turn to, where to go
I just don't know
Red tape, too late

SUICIDE

Mothers' worry just too great
There was no justice
Too bad I know this

Son of my heart you worry me so
Don't be alone . son
Come on home

The evening brings on my fears
On my pillow I cry so many tears
Help us please I cried for years
Who to turn to
Where to go
Bad gossip . riddled with hate
Sometimes you just need a mate
Criticism and abuse
It's was just no use

Son of my heart I miss you so
Don't be alone . son
Come on home

The evening brings on my fears
On my pillow I cry so many tears
Help us please I cried for years
Bureaucrats sit in their shadows worried about their perks
In the shadows the pusher and the pedophile lurks

BREAKING THE CHAIN ON ABUSE

One too kind can be so inviting
A mothers' anxiety heightening

Son of my heart cold wind doth blow
Don't be alone . son
Come on home

The evening brings on my fears
On my pillow I cry so many tears
Help us please I cried for years
Into the night the shadows took him
Our beautiful light now dim
People really don't know where we've been
Walk in my steps and you'll see what we mean
Why don't the bureaucrats just come clean?

Son of my heart I feel the shadows
Don't be alone . son
Come on home

The evening brings on my sorrows
Of no more tomorrows
On my pillow I cry so many tears
Of no more years
A mothers' broken heart, a son's broken spirit
We were left to pick up the pieces, to deal with it
Broken pieces shattered on the floor

SUICIDE

We put our trust in the law

Son of my heart did you just go
Don't be alone . son
Go on home

The evening brings on my fears
On my pillow I cry so many tears
Help us please I cried for years
Too little too late
They tell me it was fate
Barely seventeen,
Now never to be seen
Until you walk in my steps you cannot relate
Now my sweet child is at heaven's gate

Son of my heart I love you so
Don't be alone . son
Go on home

The evening brings on my fears
On my pillow I cry so many tears
Help us please I cried for years
Sad, bittersweet memories only left to haunt
Someone once told me I looked pale and gaunt
If only it wasn't too late
Go on home my sweet child to sweet heaven's gate

BREAKING THE CHAIN ON ABUSE

Son of my heart you need to go

Don't be alone . son..just go on home...

Notes:

Chapter 24 Bereavement

(Losing a loved One)

"I grieve for you, you leave me, so hard to move on..."- Peter Gabriel

If you are bereaved and not just from suicide . any loss

To loved ones left behind, I have much compassion . for you. Help is out there. You may or may not have lost a child to suicide .. Any loss whether husband, mother, child is extremely hard.

Suicide loss- Bearing my soul

I wasn't going to put this in. But it may help another parent going through the same thing. Losing a child to death is hard enough to bear. But losing a child to suicide . is a whole different matter altogether. We were so devastated we could not cook or clean and ate pizza for 4 days, had a pile of dirty dishes, just a fact of life. We had a couple of people come to visit which was comforting. Apart from my gorgeous friend who visited and lost her child the same way to suicide, we felt very alone. With the stigma that suicide leaves, in our own experience; people don't really front up on your doorstep with flowers or a casserole and offer their condolences in the same way as if your child was murdered or died of an illness .. Is it maybe that people unintentionally blame and judge you? Maybe...suicide brings out different feelings in people. But that is the humanness of the situation. Not having anyone there, that in itself, I found very hard to deal with; no one but my loving partner and a few close family members were there for my daughter and I. Naturally wrong or right you feel like maybe they are blaming you. Blaming when one doesn't fully know the whole true story is very unfair to the bereaved. As if losing someone you loved wasn't enough to deal with. Everyone needs a compassionate shoulder to cry on. Loving parents already blame and beat up on themselves. At the time I felt bitter, however I've grown to understand people's perceptions a lot better. Who knows if I hadn't gone through suicide bereavement, maybe I too would have been judgemental of others going through this grief?

Even now no one really wants to talk about my deceased child, I get it. I have several dear friends who have lost their children through illness/tragedy. They too have gone through the same thing, where people no longer want to speak of their child. We have a connection that has bound us together. Whenever we can, we get together and without restraint we chat away about our beautiful boys. Especially when you carried your child for nine months, wiped their tears throughout the years. Your child was such an integral part of your life- talking as if they did not exist, is never going to stop; nor should it ever. Sometimes, I get strange looks of discomfort and awkwardness from others when I speak of my son. But what if this was their child, they would want to keep speaking about their child... Everyone else has moved on but as loving mothers we can't move on completely; *our children existed*. There are also many daily reminders and reflections. If there is anything else that I have learnt, it is that we must always be compassionate and less judgemental. More love in this world is ever so necessary.

Suicide is complicated in that often the survivor- the bereaved is often blamed by others or by their *harshest critic-themselves*. You feel like it must feel to be labelled a murderer even though you are not that at all. Regarding the suicide . of my son, the first thing I did was ring suicide bereavement line. I didn't know what else to do. My intuition said to ring. On the phone line was a most caring and understanding lady- an "angel" who had so much compassion . for us. She understood our family's suffering as she also lost her son to suicide. Suicide is an epidemic, like a fast pacing disease.

Support group SOSBA was extremely helpful; the other people and families there are very caring and compassionate, having gone through suicide also, so they understand your pain. These caring people may have some important information to impart to you in your time of need. Please see **Help Contacts** at the back of the book.

Bereavement from other forms of loss of loved one
When losing a loved one to old age, murder, abduction ., accidents, abuses, brainwashing ., illnesses or suicide . all pain is relevant. I believe no person's pain is worse or more than another's pain. Pain is pain, hard to deal with, hard to cope with; it's not a competition

of who has been through more or what death is worse. It's all the same, everyone has different coping mechanisms and strength thresholds, so never pass judgement just be caring and compassionate. All that is different is the circumstances. I will say this though of suicide it leaves an indelible mark on survivors of loved ones that lasts a lifetime.

***STAR 5**

In healing a broken heart (on grief and loss)
In order to heal we can write in journals, go to counselling with your professional . therapist ., write poetry, write a book, write songs, draw, paint- find work that brings you joy. I even wrote to my son and mum even though both are deceased.

You may need to privately write letters to them whether alive, dead or estranged from you. It was a great release of pent up feelings and emotions, my pen and pad and now computer were my confidential friends. Music also got me through; I would listen to music, sing or dance. I gave myself permission to cry too and not always have to be the strong one. All of which I had to do in to facilitate in my healing, to learn, endure and grow from the experience. I had a ton of work to do on personal growth and still there is a ton more, learning and growing does not end. There are still aspects of my life for change, I still say the word "sorry" far too much for my liking and get on the defensive and worry about what people think, raised voices still bother me. All these things are residual remnants of being a once abused woman. You will see this in other abused women.

At the end of the chapter is a poem . I will share with you. It was written in order to grieve in a positive way for me to gain some perspective on loss and suffering. Yes, the world can be a cold harsh place and life can be unfair, the "system" can let you down badly too. But in the end blame gets you nowhere. I had the opportunity to take our matter further with the judicial system. However, I feel in many ways it would have held off my healing and instead I would become bitter, hardened, old and decrepit. *"Hadn't I lost enough?"* I thought, it wouldn't bring my son back and my daughter needs me. One of my internal questions was; *"At the end of the day is justice ever really found?* "You can put your life on hold but for how long...

Sometimes we want to blame the world and that's ok too for a little while. As long as one doesn't take it to the extreme and hurl abuse at others rightly or wrongly motivated. It is imperative to never stoop to becoming low; "Two wrongs don't make a right." *You are above that, instead hold your head high and know that you are a good person. You did not intentionally want for your child to lose their life and you know in your heart if you could change things you would. Know this too that the rest of the world goes on with or without you; it stops for no one. So, best we get our act together and get on with living; that is what our loved ones would want.*

There are choices you can make, you can sit in a heap at home and cry or help others. Sitting in a heap crying wasn't an option for me; it wasn't going to bring my child back. Some bereaved choose to work on the helpline for suicide . bereavement. I applaud these beautiful souls for this selfless volunteer work. Instead for me, I chose to put my all into my job as a disability support worker, which for the most part I thoroughly enjoyed. Without meaning to sound like a martyr. By doing this work put me in a caring position, there were clients who depended on me to get my act together.

My son certainly would not have wanted to see me forever sad, bitter and heartbroken. I have a beautiful daughter who needs me, and my family needed me and just as importantly I needed me. I also needed to be a good role model for my daughter, so everyone is counting on you to get your act together. It is also important for our other children to not feel they are the blame for their siblings' suicide.

I believe I am a changed, stronger and better person through my experiences and you will be too! Right or wrong I believe I will see my darling son again. That hope helps to keep me going.

Fake it till you make it! (Keep a balance .; know that you are human too!) It is very important for your healing to you and your loved ones to try and keep a smile on your face. Although trying to keep it together 24/7 and always being strong for others, isn't always easy to do. Being the strong one, can make one feel proud and responsible, it is a matter of finding a balance . too. It can be awfully tiring keeping up a happy, cheery face all of the time. Especially when one certainly doesn't feel like it, it can feel fake to do.

Please don't feel bad if you can't fake it every day, no one decent expects you to, or at least they shouldn't. As one adage says, *"Fake it till you make it!"* And make it you will!

One may need to drop their bundle for a bit and let someone else help carry the load some of the way and cry and release that tension by letting those tears flow can be a necessary relief.

Optional reading; *Here is a poem . I wrote to my son to help my healing.*

My Beloved Child

You touched my heart in the deepest way
My bond with will always remain
As your mother I will never be the same
No one will ever take your place

My saving grace
Your sister

BEREAVEMENT

She too is so beautiful like you
You will remain in my heart forever
Always I see your beautiful face
No one can take away our treasured memories
Forever I will hold dear
Never will we say goodbye
I know you are near
We all miss you
Awaiting that beautiful day
When we will again meet
I want you to know my sweet
That I love you endlessly to the deepest part of me
- *Your Ever-loving Mum xxx*

Never have I wished suicide on my child and believe it to never be a solution ever. I often wonder if he lived would he have been very mid up and lived a tortured life. This following saying as sad as it sounds says it all in a nutshell for me on how I feel about the loss of my child and of course I wish he was still alive and together we could work out his troubles. Even from infancy my child struggled and was a troubled soul. I don't regret for a moment giving birth to my two beautiful children. I do however regret the difficult life they both led. There is no joy in pity- understanding is far kinder.

"Death is easier than a wretched life; and better never to have born than to live and fare badly."

-**Aeschylus**

Notes:

Chapter 25 Planning A Safe Escape

(From A Violent Abusive Relationship Safely, whether with spouse, partner or boyfriend).

The decision to leave or stay?

It is not recommended to leave on your own without the help of police. However, in a dire situation where your life and that of your children are threatened you may have to leave with just your clothes on your back.

Ultimately the decision to stay or leave though is totally yours. I cannot tell you to stay or leave, you need to make that decision yourself. In order to make sound decisions you may have to weigh up all the pros and cons. Should you decide to leave, don't leave it till it's too late. If your situation becomes threatening yours and your children's safety is paramount. I know it's hard to do, but you really must become decisive.

There is no room for **"sentimentality ."**, saying *"Oh he is their father"* or *"We've been together nearly twenty years!"* **Twenty years are you kidding me, twenty terrible years. A twenty-year sentence for what!** Get real! Wouldn't you rather your children and yourself safe? Remember you are the adult. Therefore, it is your decision, not a decision for a child to make. It is important not to ask your children by burdening them with adult decisions. If you stay, there could be detrimental . effects on your family. Do not leave without the children take them **"all"** with you, do not think I'll come back for them later. If you can safely take your pets take them too, they're your family, they're victims too.

The other side of the coin is leaving . can also be a most dangerous time for you and your children. *"Should you decide to leave, do it as safely as you possibly can."* Know though in life some risks need to be taken. Lives have been lost too by taking steps to leave, so you must be careful. However, suffering a life of abuse is a life not worth living either. So, it is a matter of taking the lesser of two evils, if there even is such a thing.

Note Well: - *A defeatist attitude . can be your stumbling block,* "do not let it." Never dwell in the negative. It's true nothing is ever easy, but *don't let that stop you from freeing yourself*, it certainly is *not impossible.*

*STAR 5

Help is available

Since I first started writing this book in 2006 there has been a fantastic free new mobile/cell phone app for women to use in a domestic violence emergency. It is put out by Robin Mc Graw called "When Georgia Smiled" See robinmcgrawrevelation.com www.drphil.com or whengeorgiasmiled.org

Please also see the "Aspire Initiative" Domestic Violence Education Initiative also put out by Phil and Robin McGraw, it is full of great helpful and sound advice.

What to do with the family pets (They too are important!)

Sadly, the children and the pets seem to be the common denominator . in abusive relationships as being the most vulnerable, as we experienced seeing our beloved animals abused. Pets like children too are innocent . and can be caught up in the middle of all this drama and their safety is also at stake. But you must put your children and yourself first. Realise taking your pets with you could make your departure much more complicated, if you should decide to. Pets will not be welcome at a shelter or motel. Your children will fret for their pets and the pets also fret for you. If you can reassure your children that your pets will be fine soon. Yes, your pets will be at risk if you leave them behind. If you can take them with you without slowing you down, then obviously do so. Know that it may not be realistic to do so easily and safely.

All in all, it is such a devastating time for pets too. If you can go and retrieve your pets, ensure you take the police . with you as soon as practicable. Do not go alone . without police escort. I strongly advise you not to take friends as escorts, especially if it is a dangerous or unstable situation. Otherwise state your case to the RSPCA (in Australia) ASPCA (in the United States) and they can retrieve them for you or they can find the pets good safe homes.

PLANNING A SAFE ESCAPE

Where to go for shelter . and protection .

On where to go, this needs to be firm and clear in your mind before setting out into the big world. Living on the street or in a car is no place for you and your children. It is not safe or healthy ..

If there is no one you can stay with short term, then there are domestic violence refuge shelters you can stay in with other mothers in similar situations.

I would strongly advise if possible not to stay with friends and family because this will be the first place the abuser will look (stalk) and then you have made no headway you will be back to where you started and the punishment of you leaving . can be far worse than you experienced before. Not to mention involving others, your family or friends you could run the risk of unintentionally putting their lives in jeopardy. Please see **Help Contacts at back of this book.**

"Be very careful not to leave trails . or the predator will sniff you out and find you and then it really does get dangerous for 'all' of you. "

A safe destination

A good safe option is going to a refuge. Refuges/hostels, emergency shelters are designed in such a way to help you in your time of need. If you go to Lifeline or Salvation Army, they can direct you to where to go. Most refuges do not disclose their address in order to keep you privately hidden from harm .'s way, so the abuser cannot come into contact with you and your children. They are used to this; they have helped numerous women and children out. Once you have made the decision to leave, do not fall back on your resolve. If you go back to him, the consequences will be much worse for you all.

With refuges you will find all information about you and your children are kept confidential for your safety. Refuges are similar to self-contained units with beds for you and your children. You may have to share a bathroom and commune kitchen with others. Refuges may not be up to the standard you are used to living in, they are basic and practical ., maybe not decorated. But at least they are safe, the priority is yours and your children's safety. You may have to stay there from one week or for several weeks until you can find your own safe housing. This may be able to be sought through your Social . Security; in Australia we call it Centrelink. Ask to speak to a Social . Worker there who will be able to help you by assisting you to find emergency government housing or eventually as Housing Commission Accommodation.

There will however be a waiting list, so you will need to be patient till something becomes available for you. Also, you cannot be overly choosy about accommodation. . As often the department is doing the best they can with the resources available to them and there are many others also in similar situations to yourself.

In the meantime, you may have to rent for a while or continue staying at the shelter till something comes along.

Your Social . Worker can also assist you with finding whatever payments you may be eligible for, such as Rent Assistance, Job Assistance and anything else available to you.

When to leave

There will only be limited windows of opportunity for you to leave safely. Try to be ready at any given moment that he goes out, whether to the shops, to work or interstate or overseas. Be sensible if he is only going out for 5 minutes this may not be long enough for you. You do not need him to catch what you are doing then this defeats . the whole purpose of what you are trying to achieve, getting out safely. This can put you in a perilous situation. ***Timing and planning is key. *STAR 5***

How to safely leave

Try to plan your leaving . if possible, sometimes it is not possible to plan. You may have to be opportunistic and leave then and there on the spot. My children and I had no choice but to leave with only the clothes on our back, that is how volatile the situation was. I wanted to take our pets but couldn't.

If you can plan your leaving by doing a little packing and arranging when he is asleep or out. But be very careful as he or the children may be curious . or suspicious .. Don't flee on foot. If you can prepare with the police . in advance and have them safely escort you from your home to a refuge. Or if you have to do it alone . use a taxi but don't give the cab driver your destination, give it to him after you are safely in the cab. Don't book cab on landline phone.

Remember to have with you your ID, bills with your name attached, Medicare card, driver's license, passport, bank account details- which can make up 100 points which enables you to open a bank account. Have enough money . for essentials.

Don't tell the children you are all going to leave
You can answer their questions later. Your children may unintentionally let the cat out of the bag by letting it slip that you are planning on leaving .(so best not to pre-warn them). If they accidentally let it slip you are all in very real danger, you don't need him to know.

Precautions to take list (don't leave trails . that can be followed by the abuser): -

- Don't answer your cell phone as he may be able to trace it, get a new sim card and new phone number.

PLANNING A SAFE ESCAPE

- Be careful not to leave a communication . trail by telling too many people what you are doing. Better still tell only the police. Later you can tell family or trusted friends.

- Do not use your eftpos card or credit cards. Use cash only, being careful not to leave a paper trail as that will lead him straight to you.

- Do not go back to your home unless you have a police officer . escort you at all times.

- Change your email address so you don't leave a communication . trail that will lead the abuser right to you.

"All this may sound like paranoia, but it is not, you cannot be careful enough; this is for yours and your children's safety and future."

What to pack

Make yourself a check list, "planning is key". Keep this checklist in a safe secret spot so the abuser doesn't find it and get suspicious .. Try not to carry too much, take just what you need, as you may have to carry baby and hold your children's hands, so your arms will already be full. You could pack a knapsack for each of the children, so this way you are not carrying everything on your own.

Warm clothes, torch, a few changes of seasonal clothes for weather changes for each person, several nappies, bottle, cooled boiled water and formula if you have a baby, pacifier (dummy), wet wipes, underclothes, suitable footwear, hats, a couple of the children's favourite toys and reading and activity books . for their security and to keep them occupied, hairbrushes, cleaning wipes, sanitary items, spectacles, sunglasses, prescriptions, medication . for you and children, asthma puffers, car and house keys, mobile phone, purse, Medicare cards, pension cards, healthcare cards, document the abuse any bruises . or cuts . etc take photo evidence.

Ensure you write down any details of the abuse, bank details and cards, passports, birth certificates, all forms of I.D., documents that show you own half of everything, photos', DVDs anything sentimental (as he may destroy these) money . notes and coins, however do not use credit cards or eftpos card as he can trace where you are, important use cash only- enough in case you need to get a night in a motel and for food and essentials, withdraw half of what's yours out of the account because he may withdraw all of it, so you will find it hard to survive and you don't need to end up crawling back to him-which is the last thing you want to do. If you leave such items as soap, don't go back and get it, instead buy more (it's cheap enough), if you need paperwork don't go back alone ., instead have the police . accompany you, don't put yourself back in danger. Later you can buy other essentials. More clothes, towels, bed linen can be bought at the second-hand shop, right now money

. counts. You need to make it go the distance. Important: -Pack this book and your Action Planner Journal. ***STAR 5**

When and how to explain to your children what is happening?

Only after you have left, comfort and reassure your children that everything will be alright. If you can take them to Mc Donald's (not the local one though) this will cheer them up for a little while; biding you some time to think clearly to plan your next step. It is likely that well before you were ready to leave; your children were ready to go. You are not the only one who was tired of the abusive life. That is what I found out from my children.

What arrangements need to be made?

Open a new bank account so any payments can go straight in, but don't close your other account yet. You will need to go to your Social . Security Welfare office to explain that you have separated. Ensure you are able to make an appointment with the Social . Worker. They will be a great help to you right now. You may be eligible for rent assistance and other payments. In Australia, you may also be eligible for housing commission accommodation .. You can also put privacy clauses on your details with Social Security and other departments to protect your contact details going into the abusers' hands.

"Paranoia it is not, you cannot be careful enough; this is for yours and your children's safety and future."

Chapter 26 Protection Orders

Stalking

Some abusers stalk their victims to try and gain back control or punish you for leaving . them. Stalking is a crime. This is why it is important to cover your tracks . well when you leave a relationship .. Do not leave a forwarding address; you can get yourself a P O Box address, so he doesn't know where you've gone. The police . should protect you, so you shouldn't have to leave your family and friends.

*STAR 5

AVO/ DVO/ Stalking Orders Domestic Violence Protection Order

I'll be honest . with you I don't put much stock in these orders. But they do somewhat provide some marginal protection, which is better than no protection at all. We've had good and bad experience with our police, as in everything there is good and bad. We don't do ourselves any favours when we run down law enforcement, they often have a difficult job. Before we let off a slurry of abuse at our police, know this that our police law enforcement is stretched and can only do so much if our courts don't enforce these orders. It can be frustrating for all involved. However, in saying that I did have one unhelpful officer say each time I made a statement for a dv order that my ex kept breaching, **"Ahh...we're chopping down another tree are we."** I was astounded and not amused-wasn't this his job. More paperwork for

PROTECTION ORDERS

him, more fear and anxiety for my family and I. I then had an impromptu meeting by bumping into this officer in a shopping centre after my son's death (which he knew about) and he could not look me in the eye and avoided all eye contact. So, the frustrations certainly are there for the victims, it isn't always a fair system. There is good and bad in every system.

In Australia, you can pick up these DVO/ AVO forms from the Magistrate Courts and fill them out and take the forms to your police . station. You may have to make a statement on how it impacted on you all and the situation that occurred to enable you to receive an order for your protection. If you have trouble filling in forms, always ask for help. Your ex (abuser) will have an order served on him. It will then go to court to be heard. You may be allowed to have a support . person attend with you, best to ask first. There are also private interview rooms you can go in if you fear violence .. But you must let the court staff or your lawyer . know. These orders may say the defendant (Abuser) is not able to come within so many metres of you or your residence or workplace .. If the abuser breaches . you by coming within that distance as stipulated in the order, then the police need to be contacted immediately.

Having witnesses there to witness the situation will be helpful. Also remember if this order is to protect you then don't you go contacting him. Otherwise you forfeit the order; you will not be taken seriously. While you are at court ensure there is someone responsible and reliable to pick your children up from school . and to mind them and ensure their teachers are aware of the situation.

STAR 5 Please see **Help Contacts page at back of book.**

"Never, never be afraid to do what's right, especially if the well-being of a person or animal is at stake. Society .'s punishments . are small compared to the wounds we inflict on our soul when we look the other way."

-Martin Luther King Jr.

PROTECTION ORDERS

Notes:

Chapter 27 Legal Advice

Lawyers

When deciding to divorce . you will need to see a lawyer . as soon as practicable. If you are staying at a refuge they may be able to guide you in the right direction and advise . you of a good lawyer that practices in Family law.

You may also be eligible for Legal Aid. Apply for it as soon as possible, otherwise your partner may get in first and apply for Legal Aid assistance. Which will then mean you will have to pay full costs, so keep on your toes and get in first. Why? Because Legal Aid cannot cover costs for both partners from one relationship .. I do not know about the legal system out of Australia. You will need to check the system in your own country. From time to time laws change so keep updated.

*STAR 5

Court system for breaches for DVO/AVO/ stalking breaches

A Prosecutor will handle your case and fight in your defence. In Australia, usually you will not have to hire a lawyer . or barrister unless in unusual circumstances.

Something I found disconcerting; in fact, most alarming in the Family Court system in particular is, when the abuser chooses not to lawyer-up and instead fight his own case and then interrogate the victim. He literally gets a green light to abuse and terrorise the victim. The irony being the victim leaves an abusive relationship just to be further abused in court with no protection from the courts. The victim is courageous enough to leave abuse only to find the abuse continues. The courts should be courageous and compassionate enough to protect the victim. I experienced such with my ex and further abuse was allowed by the courts. So, the abuser continues to abuse and intimidate the victim, extremely unfair court proceedings. This perpetuating abuse needs to be stopped and there needs to be more thought for the victims of abuse in court situations. Some effort has been made by the judicial system, however, still not near enough.

Custody .

This can be the most heartbreaking situation of all. The decision of which parents the children should live with on a temporary or permanent basis is made by the courts (judicial . system). Often it can be out of your hands. The law is not always fair here to children and parents. In saying this, still do your utmost to follow the law to the letter and be the best parent you can be. Never run the other parent down to the child. Remember no matter how bad this parent is, this still is the child's parent-right or wrong. Children can have feelings for the other parent no matter how wrong the other parent is. I know it sounds crazy, believe me I do understand.

You can imagine how hard it must be for the judge to deliver the best call of judgment . without really knowing the parents. I would not envy their position at all. They are guided by stringent laws and regulations when delivering their judgments. Most judges are just, but not all, this is the error of being human, no man is perfect. I know there is no comfort in saying this, just the harsh reality of it. As I said earlier; *life can be unpredictable ., it is not always fair.*

*STAR 5

To parents/caregivers

Try not to get caught up in the whole *"he said, she said"*-because in the end *it's not all about you*, "it's about the children and their best interests." As mentioned before, do your utmost not to run down the other parent to the children. As it is already confusing and hard enough for them too, so keep children out of adult matters. Children can also be very perceptive and consequently you risk losing the respectability of your children. Also, children are not always as resilient as one might think, some children are sensitive. Respect . your children's feelings as much as you can. It can be a confusing and harrowing time for them also. In Australia, the court system does offer mediation and counselling. Do check the law in your country.

*STAR 5

LEGAL ADVICE

"You have courage enough to face it all, even if you don't feel like it right now!"

Chapter 28 Two-Fold Abuse

Brainwashing . children also a form of abuse

When parents are separating or divorcing, some parents have been known to use the anger they have against the parent who made the decision to separate. They do this by using their children as pawns or game pieces or as if in a of tug of war game. This is seriously not a game; as innocent . young lives are at stake, where the repercussions can affect them for their whole lives. It can eventually lead to tragic consequences. Firstly, it can lead to depression and if not treated in some cases, finally suicide as was in our case .. These parents that use manipulative tactics, give little thought to their children's feelings and instead use their own selfish agenda.

Murder suicides are shocking and on the rise. This can be done by cruelly punishing the other parent; threatening the parent with, **"I'll show you, you'll never see your children again." "They belong to me now."**

Children are not possessions . or commodities .. The abuser sabotages the children's relationship . with the other parent. Alienating children from the other parent, especially in the time of their life where children still need their parent is abuse. This is so selfish of the abuser. Children also are vulnerable . and fertile soil and their brains are sponges that can absorb even distorted information. Often children can feel confused and incorrectly and wrongly feel responsible that they are to blame, as if it is their fault that their parents are fighting or separating. This is such a heavy burden for ones so young to carry.

*STAR 5

Adult children abusing grandparents, relatives and children

This is a very unfair situation on so many levels, relatives and the children can be abused by being denied time and attention . with each other due to the selfishness of the abuser running their own agenda. Thereby, in the end, it is the children that miss out on nurturing relationships with all relatives. Grandparents, aunts and uncles are deprived of these important relationships also.

There are no winners only losers. There are situations too where older adult children with young children, who expect their older parents (the Grandparents) to look after their children. These adult children expect to be rescued out of trouble by constantly loaning money . for their bills/drugs etc and never paying money back, mooching . food, still living at home, stealing and hocking goods. This is selfish and irresponsible of the adult children to do to their children's grandparents, not to mention to the children also. Then if things should not go their (adult children's) way they then blackmail . them with taunts of, *"If you don't do this or that for me you will never see your grandchildren again!"* -this is abuse.

There seems to be an expectation by these immature adults that the world owes them something for nothing. However, the adage that John F Kennedy said in his inaugural . address*," Ask not what your country can do for you but rather what can you do for your country!"* - is in my mind how these young adults should in fact be thinking. Whether these adult children have arrived this way due to being overindulged . in their childhoods . may be debatable? I am a firm believer that songs are great storytellers. A great song that says it all to a 'T' is the song by The Eagles called *"Get Over it!"* If you get a chance listen to it or read the lyrics, it's a classic! Bless their hearts these well-meaning parents of entitled over-indulged mooching adult children, they as parents did what they believed to be the best at the time. Thinking mainly with their hearts, that's what loving parents do, but we need to be careful not to let our hearts rule our head. No one said child rearing was easy. Of course, we want to believe our children should get the very best, of course, we don't want them to do without- but are they... Of course, we want them to have what we didn't, of course, we want to believe our children are angels-but are they... However, in saying this we are not doing them any favours by continually giving the green light on everything.

These adult children need to learn to stand on their own two feet and take responsibility for their own actions and not put that on their older parents. They need to get a job, pay their tas, fines and bills from their own pay packet, like their own parents had to do. Nothing in this world is free; it all takes hard work and grit.

To use blackmail . to deny . children of their grandparents and vice-versa is very immature, wrong, selfish, spiteful, unfair and not to mention mean-spirited. It is time for these adult children to grow up and start acting their age by taking on their own responsibilities .. The young children of adult children are used as pawns or as hostages, this is so very abusive. Having everyone walking on egg shells is extremely unacceptable behaviour.

Grandparents can often become unintentional enablers to the unacceptable behaviours of their grown adult children; due to their feeling sorry and pity for their grandchildren they often feel caught in this game of blackmail .. Such grandparents in a sense really need to be cruel to be kind and rein in their constant emotional, physical . and financial giving and teach their grown children to stand on their own feet and stop rescuing them. This may seem unfair at first to their grandchildren but in the long run, this is the best and only way. These parents by giving in to their adult children; by giving money . and saving them constantly from all their problems are enabling this "abusive mooching ." behaviour to continue. Later these parents after feeling like a doormat. They could go on to feel numb and defeated-at a loss, they did what they knew how at the time.

There is a support . group called, "Tough Love", that has helped many families with problems just like this. You may find them on the internet or in your telephone directory. I have been involved . with this group and found much care . and support there with people who know and understand your situation as they have also been there. Your situation is not unique, you are not alone .. This group "Tough Love" is mainly for people with family members (teenagers and young adults) that are challenging to care for. Seek help and support, as it is there. Do not try to do this alone. There are trained people who know just what to do to help. All is not lost. But the first step is up to you.

*STAR 5

Abusers do not have the right to: -

- To physically injure, maim or kill their loved ones or anybody else.

- To emotionally abuse their loved ones with shouting, yelling, screaming, taunts, blackmail ., threaten, swearing, demeaning behaviour-put downs, belittling

- To deny . and neglect loved ones of healthy . food, safe shelter, adequate clothing and education and put it on others to do.

- To deny . loved ones of love, care ., attention . and affection ..

TWO-FOLD ABUSE

- To deny . loved ones from friendship ., socialisation, recreation and rest.

- To monopolise . a loved one's time.

- To alienate . their children from other family members ie., mothers, fathers, grandparents, aunts and uncles.

- To be disrespectful . to loved ones.

Children have the right to: -

- Enjoy regular quality time and nurturing from their grandparents and relatives.

- Not be unfairly used as a pawn in a game with relatives.

- To be able to receive gifts for special occasions.

Loving grandparents and relatives have the right to:

- Enjoy quality time with their grandchildren, nephews and nieces.

- Be able to nurture and be good role models for grandchildren, nephews and nieces.

- Lavish their grandchildren, nephews and nieces with love and gifts for special occasions.

***STAR 5**

Chapter 29 Protection For Your Children

(After Leaving an Abusive Relationship)

Access visits

Access visits can be arranged and/or court ordered by the Family Court. The access visits can happen either at a relative's home, park, or community centre or even a place where both parties are in agreement with. *High vigilance access visits are also available* where a mediator is able to supervise . and keep close watch on appropriate interaction between parent and children. This is usually done when previous access rules and regulations have been breached by the parent and if there is a risk of a parent acting inappropriately or there is risk of abduction . of the children.

*STAR 5

Abduction .

Abduction . has got to be the most devastating . thing to happen to loving parents and is equally devastating and confusing to the child/ children also. The grief is all-consuming. Know that this can happen, and in some instances, you may never be able to see your child/ children again. I say this not to scare you but to make you aware. The crime could be done by a complete stranger; your ex- spouse or one of the parents' friends or relatives. Dire consequences may occur in some situations such as abuse or death.

PROTECTION FOR YOUR CHILDREN

When and where can abduction . happen? (At school ., at a caregiver's home, access visits)

Abduction . can happen at school . or on child access visits or anywhere for that matter. (I nearly lost both my children to abduction by their father). It leaves the child and the other parent helpless .. Normally a child cannot be reported missing before 24 hours of being missing. These 24 hours are the most critical if you are to get your child back. Most sadly, I lost my son this way. Teach your children to even be careful of parked vans/SUVS in inconspicuous places or near parks, schools and shops. If they see a suspicious van for the child to walk across the road away from the van or in the opposite direction. A child could be grabbed quickly and easily and pulled into a van. Parentsneed to think ahead and teach children to 'think on their feet.' Encourage them to go to shops or school and ask for help to ring you or the police.

*STAR 5

At school .

You need to be aware that this can possibly happen to you. If your children attend school ., alert the teachers, administration staff and school principals that this is could be a possible occurrence. Give them ample information about the abuser. You could give the staff a photo of the other parent or abductor if you have photos and any relevant documents such as your custody papers, next of kin information and your contact details. You will need to tell the school staff not to allow the children to go home or leave the school grounds with anyone other than yourself, unless you otherwise give permission. Also, the abductor whether it is your ex- the children's father or someone else could be sitting outside waiting for the children when school is dismissed. They can be cunning, so you need to be steps ahead. Give your child a **password** that only someone trusted can have. There are **tracking watches** that sound great and could be worthwhile investing in. The child can wear their watch, so parents/caregivers can track the location of their child should they become lost. There is one called TicTocTrack, it also has alarms. Not sure of all the features, you'll need to research. Personally, I don't believe in just relying alone on these gadgets as a stand-alone safety tool to keep your child/children safe. It can give a false sense of security; it really is not enough. Don't expect a watch or mobile/cell phone to mind your child. It is far better to educate, equip and empower your child against stranger-danger and abuse.

It is by far safer if you can pick your children up from school yourself each day, especially if you know this could be a real and possible threat. However, in your absence you need to teach your children that they are not to go with anyone else or go in the car with anyone no matter what story the abductor gives them, unless you tell them otherwise. In case of abduction . tell your children to run away from the person and not to talk to the person and go straight to the office and have the school contact you immediately.

When your children are in the care . of others

You need to tell the caregivers or sitter not to allow the children to go with anyone else no matter what story is given by the abductor and for them to ring you and the police . straight away. It is very important too, for you to inform the police of any possibility of abduction . of your children, also if you have photos give them a copy to put in your file along with your phone number should they need to contact you in an emergency. You must ensure that the caregiver is aware of the whole situation and can be alert and on guard should this occur. Hopefully in your situation it doesn't happen. At least you can be aware and on the ready, prepared should such a situation occur.

*STAR 5

"Despite adversity we can still do our best to teach our children how to be self- sufficient in the world and caring decent human beings."

- N J Lutter

Chapter 30 A New Life

Making a new start

You've made the break, now you're ready to look for a new home. Now take a breather; don't let others confuse you with their well-meaning advice .. In the meantime, educate yourself. There are people that have trouble keeping secrets or they think they know what's best for you. Don't tell people you can't really trust where you are going or living.

Charity stores or community services can give you vouchers or food hampers to get you through these tough times. Don't be ashamed to ask for help, drop your pride, and freely accept help. In time, you can pay forward as there may come a time in the future where you can repay . the favour and help others. But right now, help yourself and your children first, as they say, *"Charity begins at home."* These services have seen many women in similar circumstances to yours. You are not the first and unfortunately you won't be the last.

Change to another state or suburb and another school . put some distance between your abuser and yourself for safety. But "do not isolate yourself". When you do find a safe home, try to ensure your children are as secure and settled as quickly as possible. You can do this by reading or playing with them; giving them much love, affection . and attention .. Make sure you fix up their rooms first. Ensure their rooms are comfortable with a clean made bed, some books . and toys, decorate their room as best you can financially; ensuring too that they have ample clean comfortable clothes for year-round climatic conditions.

Settle your children into their schools well; see their teachers and principals and get them on your side, but don't spend your time running down your ex. Why? Because you'll lose their credibility; you'll need every bit of support . you can get. Ensure your children are receiving all their nutritional needs. Let this be the last time you and your children suffer from neglect and abuse.

In time, after you are all settled in, you can start socialising yourself. You can meet other people; your self-esteem will improve and even more so when you find work. When settled, find suitable employment, you will need an income to get you on your feet also. Don't be fussy about what work, later you can do a course to improve your employment prospects. Ensure you provide adequate food, clothing, shelter, education and medical care . and counselling for your children and yourself.

Cover your tracks . well, remember he is a predator and will try and hunt you out. Leave no traces . or trails ., do not leave a forwarding address. You can obtain a P O Box address, so the abuser doesn't have your forwarding address. Do your best not to involve others especially as you know he is dangerous. Have an unlisted phone number or get yourself a mobile phone. Be careful and selective as to who you give your contact details to. You may have to leave your old friends behind. Now with Facebook and Twitter be very careful what you put up on your posts, put on privacy settings. Don't worry, you can make new friends and so can your children. Some people opt to change their names also; sacrifices such as this may need to be made. You need to do whatever it takes without breaking the law.

*STAR 5

Counselling . for family

Change from your local family doctor. You will need a new doctor all traces . of your past need to be left behind, if you are to cover you tracks . well. Counselling . for your children, should be your priority. Your new doctor can organize some counselling for you or the shelter where you are staying will often have relevant information on contacts for counsellors.

Optional reading; *Here is song I wrote with help from my good friend Peter Dobe, we actually put it to music* (of my experiences, it was a very healing process. You too, may find music therapeutic).

"You Freed Me" Lyrics by Natalie Lutter and Music by Peter Dobe

Love never meant much before,
Loud voices and hurtful words.
Tears I had for years and years

A NEW LIFE

A new life unfolds
You unlocked my heart
You found the key
You freed me

You opened the door you freed me
I'm on a journey now
Now that you set me free
You freed me

I will be happy now
Now that you set me free
You freed me

Love never meant much before,
Loud voices and hurtful words.
Tears I had for years and years

A new life unfolds
You unlocked my heart
You found the key
You freed me
You opened the door you freed me

BREAKING THE CHAIN ON ABUSE

I'm on a journey now

Now that you set me free

You freed me

I will be happy now

Now that you set me free

You freed me

A NEW LIFE

"You are never too old to set another goal,

Or dream a new dream."

-C. S. Lewis

Chapter 31 Workplace Abuse

What is abuse in the workplace .?

- Abuse can come in many subtle forms such as heavy workloads ., overtime . without being paid, no resting periods or meal breaks.
- Or abuse can come in more obvious forms.
- Abuse from our bosses, managers.
- Sexual harassment
- Expecting you to carry heavy loads which put you at risk health wise of affecting your back, hips.
- Working in sweat shops under gruelling conditions for ridiculously low wages.
- Putting you in unsanitary . situations where you have to handle blood, bacteria or mould spores without protective clothing, equipment or lacking experience.
- Putting you in dangerous and hazardous situations with poisons, toxins without proper safety protective clothing and equipment.
- Putting you in danger by putting you in a precarious . situation that threatens your safety.

- Having you work in areas where you have not been given training for, which can put you at risk.

- Not coming to your aid when you are in a dangerous situation.

- Being grossly underpaid below the award wage or pay inequality due to gender.

- Bullying/Gossip

*STAR 5

What can you do to help yourself (You owe it to yourself to know your rights?)

- Do your research; educate yourself on your rights . and workplace ., health and safety regulations.

- Know what your wages . or salary . should be; whether there is an award rate, hourly rate, holiday pay, sick pay, maternity leave etc.

- Make yourself aware of proper protocol; work hours-overtime ., public holiday rates.

- Adequate and regular breaks for rest and meals.

- Realistic time off for medical appointments, bereavement.

- Unrealistic expectations of your boss, manager.

- Read your contract and clarify and query anything that concerns/ worries you.

You could be discriminated against for: -
- Your religious . faith
- Your gender (male/female/transgender .)
- Your race/culture .
- Your build, height, weight
- Your sexual . orientation (preference- gay, bisexual, transgender .)
- Sexual harassment
- Being attractive/being ugly .
- Unfair dismissal
- Being pregnant .
- Your beliefs
- You may be bullied or ostracised.

*STAR 5

There are things you can do to lessen the chance of discrimination and unwanted predatory behaviour

Even though we may be innocent . in the event of discrimination .. We still have a responsibility into our actions for our own well-being. One way to avoid some of the negativity . of discrimination is to keep your private life "private"- keep it apart from your workplace ., if you think it may influence conflict .. Although you should not have to do that. You should really be free to be yourself. However, it is not a perfect or predictable world we live in.

Realistically, not everyone sees things as you do. Everyone has their own beliefs and value systems. Therefore, some things though could be better off being kept private, especially if you moonlight as an exotic dancer or if in your past time you are swinger or beach nudist. These behaviours can *be like a neon light shining, allowing the bully to set you out from the rest of the herd, so don't be so obvious.* There is no excuse for this abuse, but there is something you can do to help yourself in a practical . way. Know that anything too unusual and controversial can set you up for conflicts whether right or wrong.

This is not so much work-related, however, how you dress provocatively could bringing on unwanted attention. In saying that, one should be able to dress attractively and as they choose without being called a whore and treated poorly. Though realistically, in the world we live in, unfortunately it doesn't take much to bring on unwanted attention or gossip. We need to respect ourselves in that we protect ourselves responsibly.

*STAR 5

Chapter 32 Emotional Growth and Planning

(For the future)

Domestic Violence Support Groups

It is important to break the cycle/chain of abuse, so your children learn a different and better way of living. You also need to not pick up the same old pattern of finding future abusive partners and set a good model for your children. That is why it is important to recognise the patterns and stop it in its tracks .. You will find this immensely important to yours and your children's lives and future generations, grandchildren and so on. If you learn nothing else from this book and only go away with this information and seek professional counselling, attend self-help workshops... then my time writing this book will have had the effect in helping you and will have not been written in vain.

At support . groups, you will find other women who have been through similar situations to yourself. There you will find others there that you can relate to. Some women will be going through different stages of healing to you and then there will be others going through the exact same situation as you. There you will also be able to make friends and you can support each other by building each other up. There you will also be able to learn a different way of being, as well as vital information to help you.

You may find if you have been abused before and still find yourself in more abusive relationships and abusive situations despite leaving the abusive relationship due to your lack of self-esteem. Being shy, timid, trusting and kind-hearted, predators . can seek you out and take advantage of you. They know who they can abuse. You could feel you have a sign that labels you "victim" or neon lights that set you out from the crowd and you may well have.

My belief is predators are experts, at watching for signs of weakness ., meekness ., naivety ., shyness ., they can smell fear and vulnerability. That being said, until you strengthen up and your self-esteem improves, you will always be a "victim"- "target" for predators. As you will unwittingly attract more abusive situations your way. That is why it is so important to seek out self-improvement courses and therapy. You may find yourself again in destructive . relationships with others such as family, friends and/or work colleagues. I may have mentioned this earlier, but simply because of the amount of time spent with abusers/predators I have even come to know and recognise a 'telling' look of a predator with their eyes. They often have a predatory gaze not that different to a predatory animal's gaze one sees when watching a documentary.

Friendship . Abuse

Kind, caring, generous and good decent people can be abused by their friends. There can even be abuse in friendships. Sometimes one can be too good a friend and not expect anything in return. This is not true friendship .. For years I gave and gave of myself and never really expected anything back in return.

One friend brought into our home a dirty ditty tape recording and played it in front of our children. She knew very well that our religious . teachings went against that. Despite that she still did it, without even asking our permission. Obviously, she did it to get a rise out of me; it was a calculated move on her part. I felt very annoyed and disrespected. On another occasion knowing we could not have blood products due to our religion, I saw her sneaking blood from the meat juices as a base for gravy she was making for us during entertaining. Another time she made fun of my baby because he was slow in talking, which naturally hurt. I loaned things to her over the years, did babysitting, cleaned her home for nothing just because I cared. Nothing was ever reciprocated, instead I was desperate for friendship and chose to overlook and tolerate this. Thinking things would improve but they never did. She took our friendship . for granted, that I would always keep giving. I realised the friendship was not mutual, the friendship eventually ran its course.

Another so-called friend smoked cigarettes in my home regularly knowing my feelings. I also had a dear friend please do not smoke sign in our home, especially since I am an asthmatic and particularly my child's young lungs don't need damage from passive smoking. I then found she smoked marijuana in my home whilst we were away on a working trip, the house reeked of dope. She had oil burners placed around our home which I never used, and she spilt coffee all over my stove and did not bother to clean it up and left the stove on whilst we were away on the same trip, which could easily have resulted in a fire. I was livid. She also spoke in a degrading way about my son, which appalled me, that was the final straw. I cannot fathom nastiness it doesn't dwell in me. However, abusive people just know who to abuse. They do it to make themselves feel better. If they can push you around they will. One can attract users and abusers. Basically, you can unwittingly teach people how to treat you and settle for less because you don't believe you deserve any better.

Sometimes we need to declutter . our lives from negative people that do not treat us with respect, . especially in our own homes. Another thing- think good and hard before going into a business with friends (unless you have a strong relationship built on loyalty and trust), as they rarely ever work. Someone always ends up hurt or feels used and abused. It is up to us to draw the line in the sand that isn't to be crossed we need to be clear about what is and isn't acceptable in our friendships. We need to set boundaries and limits . if we are not to be abused. Some friendships sadly just run their course and you find you have evolved and outgrown that relationship. Or maybe it was never truly a friendship to begin with.

BREAKING THE CHAIN ON ABUSE

How to know if a friend is true or not: -

- Is always loaning money . from you.
- Is always asking for things.
- Is rude and disrespectful . to you and your guests.
- Leaves you out of things.
- Does not seem a two-way relationship- no reciprocation.
- Is sneaky.
- Is always snooping ./prying . into your private personal life; i.e., reading bills, letters, diary, snoops in your drawers, eavesdropping on phone calls, asking you private and personal questions that you don't wish to share.
- Flirtatious . behaviour with your or your partner or family member.
- Never returns the items you loan or gives it back in a poor state.
- Never pays you back after borrowing money. .
- Always expects favours.
- Immature behaviour- puts you down, jokes and belittles you, especially in front of others.
- Disregards your values.

EMOTIONAL GROWTH AND PLANNING

- Tramples over your feelings.

- You ask how they are and they never seem to want to know or care . what you might be going through. Conversations always circle back to what they are going through. It's always about them.

- Always living in your pocket, frequently visiting.

- Takes over your home going into your fridge or your private rooms or turns up frequently without notice or ringing if they have been made aware of your wishes and limits. .

- Constantly forgets important dates to you.

- They rarely keep in touch.

- Don't go to as much trouble as you, the feeling is not mutual (let's face it they may not really like you, so no love lost).

- Is ill-mannered and does not use the doorbell- just walks in anytime (however you may be fine with that and if so then that's ok), the words- "please, thank you, can I help, sorry" seem to be missing in their vocabulary.

- Is overly familiar, stepping over the line in your family and bosses you.

- They may be stealing from you, items go missing.

- If staying in your home may not clean up after themselves; leaving . your home in a poor state or forgets to return items or gives them back to you in poor state.

- Displays a couldn't care . less attitude . toward you and your family.

- Disloyal-gossips . about you and does not stand up for you.

- Only turning up or ringing you when they want something from you.

- You always do them a good turn and they do nothing in return and when you should really need a friend to turn to, they are not there for you they are too busy or make up excuse after excuse.

- Disciplines your children against your known wishes. Abuses your children.

- Belittles and makes fun of your children.

- Takes you and the friendship . for granted and uses you.

- Is not sensitive and respectful of you.

- Is negative, draining your energy, ringing you talking for hours when they need help and quick to shut you down when you need help.

- Always bringing you all their problems to solve.

EMOTIONAL GROWTH AND PLANNING

- Puts you in precarious . situations.
- Dominates . conversation and never listens to you.
- Monopolises . your time and smothers you and expects you to be friends only exclusively with them.
- Is jealous and envious and always copying you.
- Is selfish and wants only to do what they want and never shares anything.
- The friendship . is one sided most times.
- Is regularly drunk, disorderly or stoned.
- Behaves indecently or inappropriately around you and your family.
- Yells and swears at you.
- Has poor hygiene habits.
- You have little in common.
- Discourteous-not punctual, inconsiderate
- You both have different value systems.
- If it feels too good to be true or it doesn't feel right, often your first instinct is right.
- They want to control you.

***STAR 5**

If they fit even some of the above features, alarms bells should be ringing. Even the above is predatory behaviour. Predators use and abuse *soft touch people.* It could be a good time to say good bye. As such, people obviously only want to be friends to run their own agenda. You don't need friends that are negatively impacting on you and your family; draining your energy and emotional bank balance .. If they won't stand up for you ever, then you need to stand up for you. It is amazing how we allow so-called friends to treat us; things we would not tolerate with even our own families. Take control; don't be anyone's puppet.

With any friendship you must ensure you keep a balance and not allow them to infringe . into your family bubble, unless you are so certain that they will not take you and your family for granted. Remember friendship is a two-way street; it should never be one-sided. This goes too for family members that do not show respect.

Remember there are many good and decent people out there who would treat you far better, who are deserving of your friendship .. It is important for you to go out and socialise. Don't let a couple of bad friendships put you off and turn you into a hermit .. Life is for living, loving and having fun. Try not to be paranoid .. If it's only a couple of things that bother you and it's not that big of a deal, then don't overreact and be overly sensitive. No one is perfect not even you. However, if you keep having friendships that fail and let you down, think about it- the common denominator could be you, you may be attracting the wrong kind of people in your life. Change something about what you are doing, self-respect stands for a lot.

*STAR 5

Loss of a friend

Losing a friend can be devastating .. It is one of the most painful things I personally have ever encountered. I took my friends in, like sisters. Especially if you have spent much time together and shared deep meaningful moments, bared your soul and invested so much into this relationship .. I found the experience similar to grieving the death of a person. Counselling often helps.

You may find you have trust issues after that bad experience. Know your worth as a person and a friend. Never let anyone ever use you again. Sometimes decluttering of . friendships has to occur and get rid of negative energy that keeps us down or stuck.

*STAR 5

Helpful books and resources

At your local bookshop or library there are many self-help books . that you may find useful. If you have the internet there are e books and audio books also. Sometimes in your local doctors waiting room you may find helpful brochures that are always good to read. Whilst waiting to see the doctor, I would often grab handfuls and peruse them whenever I could. You will find regularly seeing a professional . such as a psychiatrist or psychologist or counsellor will be of value to you and your children.

In Australia, we have a Medicare system where you pay either a small gap or the full amount and receive back a large amount reimbursed back to you. Personally, I believe that if you can afford to and even if you have to pay the full amount with no reimbursement, it is money . well spent.

***STAR 5*

Assertiveness and confidence building workshops

After you have settled your children and you into safe accommodation . whilst they are at school . have some 'you time'. It is time to invest some time in you. Why not attend workshops that can assist you in becoming the person you need to be for yourself, this will also go a long way in helping you in your relationships with others and it sets a good example for your children. Becoming assertive . and confident . will take you a long way in your life. No more will you and your children be abused; you will learn how to be strong, capable and confident no matter what life throws your way. You will learn a new way of living.

EMOTIONAL GROWTH AND PLANNING

*STAR 5

Healing yourself and your family: -

- Seeking counselling/therapy

- Medication- sometimes it is important to take prescribed medication ., it really can help. Your doctor may have to try you on a few different ones, until they find one that suits you.

- Reading Self Help books.

- Do volunteer work, help out at school canteen or with reading program. .

- Doing courses to heal or better oneself.

- Say positive affirmations. .

- Meditation . and Visualisation .

- Gentle exercise ie., Yoga, Tai Chi

- Nutrition

- Writing in journals, diaries, self-help workshop books- I did this religiously.

- Listen to free YouTube Motivational Speakers.

- Writing poetry, song lyrics, books. .

- Singing

- Dancing

- Hobbies

- Self-care . and pampering

- Socialising- interacting and communicating with others.

- Join a Support group.

- Initiating Support networks.

- Altruism-Volunteering and helping others.

***STAR 5**

Bettering yourself for life

Why not learn a new skill or trade and earn a diploma, certificate...? By having this, it also puts you in better stead for career . opportunities? This will serve you a lifetime, you will never have to wonder when the money . is coming in or can you pay the bills or have you enough food or clothing for your family. Self-reliance is the best tool of all. Never do you have to rely on someone who threatens yours and your children's lives again. Learn to become more assertive .. Re-invent yourself. Be the authentic you, you were meant to be! Be no one's captive!

*STAR 5

"There is one single thread binding my way together the way of the Master consists in doing one's best that is all."

-Confucius

Chapter 33 Self-Reliance

(Self Sufficiency and a Journey of Self-Discovery)

Parenting yourself

You may have to be prepared to have to re-parent yourself. Sometimes this is necessary in order to learn and grow. Some have had to sadly because they didn't have parents, or their parents were abusive, or their parents just didn't have the skills, or their parents were busy working, sick or just trying to get by each day. Some simply just did not know better and had trouble coping and parenting . as well as they would have liked to, pressures are many.

Watching such shows like Dr Phil (Mc Graw) and Oprah can help a lot. Do watch these programs you will be amazed, inspired and informed. A great deal of my personal growth and change came from watching these informative shows. They are in our lives for a reason as a learning tool. These celebrity icons have also lived challenging lives and have embarked on self-discovery journeys and so too many of their guests on their shows. Many have inspired me to be a better person for all the right reasons. Dr Phil has a great saying, he basically said if one has not been fortunate enough to have a proper upbringing he says, *"Sometimes we have to rise ourselves above our raisers."* So true, we can moan and blame our parents but at the end of the day, we are adults; now responsible for our own behaviours and excuses . just don't wash. We can't keep using the, *"I've got to blame my **parents' card**."* Many of us have had difficult upbringings and so too our parents, it doesn't in any way condone abuse it just makes it easier to understand why it occurs.

*STAR 5

Mentors . play very important roles

Sometimes we find an affinity with people apart from our parents. It is not that we don't love our parents and not that they don't love us, those of us fortunate to have the love of family. Mentors . have some wise advice . to offer if you are willing to listen and learn. My friends are not all from the select clique/circle group of my own age perse, but more so from men and women old enough to be my parents. We are often not open to listening to our parents or our partners for that matter. Not that our partners should ever have the parent role. It's a real no, no! Do not let your partner parent you.

Sometimes we can click better with people other than our parents. I believe some can have personality clashes with one's own parents, not intentionally though. As parents we need to be comfortable with that especially if our child is not in any harm . and they seem to have an affinity with someone else. We can't always be everything to everyone, all of the time. Just be grateful for the extra love and support ..

Mentors ., gurus if you like, know only too well of the pitfalls and challenges ahead. Maybe one day you can be a mentor to someone else younger and inspire and educate them to grow and learn for the betterment of themselves. You too can be Oprah, Dr Phil, Maya, Dalai Lama or the likes of Reverend T D Jakes to this younger generation on the road of life. Anything is possible!

*STAR 5

You can do anything if you put your mind to it!

One can learn how to become self-reliant how to change a tyre, hammer a nail, do car maintenance; there are DIY courses available through hardware stores. There is a song *"Anything You Can Do I Can Do Better!"* Women can do anything, if they put their mind to it. Some women have the old way of thinking that they are nothing without a man, this is in fact wrong. Why not become proactive . and self-actuating.

Learn to discover and appreciate within you, your assets, qualities and talents, who knows where it may take you! If you left school . early and did not finish your high school graduate certificate, now is the time to finish that education, if that is what you want to do. Take up a course to put you in better stead for work or learn the guitar, write poetry, write a book, sing, dance, do voluntary work anything your heart desires and teach your children to do the same. You could be well amazed at what you find on your journey.

SELF-RELIANCE

STAR 5

Optional reading; A beautiful inspirational song "Smile" written by the famous Charlie Chaplin is one that brought me great comfort.

Smile

Smile though your heart is aching
Smile even though it's breaking
When there are clouds in the sky
You'll get by
If you Smile through your pain and sorrow
Smile and maybe tomorrow

You'll see the sun come shining through for you
Light up your face with gladness
Hide every trace of sadness
Although a tear may be ever so near

That's the time you must keep on trying
Smile- What's the use of crying
You'll find that life is still worthwhile
If you just smile.

That's the time you must keep on trying,
Smile- What's the use of crying

BREAKING THE CHAIN ON ABUSE

You'll find that life is still worthwhile
If you just smile.

Smile though your heart is aching
Smile Even though it's breaking
When there are clouds in the sky- You'll get by
That's the time you must keep on trying

Smile- What's the use of crying
You'll find that life is still worthwhile
If you just smile
You'll find that life is still worthwhile
If you just smile.

SELF-RELIANCE

"If you think you can do it, or you think you can't do it, you are right."

-Henry Ford

Chapter 34 A Relationship Worth Fighting For!

(Whether it be with yourself, your children or your partner)

What about our most important relationships!

In this fast paced, ever-changing world, sometimes our most important relationships get left behind. We say we marry to commit to one another, yet divorce . is on the rise. Sometimes you see couples that split up after only a year or sometimes just months. They plan these lavishly expensive weddings; going to great expense, time and effort yet after the wedding they spend even less time and effort on their marriages. Why did they marry in the first place all their guests are no doubt wondering- do they, the couple wonder the same?

It takes two to make or break a relationship .. Both need to be committed. Think good and hard before even bringing children or pets into this equation because then there are more casualties in this calamity of commitment break up. With the family dog when there's a break up who gets the dog, you just can't slice the poor thing into equal halves. Breaking up is not only painful to the couple but the children especially and then their pets. Remember their world is turned upside down too and what happens next for the innocent . children and pets?

*STAR 5

A RELATIONSHIP WORTH FIGHTING FOR!

Preserving your relationship with your children

Your children need to be your priority. There can be much interference from others and so-called "do gooders". Some are well-intentioned and some "meddlers ."- trouble makers. We can be so caught up with so much happening, and truly not see the forest for the trees. Well-meaning advice . and good intentions and what everyone else feels best for you and your family, can lead to much confusion. You may not be emotionally, socially or spiritually strong enough to make even the most practical . decisions. However, you don't need to be pulled from pillar to post either, when you are at your most vulnerable .. Try to have your own mind on things. Learn to trust your own instincts as a parent and to believe in yourself. Although I do know it is easier said than done. In the end, it is your own decisions that you need to make.

Make your children your priority; you don't have to spend large quantities of money . to keep them happy. A baby is most happy with a cardboard box and pots and pans than a full toy box, that's not saying don't buy them toys. Books are wonderful and educational . you can read to your child at bedtime or any time, whilst sitting in the doctors' waiting room even.

Children can be easy to please and they do appreciate the small things in life if you bring them up to appreciate not being materialistic .. Spending time with them doesn't have to cost money. For instance, for dessert I would buy my children fruit trying all the exotic ones, we worked out they tried over 50 varieties we'd talk about the flavours and so on. Because of my parent's culture . we often had different foods to experience. Cooking in the kitchen is also a wonderful thing to do with kids. Both my children loved to cook, and my son would experiment in the kitchen and make lambs fry meat pies and bake bread and cakes. Other experiences were, my son would ask me to buy him instead of lollies a tin of smoked mussels or oysters and my children's Grandma would buy him crocodile steaks and my daughter would ask me to buy her olives, fruit and nuts not sweets so much, like their Mum a sweetaholic!

Spending time in nature or with cultures gives them a broader appreciation of the world we live in .. My children learnt to have a love of nature. We would often take nature walks on an almost daily basis, and we'd talk about the environment. We'd stop and try and identify birds and we collated our findings in a notebook just for our own interests. We would pick up rocks, bark from trees, feathers and shells and make collages or just put them in their treasure basket. Sometimes we'd just stop to watch ants going back and forth on trees and we'd talk about that. Every time we went to the beach we'd also bring a rubbish bag with us and tidy up the beach and pick up fishing line and soft drink cans and we'd bring tongs for more dangerous items like fishing hooks, glass and syringes, we never found syringes thank goodness.

Teaching and showing your children how to look after and appreciate their environment is so important, our children are our world's future. My adult daughter is now an Ecologist. I like to think, that I along with my partner played a small role in directing her that way.

Being a good parent also means looking after you

Put yourself first and then next your children. It is quite well known that if flying in a plane during an emergency; to save your children you need to first put on your own oxygen mask. This is so true with life. If you are not ok, you cannot possibly help anyone else. Therefore, parents need to nurture, love and care . for themselves first and foremost, for to love and nurture others adequately this is the first most important step.

*STAR 5

You are not alone

Is your relationship . with your spouse not an abusive relationship? But there is some disharmony . and it's far from the most ideal for true happiness. Are you concerned about the longevity of your relationship, but still believe it's still worth fighting for? *"What a Trooper you are!" "You sound like a lifer like me in it for keeps, though it ain't easy..."*

What is the cause of disharmony . and conflict .? A number of contributing factors, baggage from both partners, cultural differences, been a bachelor or spinster too long and now have to make accommodations for another and so on... If you know you are in a reasonably good relationship . with love still there, that it is worth keeping, then why not do your best as a couple to save it.

Sometimes we need to prioritise . our time constructively and work out what is important in our lives. That should be our relationships. We can get so run off our feet in the hustle and bustle of daily life and find we have little couple time or family time. *Why not schedule it in your busy routine in your diary ..* I've noticed *couples that play together seem to have longevity.* One of my friends had a hubby that always played golf. She felt like a golf widow. She then told me she's now playing golf with him, another friendly couple travel together and others join in community volunteering together. Do something where you both have a common interest together. So, *"If you can't beat em join em!"*

In saying that, we all need our own space and separate interests also. Too much of each other can be smothering. You may need to also *give each other space- room to breathe.* Then, at the end of a day you can both get together and share about your day; at least that's what I found helpful for our relationship .. Our relationship wasn't and isn't always sunshine and roses; we irritate the heck out of each other at times. Having our own interests certainly helped. Balance . in any relationship is paramount. *Prioritise family first and work everything in and around that*, not other things coming first because you will then find there's no time left for family. Volunteering is good, but what about family? Your family is meant to be priority, you need to keep a balance. Your partner is meant to be your best friend. *"Think about how you talk to others your friends and then how you talk to your spouse is it harsh or friendly? It should be friendly!"*

No relationship is perfect, if someone does say it is, they're lying! Do fix up what is in your own backyard first, if your relationship . is broke fix it first and then after that volunteer or do whatever interests you. If your marriage . is on the rocks the last thing you need to be doing is lobbying for a bar in your local district. Instead you need to be concentrating on your relationships, read self-help books ., go to counselling and importantly put what you've learnt to practice- *"Actions speak louder than words."*

Communication is important too, don't just hear, but truly "listen." There is a difference between hearing and listening. Also ask and paraphrase- repeat back what they are saying so they know you are acknowledging them- what has been said by your loved one. Otherwise they'll feel like they're talking to the wall. *Give them your undivided attention ..*

If your children need school . equipment or glasses, ensure they have what they need instead of going out drinking, playing the pokies and smoking at the local pub. I'm not against pubs or having a flutter at the pokies, drinking or even smoking. But don't let other vices take control over and above your family commitments. Who doesn't like a drink or flutter on the pokies, but it's keeping a balance. Don't let these things control you and affect your family. What is more important another pint of beer or your family? Budget your money . and time so your family does not do without emotionally and physically, this is just plain old good common-sense.

*STAR 5

In Summary: Balance and communication . is the key in any relationship ., by all means have a drink or two. Spend time with loved ones first and then spend time on interests important to you and share some common interests as a couple, treat your partner as a best friend.

We are ever so blessed to have television self-help programs such as Dr Phil (Mc Graw) and Oprah. I've learnt so much about relationships from watching those shows. He is someone I believe that is full of common sense. Some of his tips are; to *"Be a soft place for family to fall," "To pick your battles"*- don't be petty, and another good ole saying *"Do it until."* One of my mentors even told me sometimes we say "No" to our children or partners, just for the sake of it, because it is habit. She said we should try to use that word less and realise sometimes we say *"no'" for no good reason.* She was so right!

You'll often see couples with relationship . problems come on the Dr Phil show, he'll ask them if they've gone to marriage . counselling and often they'll say a resounding No. NO? Can they really be that serious! If your relationship is struggling it could benefit greatly from the help of professional . counselling and better communication . skills and reading self-help books ., watching Dr Phil programs seriously!

Power dominated relationships

Do you easily give your power away to keep the peace . or to save from argument? Does everything seem like a power struggle? It can be all too familiar. Try to keep your relationship . on an even keel; your partner needs to be your equal. Have an adult to adult relationship, not where you are the child and your partner the parent, or vice-versa. This is far from conducive to your relationship, it will cause problems with your relationship.

Sometimes we feel the need to keep quiet not challenge anyone on questions, in order not to rock the domestic boat. But this just ends up with you feeling resentful . and walking on eggshells. *You need to be empowered.*

When you hear of people that have been together ten years or thirty years and they are trying to get their relationship . from nine years or 29 years to the round figure of 30 years. Still they know their marriage . or relationship is fraught with arguments and great difficulties. Sentimentality needs to go from their minds. It is better not to be with someone for ten or thirty years of miserable existence, living a lie. *Sentimentality can be so impractical.*

***STAR 5**

Do you feel you may have jumped in too soon?
It's only natural you may feel you need a companion .. You may need to strengthen your self-esteem and work on yourself first before getting involved . with anyone. Also, you need to give yourself and children time to heal and emotionally grow. Otherwise if you both have baggage to bring in the relationship, it is not the best start.

A *relationship with yourself* (the most important one of all!)

"Know your worth!" At the end of the day always remember you are as good as anyone else, no one is better than you, one's IQ doesn't make them smarter than you. You are their equal! We all have differing strengths ., qualities and weaknesses, we are all unique! Never judge others or try to compete, you'll come out the loser. Be consistent and true to yourself. Know your own strengths and limits . and work with that.

To become a well-rounded person, try if you can to understand and respect . the differences in people of all colour, race, beliefs, age, gender, pretty or not, friendly or not (they could be having a bad day). For if your house was ever on fire and heaven forbid; you would like to think that they would help you in your time of need in rescuing you from the fire and vice-versa.

***STAR 5**

You don't necessarily need a relationship to be happy or fulfilled
Solitude...Ahh...Peace, silence can be golden for many. Many people are happier being alone ., dancing to their own tune. Cooking if they feel like it, eating when they want to, leaving . the toilet seat up. They enjoy their solitude and turn their music up or down to suit them and not anyone else.

When you live alone . you can be selfish and drink straight out of the milk carton if you choose, watch what program they want to watch on TV. Life is what you make it. The choice is simply yours. *To each his own.* Maybe even your married friends sometimes envy you somewhat!

***STAR 5**

Questions to ask yourself before committing to a relationship .:-
- Can I financially afford . a long-term relationship? .
- Do I really know what a commitment entails?
- Am I responsible enough?

- How does my family feel about my new boyfriend? Will I have supportive family?
- Do I know if the other person wants children?
- Will I want children with this person?
- Am I willing to cooperate . and communicate . with a partner?
- Do I work all day, or often work abroad which means I have little time to commit?
- Have I the time and energy to sustain a long-term relationship .?
- Am I too selfish and preoccupied, or too busy or too forgetful and sometimes lazy and therefore likely to neglect a long-term partner/relationship .?
- Am I too impulsive?
- Am I committed enough? Is having a relationship . a short time novelty that I may not want for long term?
- Do I know what I'm getting into?
- Am I patient and not have anger issues or any addictions ., therefore putting future relationships at risk of abuse or neglect? (If you have anger issues or emotional baggage it is important to get those addressed adequately by a

professional . therapist . before taking on any large commitment)

- Am I prepared to be in a relationship . for the long haul?

STAR 5

"A good relationship is when someone accepts your past, supports your present, and encourages your future!"

-Martin Luther King Jr

Chapter 35 There Is No Greater Love

(-Than the One of Loving Yourself)

Unburdening yourself (When the going gets tough)

Remember you are important too. Don't forget to eat healthy ., be kind to yourself, and even pamper yourself. Fitness . is also important. Social . time and "you time" also. Some people are very good at doing this and some are not. I fell into the last category. I'm still learning!

Whenever we are feeling overwhelmed or alone . for any reason, we need not fret. There are coping mechanisms you can use, which I did speak about earlier.

Not everyone is motivated to write, if you are not a writer, why not instead grab yourself a tape recorder and instead talk onto the tape about your feelings or concerns and keep it in a safe spot if it is confidential to you. There are many ways you can unburden yourself. You could try singing, writing, dancing, yoga, tai chi, martial arts, painting, volunteering the choice is yours. Look after your skin and hair, tend your garden. Seek counselling/ therapy, join support groups if you need to. Down the track, why not educate yourself. In the meantime, each day you could practise meditation, visualisation and affirmations and notice how your life changes for the better.

THERE IS NO GREATER LOVE

The song made famous by Whitney Houston, *"The Greatest Love of All"* resonates well with love and respect of self. It tells us that the greatest love of all is the love we have for ourselves. For only after loving ourselves can we truly love others properly.

STAR 5

Chapter 36 Forgiveness

What of forgiveness .?

If we have let someone down we must strive to do better, beating ourselves up constantly helps no one.

On forgiveness I can only speak from my own experience. Forgiveness . is a personal thing, whether to forgive or not. It is a religious or spiritual thing to many. I am a spiritual person however; to me, I forgive those worth forgiving, and I am at peace with that. I refuse to feel guilty . because I can't forgive certain people; after all I am only human. Maybe to some it takes a big person to forgive. For me I forgive those who truly regret their transgressions . toward me. I also believe forgiveness is a process, it takes time to do, not an overnight situation. Also, it is hard to forgive someone who keeps on doing the wrong thing time and again. However, in saying that, forgiveness is essentially meant so that we can move forward and not remain stuck. No good comes from hanging onto grudges; you only ending up hurting yourself.

The most important one to forgive is yourself; if you feel you need to and move on with your life. I found forgiving myself the hardest part of forgiveness; we are our own harshest critics. I have for the most part forgiven myself, if I hadn't I would surely have gone insane, for my own sanity sake I have had to. There are still some of my actions that I have still some unfinished business with. The

FORGIVENESS

intricate patterns of the mind can be confusing, that is why I leave it to the professionals . to deal with. Who knows! I may for the rest of my life have to continue to see these wonderful professionals who have helped give me back my life.

With my tormenters, to me what they did was inexcusable ., disgusting . and unforgivable .. The anger I hold toward them I have harnessed and vented into positive ways to help others in similar situations. Yes, whilst it may be true that "abusers" may have been "victims" in their youth, it does not excuse their actions now as adults. As I have not done the same to others despite being abused and there are many millions also who have not abused others despite having been abused themselves. I can't undo what has happened to me, what's done is done, and I have had to deal with it and go on to lead the rest of my life as normally as is possible. Do I believe it affected my life in a traumatic . way? Yes, I sincerely believe so. It affected my very being to the core, affecting my decision-making and choices. Through my victim mentality, I likely unintentionally and subconsciously chose an abusive pattern through my life at times when I was quite vulnerable . and naïve. However, now I am far stronger and feel I have much more control over my life.

One can say, *"Woe is me!"* Or... they can say *"Life happens"*, make a change *because change is always possible if you want something bad enough* and move on. I get very bothered when I hear people complain about their situation and then do nothing about it to change it. If you don't like something change it. It can be hard to take the first step; it is kind of like going into a cold swimming pool and being afraid to put your head under the water. Take the plunge! Unless you do- nothing changes.

Regarding my son's suicide ., people have asked me, shouldn't I be angry at my son and will I ever forgive him? In fact, I have blamed myself for missing the signs and what if I'd done this or that- all the *'what ifs?'* Never have I ever been angry at my son for taking his life. My child must have been in what can only be seen in his eyes as inescapable ., unending . and unbearable . emotional pain, to take his own life. His suffering would have been tremendous and even if some of this action was with spite, it really takes a troubled mind to do this. I have no need to be angry at him, therefore no need to have to forgive him. If anything, I have nothing but the deepest compassion . for my son. From his suffering I have felt a pain so raw; it literally rocks me to my core to know my son suffered so much. It is another reason I write this book, so no other child suffers so.

With my own parents they were extremely strict with us growing up. As a parent myself I can understand a lot better why they did what they did. Some of it fair and some of it unfair, right or wrong.

FORGIVENESS

My parents had life threatening illnesses during our teenage years. At times they were not always able to be there for us or look after us. My father also being a shift worker. Life was not easy for them also, they had many hardships and their childhoods . were fraught with difficulties. There is probably much I don't know about their own sufferings. I guess that's why I don't get overly upset.

My parents' real intentions were good, to give us a better life than they had. They punished us the way they were punished, right or wrong it happened, and we can't get twisted and bitter over it. Otherwise what kind of lives would we have? I know they loved us in their own way. Like many well-intentioned parents they had their own set of difficulties. Therefore, I don't believe I need to forgive them either. Dad in conversation in his own way apologised for the life I lived and his many regrets of how it should have been. The word sorry never came out, but I know what he was trying to say, that he was sorry. A lot of people find it hard to apologise, but in their actions, their own way, they may be saying sorry.

I was recently told my Mother wanted me to forgive her and Dad, so if it is important to them both, then of course I forgive them both. Years ago, with emotional immaturity I blamed them both, so ask me years earlier and I might have said differently. **But we must also remember as adults we are also responsible for our own**

growth, change and choices and cannot forever blame our parents.

People can change for the better, *not all* but "some" people. It is sad that it can take a crisis for people to change or for them to be at deaths door. But at least change is happening and for that we need to be ever so grateful.

I am ever so grateful that I was able to have a very good and close relationship . with my darling mum years before she passed away. My only regret now is that I listened to her when she said not to connect her tv in hospital whilst she was sick. It would have been dreadful for her to sit and think about her failing health. Thankfully not the worst regret to have. Now I have a wonderful relationship with my darling dad too.

My only regret would be to not have had more time with him if he were not to live long. So, life is short, treasure what you have before it's gone, the day, the time we may not know- our loved ones can go anytime, or we can go anytime. Make your regrets few. Life can be unpredictable .. One can never be fully prepared in losing a loved one.

When you have a better understanding of a person it helps you to keep a better perspective. I myself have made way too many mistakes too, with still much to learn, my daughter is one of my greatest teachers and my dearly departed son included. I have had to apologise to my children for the hardships they endured.

A person's upbringing can show a lot of why a person is a certain way, *it doesn't condone actions* but more so makes one *better able to understand and make sense of what makes people tick.* I don't so much blame others such as my parents; my life has just been one of unfortunate circumstances. Was it fate, I'm not sure. Maybe I've gone through what I have so I can help others, which is the way I like to see it. Then at least all our suffering was not all in vain.

Silent . treatment/ Holding grudges

Silent treatment and grudge holding . are seriously a waste of precious energy, emotion and time and in and of itself can be abusive, not to mention what it does to the person bearing the grudge. Whilst one is dishing out silent treatment to punish another all they are really doing is punishing themselves; because the other person has moved on. So, the effect that the 'instigator of silent treatment' wants to dish out has in a sense backfired and not had the effect that they had hoped for. And for the most part people do not understand silent treatment, so they just forget about it and move on. May I suggest 'silent treatment instigators', "let it go," before you give yourself an ulcer. Letting go of that anger and release it, is freeing. Holding onto grudges for days and years is of no benefit to anyone particularly the grudge holder they end up being the losers in this bizarre behaviour. You may never be able to forgive; but you must for your own health and sanity sake move on, move forward. Anger whilst a relevant emotion at relevant times can be irrelevant and counterproductive at other times ..

FORGIVENESS

"To err is human; To forgive, is divine"- **Alexander Pope**

Epilogue

(The Climax on Government Responsibilities due to the breakdown of families)

"I'm going to get bold and opinionated here! Why? Because I can!" So please bear with me while I have a long overdue rant. I'm going to say it like it is. Apologies if I step on anyone's toes, but it isn't about just us; but the world as a whole. Not everyone is going to agree with me and that is fine.

Personally, I would like to see educational . courses on the following life skills *(not particularly in schools, however just as one would sit for drivers' license this could be made mandatory):*

- Relationship Communication Skills
- Awareness and Prevention of Domestic Violence
- Bullying (Children and Adults)
- Sexual Abuse (Children and Adults)
- Dangers of Slavery and Prostitution
- Stranger Danger/Abductions/Stalking/Muggings/Thuggery
- Responsibility of actions and consequences

- Law and Gaol (Jail terms) because most don't know how long jail terms are for. (Citizens/Society- even our youth need to know how long our jail terms are)

- All Addictions. Also driving under the influence of drink/drug taking. .

- Personal Self-Care- Hygiene, Health/Fitness ., Eating Disorders, Contraception, STD's (Sexually Transmitted Diseases)

- All forms of abuse in general.

- Equality

- Prejudices ie., Racism ., Homosexuality ., Transgender ., Religion . and Cultural tolerance and respect

- Pregnancy and choices; Responsibilities, Conscience, Abortion, Adoption, Prenatal Care, Post Natal Depression . Mental Health Issues- Schizophrenia, Manic Depression etc

- Repercussions of abuse- Depression ./Suicide/Murder/Maiming/ Carnal Knowledge

- Personal Safety, Personal Space, Self Defence

- Parenting Skills- being responsible

- Meditation ., visualisation, stress relief, emotions such as forgiveness.

- Human Compassion toward family, friends, society
- Pet Care
- Mindful Thinking ridding the mind of apathy.
- Financial Planning, Saving and Budgeting
- Future Goal Planning
- Self Sufficiency Life Skills (i.e., how to change a tyre, parenting . skills, employment skills, growing vegetables, what is work ethic, how to apply for a job- for some years some of this has already been partially covered in schools)
- Our main problem is values have lost traction; respect and the importance of this attribute to be taught within families and society.
- Altruism
- Love and Compassion for our Elderly, Disabled, Sick and the Poor (Homeless etc)

All of the above needs to be a mandatory part of the educational . curriculum worldwide taught by professionals .. Not certain how it can come about, but it needs to happen in some way. I'm not on some passionate crusade, I'm being practical ., it is a real problem that needs focus. Realistically, this is not a perfect world, so not all the world's problems can be fid completely, but we can all work toward a better outcome for many. I can't say this strong enough, it is the system that we have entrusted our precious children with. Therefore, we need to ensure they do right by us. Government authorities cannot be afraid to broach those touchy subjects for fear of upsetting. Upsetting who? The criminal?? Governments cannot afford to not hide . their heads in the sand for another day. Safeguards need to be put in place pronto, if our world is to ever stand a real chance! I can't stress this enough, this is of "utmost" importance.

Idealistically, all parents should be responsible in the day to day care . of their children teaching them life skills, manners and so on. However, truthfully it is never going to be a perfect world or an easy world. Essentially it is "not" the role of teachers, however, what do we do for the children that unfortunately did not ask to be born into a dysfunctional family?

There are families, where parents are working several jobs just to make ends meet, there are single parent families doing it tough too, and parents that are clueless and there are of course, the negligent.

We need to pay our teachers more; they have one of the hardest jobs of all! These wonderful humans are often not just in the role of teachers but have had to be parents, friends, nurses, therapists and more. If we are to ever get a handle on spiralling cycles of violence . and all things horrendous! To not have safe guards and education on these most important matters in our education . systems to put it bluntly, is just woeful. We are otherwise just wasting precious time, resources and money . on expensive luncheons and trips away for our politicians. We need to get real, misuse of taxpayer's money is abuse to society; the governments . in general when their intentions are off, are guilty of having blood on their hands. We need to toughen gun control just look how well the countries that have toughened gun control are thriving; thereby lessening their abuse footprint on humanity and nature. We need to invest more dollars into mental health. We need to educate, equip and empower.

The 3 R's (reading, writing and arithmetic) are simply- just not enough, that is overwhelmingly glaringly obvious. As I believe it to be the real truth; there really does need to be the 3 E's Educate, Equip and Empower in order to effect lack of suffering and I have made this the motto to which I have chosen to live by. Once and for all we have got to get it right; it isn't rocket science. While I hear you say it's our parents that need to teach children about the big world. Whilst that is ever so true, however, there are parents who lack. Why...why should children be the victims of this? Children are everyone's responsibility community and government; it really does take a village. Yes, our teachers are understandably already tad out mentally, emotionally and physically with what is already on their workload, as said earlier we need to pay them more, bring in more teachers. That is why *"to sweeten the pot,"* our govts need to inject money . into our education system. It is our responsibility as a society, a community, a nation to tell our governments . this; we have a voice that needs to be heard. People tell your governments . this, get on your soapbox! We let our governments . off the hook far too easily; this is their obligation and accountability. While pollies go to their various luncheons, our children are dying daily on so many levels emotionally, mentally, spiritually and physically. Our governments . are quick to point out to all that there is no such thing as a free lunch. A tad hypocritical . one might think? So, let's make our governments . work for their supper, no more free lunches! **We too need to support the government bodies that are doing the right thing!**

Our government can at least ensure our youth are taught correctly, using our taxpayer's money we've given and entrusted to them to use appropriately. Blood is on our hands if we don't get this right! Let's not sugar-coat this, our governments . need to have a conscience and be accountable they took on the responsibility of running our countries; anything less is unacceptable and is in all honesty nothing but fraudulent abuse to our society. Until we get real, until our governments stop procrastinating and "umming and ahhing," worrying about who they might offend and of being politically correct with their words and laws instead be politically correct by being strong, forthright and doing what's right once and for all; otherwise our world is headed for disaster. It is so evident;

however, it is not too late. It is only too late if they don't get onto it right away! Our world leaders really need to be the superheroes for its citizens. "Someone needs to take the helm of the world ship and steer it into calm waters."

Literally the likes of Nelson Mandela, Oprah Winfrey and Dr Phil Mc Graw & Robyn Mc Graw, Dalai Lama and the Mother Theresa's of the world are the ones who should be our political advisors and consulted by our world leaders, governments . for wise advice . on how to run our countries properly! These are people with their fingers on the pulse. They are a wonderful example of humanitarians. As they say, *"It takes a village."* I'm sure you get the gist, but *does our "governments" get the gist?? "A wake-up call is needed right now, it is that much of a crisis now!"* This world needs professional . help now *not tomorrow*! Common sense must prevail here or what is the point of anything! "Otherwise we are slowly committing suicide . of our world every precious second that is wasted!" I know of no other animal that kills off and maim their own species like mankind does, **an epidemic that *"must"* be stopped**.

The Judicial system is in a mess

Our laws are unbelievably and ridiculously slack, far too lenient. A child murdered loses 60/70 years of their life and the perpetrator gets 15/20 years the scales do not weigh in favour of the child that

EPILOGUE

is for sure! Life no longer means life, it's only a mere 20 years in jail with parole- hardly a deterrent to offenders, let alone a punishment for such abhorrent crimes. Rape of a child is murder of their very soul, it should be a life term for the term of their natural life- no parole. Such a kick in the teeth for families of victims of murder and assault. As if it isn't a hard-enough loss already, losing their loved ones in such a final way (death or maiming) and for their child to have suffered so horrendously. We cannot fathom the judicial systems logic! This is likely why our world is in the sorry state it is in... Laws need changing. Our judicial system needs a complete overhaul. Countries where there is a low crime rate, low unemployment rate etc need to show failing governments just how it's done.

I implore those of you who are able-bodied, have the right contacts or have time, money ., resources to <u>do something</u> immediately about this most critical situation; together we "can".

Of course, there are many great politicians out there doing a great job and they really need to be supported by us all. However, there are other politicians within our governments . not doing what is right, abusing our system and its people?? Our sick, frail and dependant- children, disabled and elderly are the ones suffering from all this obvious financial and social lack. Our schools, health systems need all the help they can get. There are children to be loved, cared for, fed, educated, saved and housed. If you know the likes of wealthy people, spread the word to them, as no more time can pass you already know that. Such people I'm sure would be pleased to help and be humanitarians. Sometimes it takes one to ask people of such high profile and status. Addressing the wealthy of the world, why don't you do something good for our world and adopt a child in need, you surely can afford . it and it will be most rewarding and/or donate too. We can get up off our behinds and do something for our families, our communities, our environment. The world waits for no one, don't wait for someone else who is dragging the chain, be proactive. Just to be able to have a conscience and be able to sleep . at night knowing every able-bodied person on this earth is doing all they can for mankind and nature in their own way. We don't need to keep having more babies, unless we're prepared for the long haul. In my own idealistic design; we need to tidy up the world's orphanages, each rich but loving couple adopting a baby or two if possible. It may not solve all the world's problems but it's a start. We need to look after our most vulnerable; our world's babies, children, our elderly, our disabled, our homeless, our sick, our dying, our frail, our pets, our fauna, our environment. It's in a shocking deplorable mess!

Lack of Priorities
Whilst they are quick to tell the public to tighten up the budget. What about taxpayer's money is it being spent wisely? Some

politicians are worrying about what Christmas decorations we should put up in the main street in our city! I mean really? Let's get our priorities straight and right! If we don't look after the world we've got there will be no world, no world to worry about what Christmas decorations to put up! It really is just that **"CRITICAL!"**.

"Now are you sitting down?" Brace yourself! Some idiocrasy has occurred. In excess of **"$740 BILLION AND COUNTING"** has been spent worldwide on Olympic games. I love sports! I'm no Negative Nancy; I'm not against the games. No reason why we still can't have them. But really at such a cost detrimental to our citizens. Where are our world's priorities? How many people could that feed, how many homeless can be helped, better mental health options, adequate schooling, housing etc? The government puts the public on tight budgets; pensioners are struggling on their meagre benefits but the govt is tightening their belts in the wrong area. Not forgetting that taxpayers are footing the bill! Governments are saying we have no money for our healthcare and education systems, so we'll tighten up on pensioners, the ones who can ill afford to be tightened up on? This is nothing short of shameful. The world governments and the UN really need to have a good sit down and sort this diabolical mess out pronto!!!

"WOW...IS OUR EVENING NEWS NOT EVIDENCE ENOUGH OF THE CRITICAL STATE OUR WORLD IS IN!"

It all starts with us. "Let us break the chain of abuse!" We need to picket, we need to protest, pound the pavements, do petitions, write letter after letter to our govts; go to our media for exposure, get elected, we need to do everything in our power, we need to crusade against what we know is not right! "United we stand, divided we fall." It takes more than one or two people to get things done. Until then nothing will get done, we can whinge, whine, complain bitterly and lament. I don't particularly think it is getting any worse, but it certainly isn't getting any better. In past decades, as a society we were good at turning a blind eye. We were more tolerant; didn't like scandal and we were not as learned as we are now. That is why violence and crime did not seem as prevalent back then. We know better, so we should do better.

We have got to get serious, **REALLY SERIOUS!** **"What are 'we' really prepared to do to change things? And I mean 'really' change things 'no more Band-Aids,' we need a 'no nonsense full-proof system,' as full proof as is possible in our human error world"** *Our very lives depend on it as much as the air we breathe!* Our children depend on "us" to make the right decisions! Why are we continually letting them down?? Why!! We keep saying our children are our future, why then are we killing them off and killing their future?? What kind of world are we leaving them. We have to be prepared to put our money . where our mouth is.

EPILOGUE

Out of The Box Thinking

Now I'm going to divert us in a slightly different direction here. We have got to think 'outside the box.' Creative and critical thinkers are needed in government. For example, we have Japan with it tight gun control with great results of low crime rate. Guns in the hands of youth and the mentally unstable is an 'accident waiting to happen.' Call me naïve but I don't totally understand guns, especially when one has had one held to their head by their ex.

Regarding out of the box thinking, there is the example of holding childcare centres in aged care facilities where children bring joy to the elderly and the elderly in turn able to grandparent children that require such attention- it appears a win/win. It is unusual **"out of the box thinking"** but it all appears to work. Right now, in our countries rife with violence obviously we are doing something wrong. **Albert Einstein** said ever so eloquently, ***"Insanity is doing the same thing over and over but expecting different results."*** We must be prepared to change our outdated laws, systems, governments, judicial system; it is not fairing us well.

I know of friends who choose not to watch the evening news because it is full of homicide and mayhem. People have had a gutful of violence and cannot stomach it. In one sense that is not good because the evening news keeps us informed. However, you could hardly blame them. Dare we tell our government how to do anything. Violence in our homes and communities is so easily attainable it comes through social media and television. How many people with severe mental illness and how many children with undeveloped immature brains are subjected to watching such violence on an almost daily basis along with violent computer games. With the real concern that they too can mimic/act out what they witness in their living rooms into their real lives. Copycat criminal behaviour is not unheard of. From my own experience my abusive ex would become more violent toward us his family after watching violent television programs.

More money needs to be injected into mental health services and violence minimised

We need to get to the grass roots of the problem and it doesn't take an Einstein to work that out. Mental health is the common denominator in why people continue to disrespect and abuse. You have to even wonder how mentally stable are some of our world leaders at the helm of the world ship! Who we are entrusting with our very lives? We need to protect our mental psyche; a lot of violent programs are very dark and really do mess with the mind. I'm no negative Nancy, I loved watching Dexter and have watched every episode, because of the intriguing story line. But it doesn't take a rocket scientist to work out that this stuff really can go into the wrong hands and minds.

To minimise violence in our world maybe we need to make extreme violent television programs not so readily available just as it has been done with pornographic movies. Maybe it needs to be made for pay tv, DVDs? Geez, I'm going to upset some, but we just can't ignore the facts- that speak for themselves. Maybe we need ratings on violent programs, on the levels of violence so we can make an informed decision with regards to entertainment. There are so many decent wholesome, uplifting and still entertaining television programs and computer games that will not corrupt the mind. We concern ourselves with winning the war on plastic, drugs and junk food for our wellbeing and environment. But what about the junk food (violence) we feed our minds? Nothing wrong with some of these things in moderation, we just need a balance. Most of us are balanced and alcohol, violent shows, guns etc., do not present as a problem; however, there are those with fragile unstable minds and young impressionable minds that need to be considered here. Realistically, as people will continue to source plastic, drugs, junk food, alcohol, pornography and violence; we will never completely win the war on these things not good for our wellbeing and environment. But we can certainly reduce what we and our children are exposed to and take some responsibility.

Our government and law enforcement crack down on drugs, it won't solve the problem but hopefully it is curbing it, and that is all we can do with violence also. We really should have the rights and choice to be able to turn on our televisions and not be subjected to violence. The world is a sadly obscure sinister place where we do need to keep our wits about us. As 'off the wall' and farfetched as this may sound; just as we have random breath tests, maybe we need random welfare checks on homes by law enforcement and child welfare? If there is nothing to hide, what is the problem? Far too many children worldwide have endured horrific abuse/neglect and masses of children go missing also. Murders, neglect and abuse may not fully be stopped but could quite certainly be minimised. We can't just expect neighbours to know everything that is going on next door. Far too many adults have proven time and again that they cannot be trusted. What is more important the home privacy or protection of all children? Better still, we need to get down to grass roots and ensure mental health stability- better nutrition, lessening availability of mind-altering compounds (drugs/alcohol), violent programs and guns to the mentally unstable and put up tougher laws. Short of implementing such extraordinary systems in place as earlier mentioned, how else do we deal with abuse and missing children? Can such eclectic systems really be totally foolproof? Maybe... maybe not entirely...really **the key lies in prevention.**

EPILOGUE

What can communities do!

Maybe you are already doing it with your work, if so wonderful! If you have a crusade you believe in, jump up on your soapbox too! There are many areas that need attention ie., mental health, education, domestic violence, animal cruelty, child sexual abuse, environmental conservation, equal rights, equal pay, healthcare system, poverty, the list is endless, but it is far from hopeless. The attitude needs to be, **"We Can, And We Will!"** Even if we do something as small as helping out at school with a reading program or helping pick up rubbish on our beaches, visiting a nursing home it all helps, and it really isn't a small thing in the bigger scheme of things. If you have a talent utilise it for the betterment of all if you can. All our circumstances are different as to how much one can help, but if the we can somehow get ourselves on the same page with the same vision a better future for some is achievable. Of course, we can't save the world, but we can help where and when we can.

The Harsh Realities

We will never save the world or each person.

There will always be pedophiles, murderers, abusers, plastic, pollution, disease; but we can help minimise the impact on our world.

"Be the change you wish to see in the world."- **Mahatma Gandhi**

We can give up and say it's all up to our governments. But what about the role we can play to help bring about change? It isn't just up to the government. We are all responsible for positive change. Most of us are good at keeping our homes in reasonable shape, but what about our world, isn't that our home too?

Numerous already selflessly volunteer their valuable time. For those who haven't volunteered, mentored or donated before because they haven't had the time, why not make the time, "crusade." *Mentor or volunteer in your community.* Understandably some cannot due to health and commitments. Just as my favourite band **The Eagles** made famous their song ***"Do Something!"*** – with the message that we all need to be worthy of the breathing space we take up, this song is so apt it has literally stayed with me and plays continually in my head telling me to "do something." Maybe now that song will stop playing in my head and I can rest assured that something may be done, as uncannily enough, a happy coincidence, 'synchronicity' call it what you will; I just noticed we recently have a new campaign in Australia called ***"Do Something!"*** *Whilst it is great to see the governments new initiative on encouraging society and community to volunteer and become involved; personally, I would like to see more governmental change also; not just the government telling its people to **"do something"**, the government also needs to **"do something"**.* Hand in hand the government and its people can

EPILOGUE

work together to bring about this vital change; ***"Together We Can Help Break The Chain On Abuse!"***

"When there is a lack of honour in government, the morals of the whole people are poisoned."-**Herbert Hoover**

EPILOGUE

"Whether in your work, mentoring, volunteering or even donating. <u>'Make your life matter!'</u> What are you passionate about? Is it the environment, animal welfare, the arts, education, the vulnerable- elderly, sick, disabled, homeless or is it injustice, health, fitness, peace etc? Some of you are already doing this- You are truly priceless! Whatever it is, make your mark on society. Have you a talent, use it, teach, help!"

-N J Lutter

Summary

We need to do the following if anything is to ever change for the better: -

1. Better mental health facilities and programs. Healthy minds for healthy lives!

2. Money injected into mental health and education.

3. Teach life skills.

4. Tighter gun control. It is not the guns but the people using them. So, if we tighten the gun laws so guns do not fall into the wrong hands. We need to look at Japan's gun laws as a good example.

5. Tougher jail (gaol) sentences and enforcing laws.

6. Educate, equip and empower our citizens young and old of prevention and awareness of all types of abuse and violence. You'd protect your family against evil and harm by educating; so why wouldn't the govt do the same with its citizens?

SUMMARY

7. If it is said statistically that Norway has the best successful mental health programs and that Singapore and Japan are seen as some of the safest countries in the world; Thailand and Norway as having the lowest unemployment rates; and that North America has the lowest rate of domestic violence, and the happiest countries being Denmark, Switzerland and Netherlands; then why are we not consulting with these countries? We need to know why these countries are thriving in these areas and consult with them in order to do it better. Take a leaf out of their book.

8. And I'm being serious here. Last but not least our world leaders need to consult advisors such as the likes of Dr Phil McGraw, Dalai Lama, Nelson Mandela, Mother Theresa (deceased- 'all are examples only') etc

9. It would seem that there may be some wrong people obviously running the show. What are their agendas?

*STAR 5

Worldwide Statistics

Facts and figures on how many of our world's children are exploited (abused) annually (years 2000-2006)

- Did you know that as many as 77 countries sanction violent . punishment of children who were found guilty of minor or major crimes? In some of these countries the punishments . ranged from execution to corporal retribution including caning, flogging, stoning or amputation.
- Did you know that up to 53,000 children are murdered worldwide each year as documented by *World Health Organisation?*
- Did you know it is estimated that 150 million girls and 73 million boys under the age of 18 experienced some form of forced sexual . intercourse or violence . as documented by the *World Health Organisation 2004?*
- Did you know that 40 per cent of soldiers in the Democratic Republic of Congo are children? 11,000 children are yet to be disarmed, this is according to *Amnesty International.*
- Did you know that the highest child homicide rates occur in adolescents, especially boys, aged 15-17 years and among children 0 to 4 years old? (*Global Estimates of Health Consequences due to Violence against Children*, WHO 2006)

WORLDWIDE STATISTICS

- Did you know it is estimated that the number of street children worldwide is 100 million children and it is ever increasing each year with the population growing.
- Did you know that up to 275 million children worldwide are estimated to witness domestic violenceannually? *(UNICEF, 2006)*
- Did you know that in 2004, 250 million children between the ages of 5 and 14 were involved . in child labour, of whom 126 million were in hazardous work? In 2000, it was estimated that 5.7 million were in forced or bonded labour, 1.8 million in prostitution and pornography, and 1.2 million were victims of trafficking as sex . workers, a modern form of slavery. (*International Labour Organisation Office*, 2006)
- Did you know it is estimated that between 100 and 140 million girls and women in the world have undergone some form of female genital mutilation/cutting? (*UNICEF Innocenti Research Centre*, 2005)
- Did you know it is estimated that annually that one million children all over the world are sold or "trafficked" internationally and across borders into illegal sex . trade. (*UNICEF Convention on the Rights of Children*)
- Did you know it is estimated that 40 million children below the age of 15 are subjected to child abuse each year? (*World Health Organization (WHO)* 2001)

- Did you know it is estimated that throughout the world up to 80 to 98 % of children suffer physical . punishment in their homes, with a third or more experiencing severe punishment resulting from the use of implements? *(World Health Organization (WHO) 2001)*
- Did you know that the thirds highest leading cause of death in the world with adolescents is Suicide? (*WHO*, 2002)
- Did you know it has been estimated that, through the use of limited country-level data, that almost 53,000 children died worldwide in 2002 as a result of homicide? *(WHO, 2002)*

STAR 5

WORLDWIDE STATISTICS

"Imagine all the people living life in peace! You may say I'm a dreamer but I'm not the only one."

- John Lennon

Final Summary

"Six actions I find totally unhelpful and on the negative that seems to stifle us in improving ourselves and others are:

1. Denial .
2. Blame
3. Holding Grudges
4. Can't   As my Grandmother taught me, *"There is no such word as **'can't'** in her dictionary!"*
5. I Don't Know
6. What If

Our lives would improve greatly, if we could just rid ourselves of those negatives words and actions and instead replace these words and actions with:

1. I can!
2. I'm sorry!
3. Too easy!
4. I will help!
5. Good on you!
6. I love you!

Realise help can be sought and there is "No Excuse for Abuse!"

FINAL SUMMARY

"May you and your families live a long, happy and healthy . life!"

-N J Lutter

Resources

Other Books by N J Lutter

"My Body Is Mine, Not Yours!" (Part 2) comes with accompanying **"The 3 E's Caregivers and Educational Instructional Companion Guide" (Part 1)** for caregivers and children on the awareness . and prevention . of child sexual . abuse which is a handbook for to be responsibly supervised with a therapists ., educators and caregivers. **"Absolutely No Excuse For Abuse!"** with companion **Action Planner Journal** was written for the abused who want to seek help. **"Conquering Cancer Fears!"**

Unchecked feelings and emotions can build up pressure like in a pressure cooker and then if the release valve is not slowly opened emotions could explode in ways we never realised, so it is very important to seek professional . help and advice . as soon as possible.

It is also important to have some strategies in place to help us deal with our emotions. Hence, I have written some journals on emotions that are a tool to compliment your counselling. You can then share your journal with your loved one or therapist .. With journals we can either communicate . if we wish in it or get in touch with our feelings. It is equally important to have a safe outlet where we can vent our feelings without harming ourselves or others, which is all about our most important relationships with ourselves, our partners and children. "Build stronger and happier relationships for a lifetime!"

References

Dirie, Waris *Desert Flower* William Morrow Paperbacks (September 22, 1999)

htpp://warisdirie.wordpress.com/about/

The Psyche Mind

World Health Organization (WHO) 2001-2005

UN Commission on Human Rights

Amnesty International

Save the Children

Family Violence Prevention Fund

Worldwide Emergency Contact Phone Numbers http://www.sccfd.org/travel.html

Esafety.gov.au

REFERENCES

"The true character of a society is revealed in how it treats its children."

-Nelson Mandela

Help Contacts Worldwide

In Australia

Queensland

Esafety.gov.au

Survivors of Child Abuse www.snapaustralia.org

Domestic Violence Support Groups-

DVconnect womensline

Free call 1800 811 811

Phone line for women, children and young people. 24 hours, 7 days

DVconnect mensline Free call 1800 600 636

Phone line for men 9.00am to 12.00pm, 7 days

Tough Love Support Group http://www.toughlove.org.au/

Survivors of Suicide Bereavement Australia SOSBA www.sosbsa.org.au

Advocates of Sexual Child Abuse www.asca.org.au/

Domestic Violence Telephone Service www.dvconnect.org Ph. 1800 811 811 or TTY: 1800 812-225 1800 811 811

Brisbane Domestic Violence Advocacy Service (BDVAS) www.dvrc.org.au/advocacy-service.html Ph (07) 3217 2544

DV Connect Mensline www.dvconnect.org Ph. 1800 600 636 7am - midnight, 7 days a week.

Brisbane Rape & Incest Survivors Support Centre www.brissc.com.au Ph. (07) 3391-0004, country Ph. 1800 242526

NATIONWIDE (For all states) PANDA Postnatal/ Postpartum Depression-Panda.org.au 1300 726 306/gidgetfoundation.org.au /Sane.org /Cope.org.au

HELP CONTACTS WORLDWIDE

Beyond Blue 1300 224 636

New South Wales

DoCS Domestic Violence Line www.community.nsw.gov.au/ (24hour) phone 1800 656 463 or TTY: 1800671442

Violence Against Women Confidential Hotline phone 1800 200 526 (24-hour state-wide free call)

Domestic Violence Advocacy Service DVAS phone 1800-810-784 or (02) 9637-3741 (weekdays)

Another Closet DV in gay and lesbian relationships

ACON 's Lesbian and Gay Anti-Violence Project phone 1800 063 060 or 9206 2066 Monday to Friday 10.00am – 6.00pm

Immigrant Women's Speakout Association www.speakout.org.au phone Mon-Fri 9.30 -5 (02) 9635-8022

Dympna House For survivors of sexual . abuse. Mon-Fri. Ph. 1800-654-119 or (02) 9797-6733

Women's Legal Resource Centre www.womenslegalnsw.asn.au phone 1800 639 784

Violence Against Women Confidential Hotline

1800 200 526 (24-hour state-wide free call)

Victoria

Women's Domestic Violence Crisis Service of Victoria (24hour) **Crisis line** phone 9373-0123 Melbourne, or country toll free 1800 015 188

Domestic Violence Resource Centre (Vic) http://dvrcv.org.au/ Melbourne phone 9486-9866 9am - 5pm Mon-Fri.

BREAKING THE CHAIN ON ABUSE

Centre Against Sexual Assault (CASA) http://www.casa.org.au/ phone 1800 806292 (24 hours)

Child Protection Crisis Line phone toll free (24 hours) 131-278

Immigrant Women's Domestic Violence Service www.iwdvs.org.au phone Mon-Fri 9-5. Ph. 8413-6800

Gay and Lesbian Switchboard www.vicnet.net.au/~glswitch/ 9827.8544 (Melbourne) 1800.631.493 (country)

ACT

Domestic Violence Crisis Service www.dvcs.org.au phone Ph. (02) 6280-0900. TTY: (02) 6247-0893

Women's Legal Centre www.womenslegalact.org phone 1800-634-669

Family Services (protection of children from abuse) www.dhcs.act.gov.au/ phone (02)6207 1069 (North); (02)6207 1466 (South); After hours (02)6207 0720

Tasmania

Domestic Violence Crisis Service Mon-Fri 9am-Midnight, weekends 4pm-midnight. Ph. (03) 6233 2529 or 1800 633 937 (North), 1800 608 122 (State-wide).

Sexual Assault Support Services www.sass.org.au Hobart & Southern: Ph. (03) 6231 1811 (24hr - after hours (03) 6231-1817).

Launceston: Ph. (03) 6334-2740. Nth West: Ph. (03) 6431 9711.

HELP CONTACTS WORLDWIDE

Women's Legal Service Free legal advice .. Ph. 1800 682-468 or (03) 6224-0974

Child Protection Advice & Referral Service -Child and Family Services To report . child abuse Ph. 1300-737-639 (statewide), (03) 6230 7650 (Hobart)

SHE (Support, Help & Empowerment) www.she.org.au Counselling . for women affected by abusive relationships. Ph. (03) 6278-9090 (Hobart)

Yemaya: Women's Support Service Counselling . & support . for women who have experienced abusive relationships (Launceston) Ph. 03-6334-0305.

For more services in Tasmania see website: www.women.tas.gov.au

Western Australia

Women's Council for Domestic & Family Violence Services WA www.womenscouncil.com.au Admin: 9:30 – 2:30 Mon-Fri. Ph (08) 9420 7264

Women's Domestic Violence Helpline Information, referral and telephone counselling. Ph. (08) 9223 1188 or 1800 007 339 (24 hours)

Men's Domestic Violence Helpline Information, referral and telephone counselling. Ph. 9223 1199 or 1800 000 599 (24 hours)

Crisis Care Unit 24hr crisis support . (violence ., child protection, suicide ., etc). Ph. (08) 9325-1111 or 1800 199-008. TTY: (08) 9325-1232

Sexual Assault & Referral Centre Counselling ., female doctors 24hrs. Ph. (08) 9340-1828 or 9340-1820 or country callers Ph. 1800 199-888

Women's Multicultural Support and Advocacy Ph. (08) 9325-7716

BREAKING THE CHAIN ON ABUSE

Women's Council for Domestic and Family Violence Services (WA). A state-wide peak organization Ph. (08) 9420 7264.

Child Protection http://community.wa.gov.au/ (child safety page) Crisis Care on (08) 9223 1111 or 1800 199008 (freecall)
Women's Law Centre (WA) Inc Legal advice .. Inglewood, Ph: 08 9272 8800 Freecall: 1800 625 122
For a list of family violence . services in Western Australia see community.wa.gov.au/ (family violence area)

Northern Territory

Domestic Violence Counselling . Service phone Darwin, 9-5 Mon-Fri (08) 8945-6200. Alice Springs (08) 8952 6048.
Crisis Line General and domestic violence crisis counselling (24hr) phone 1800 019 116
Women's Information Centre Referrals (Alice Springs) phone (08) 8951-5880
Dawn House Crisis accommodation and support . services for women with children escaping domestic violence. (08) 8945 1388 (24 hrs).
Family & Children's Services (Child protection) www.health.nt.gov.au phone 1800 700 250
Legal Assistance www.dcls.org.au Darwin Community Legal Service Ph. 08 8982 1111.
Domestic Violence Legal Help (Alice Springs) Ph. (08) 8981 9726.

South Australia

HELP CONTACTS WORLDWIDE

Domestic Violence Helpline www.ucwadel.org.au/domesticviolence/ Ph. 1800 800 098 (24 hours)

Domestic Violence Crisis Service Ph. 1300 782 200 (24 hours). After hours Crisis Care ph. 131 611.

Yarrow Place Rape & sexual . assault service (24 hr) www.wch.sa.gov.au Ph. (08) 8226-8777 or Toll Free: 1800-817-421 After Hours: (08) 8226-8787

Women's Information Service of South Australia www.wis.sa.gov.au Ph. (08) 8303-0590 or 1800 188 158

Women's Legal Service wlssa.org.au Ph. (08) 8221-5553 legal advice . line.

Family & Youth Services (Child Abuse Report line) Ph. 131 478

AUSTRALIA EMERGENCY – POLICE, AMBULANCE, FIRE BRIGADE- RING 000 or 112 on mobile/cell phone

List of Australia-Wide Helpline and Counselling . Services

1800 RESPECT (1800 737 732) 24 hours a day, 7 days a week- A national sexual . assault, family and domestic violence counselling line for anyone who has experienced—or are at risk of—physical . or sexual violence .. This service is designed to meet the needs of people with disabilities, Indigenous Australians, young people, and callers from culturally and linguistically diverse backgrounds.

1800 MYLINE (1800 695 463) 24 hours a day, 7 days a week- A national relationships helpline for young Australians to talk to someone about the relationship . issues they may be experiencing, or if they are unclear about where to draw the line between what is, or is not, a respectful relationship.

LIFELINE-Ph: 13 11 14- A generalist and crisis telephone counselling, information and referral service, provided by trained volunteers who are supported by professional . staff.

Mensline Australia Ph: 1300 78 99 78- An Australian Government initiative providing telephone counselling and a referral service for men. It is operated by Care Ring (Personal Emergency Services Inc), and is a resource for men who need advice . on a large range of issues (e.g., relationship . support ., parenting . skills) and for those at risk of committing suicide ..

Child Abuse Prevention Service Freecall: 1800 688 009- Workers offer information, referral and ongoing support . to those affected by child abuse, concerned about the welfare of a child, or needing family or parenting . support.

Domestic Violence Helpline Freecall: 1800 800 098- Telephone counselling for victims of domestic violence and their concerned friends. Also provides information about services for those affected by domestic violence . or who are troubled by their own behaviour.

PANDA (Post and Antenatal Depression . Association) Ph: 1300 726 306 Mon–Fri: 9:00 am – 7:00 pm (AEDST- If the matter is non-urgent or after hours leave a message and the call will be returned as soon as possible.

Family Relationship Advice Line Freecall: 1800 050 321 Mon–Fri: 8:00 am – 8:00 pm (local time) Sat: 10:00 am – 4:00 pm (excluding national

HELP CONTACTS WORLDWIDE

public holidays). Instructions for deaf or speech-impaired callers can be accessed on the website. Assists families affected by relationship . or separation issues. The Advice Line provides information on family relationship issues and advice . on parenting . arrangements after separation. It can also refer callers to local services that can provide assistance.

Child Wise—National Child Abuse Prevention Help Line Freecall: 1800 99 10 99 Mon–Fri: 9am – 5pm Support service for individuals, organisations, professionals . and parents requiring assistance on child protection. A compassionate and professional . team of trained counsellors can assist with any enquiry or report . relating to child sexual . abuse.

Children and the Media: Let's Talk—Children and Media Helpline Freecall: 1800 700 357 Provides a movie review service for parents and caregivers. Before taking their children to a movie, parents are urged to phone the helpline to check whether that movie is likely to be suitable.

EMERGENCY CONTACTS WORLDWIDE

IN NEW ZEALAND

New Zealand Emergency – Police, Ambulance, Fire Brigade- Ring 111
Free domestic violence helpline 0508 744 633 (9am-11pm 7 days per week every day of the year)
Free domestic violence helpline 0508 384 357 (7.30am-11pm weekdays, 9am-11pm weekends)

IN UNITED KINGDOM

BREAKING THE CHAIN ON ABUSE

Britain Emergency – Police, Ambulance, Fire Brigade- Ring 112/999

ADULTS:

UK Free domestic violence Helpline 0808 2000 247

National Stalking Helpline 0300 636 0300

IN UNITED STATES

America Emergency – Police, Ambulance, Fire Brigade- Ring 911

National Domestic Violence Hotlines USA: 1-800-799 SAFE (7233) or 1-800-787-3224 (TTY) for the deaf

IN CANADA

Canada Emergency – Police, Ambulance, Fire Brigade- Ring 911

IN INDIA

Emergency – Police, Ambulance, Fire Brigade- Ring 108

IN PAKISTAN

Emergency – Police, Ambulance, Fire Brigade- Ring 1122

IN IRAN

Emergency – Police, Ambulance, Fire Brigade- Ring 110

IN ASIA

Emergency – Police, Ambulance, Fire Brigade- Ring 119

IN CHINA

Emergency – Police, Ambulance, Fire Brigade- Ring 120

Note Well: -

Many countries use Emergency contact phone number **112.**

Notes:

Index

A

abandoned, 277, 281, 284
Abandonment, 113
abduction, 248, 317, 349, 350, 351, 352
abortions, 113
accommodation, 329, 334, 373
addictions, 51, 86, 87, 229, 230, 232, 233, 297, 303, 393
Addictions, 58, 86, 87, 229, 232, 301, 406
adoptions, 113
advice, xviii, xxviii, 2, 3, 36, 279, 297, 339, 353, 378, 384, 411, 433, 440, 441, 442, 443, 444
affection, 33, 67, 82, 98, 127, 169, 196, 227, 234, 268, 347, 353
affirmations, 26, 374
afford, 33, 77, 91, 115, 116, 118, 121, 122, 123, 126, 232, 276, 281, 289, 392, 413
aging, 122
alcohol, 26, 32, 59, 68, 69, 233
alienate, 348
alone, xxiii, xxvi, 3, 17, 23, 32, 36, 48, 49, 62, 80, 87, 91, 94, 95, 113, 120, 134, 140, 150, 159, 174, 191, 232, 240, 246, 268, 277, 298, 304, 309, 310, 311, 312, 313, 327, 331, 333, 347, 392, 395
appreciation, 385
approval, xx
arrogant, 61
assertive, 51, 374, 375
attack, 16, 54, 283
attention, 30, 58, 98, 104, 116, 119, 129, 159, 171, 173, 175, 176, 227, 234, 248, 252, 253, 281, 282, 286, 299, 344, 347, 353, 388
attitude, 8, 60, 61, 130, 326, 369
authorities, 24, 29, 242, 257, 281, 285, 287, 288, 289
availability, 168
awareness, 1, 2, 433, 456

B

balance, 137, 320, 321, 371, 387
birth control, 124
blackmail, 54, 344, 346, 347
books, xvi, xxii, 49, 90, 121, 168, 231, 295, 333, 354, 373, 374, 375, 388, 390, 456
brainwashing, 52, 302, 317, 343
breaches, 336
bruises, 180, 257, 288, 333
budget, 107, 118, 121
bullying, 37, 237, 240, 241, 245, 256, 257, 288

C

care, 19, 22, 23, 56, 60, 66, 67, 80, 83, 98, 104, 105, 110, 116, 117, 119, 120, 127, 131, 135, 143, 162, 169, 174, 179, 190, 197, 227, 234, 239, 252, 253, 257, 258, 262, 263, 265, 267, 268, 269, 275, 276, 277, 279, 280, 281, 283, 284, 286, 288, 304, 347, 352, 354, 368, 369, 375, 386, 408
career, 375
childhoods, 345, 400
circumcision, 34, 36, 76
commodities, 343
communicate, 179, 261, 266, 393, 433
communication, 36, 107, 108, 245, 253, 332, 389, 390
communities, 8, 34, 109
companion, 391

INDEX

compassion, 3, 33, 77, 315, 317, 399
computer games, 69, 75, 78
confidence, 24, 133, 151, 256, 258
confident, 374
conflict, 273, 361, 386
consistency, xvi
contraception, 124, 125
cooperate, 120, 393
coping, xviii
cost, 92, 138, 168, 247
Counselling, 83, 195, 257, 355, 440, 441, 442
counterproductive, 31, 110, 403
courage, xxvi, 3, 22, 23, 97
Crime, *29*
culture, xxiv, 35, 36, 54, 75, 361, 385
curious, 331
custody, 340
cuts, 49, 180, 333

D

declutter, 366, 372
defeated, 53, 61, 91, 144, 159, 302
defeats, 330
defenceless, 3, 8, 133, 159, 166, 275
denial, 17, 21, 30, 31, 59, 60, 61, 79, 80, 82, 87, 91, 151, 190, 195, 232, 239, 240, 294
Denial, 141, 294, 431
denominator, 327
deny, 97, 98, 130, 142, 149, 167, 227, 234, 346, 347, 348
Depression, 92, 93, 293, 295, 406, 443
desperate, 3, 159, 161
destructive, 38, 282, 364
determination, xvi, 97
detrimental, 18, 22, 325
devastating, 159, 161, 305, 349, 372
diary, 153, 387
disability, xviii, 123, 128, 261, 267
disciplining, 33
discrimination, 361

disgusting, 82, 196, 398
disharmony, 59, 86, 174, 386
disrespectful, 98, 227, 235, 273, 348, 367
divorce, 30, 145, 166, 339, 383
Document, 153
domestic violence, xvi, 1, 30, 232, 328, 335, 363, 405, 428, 437, 438, 439, 440, 441, 442, 443, 444, 445
dominates, 370
drugs, 26, 32, 51, 59, 69, 86, 117, 233

E

educational, 168, 384, 405
embarrassment, 31, 52, 87
embezzlement, 51, 77
Emotional, 30, 34, 52, 65, 165, 225, 262
escalate, 18, 230, 237
excuses, xiv, 21, 141, 151, 377
ercise, 33, 277, 282
Extreme Hoarding, 57

F

Families, 34, 78, 232
Fitness, 395, 406
Flirtatious, 367
forgiveness, 397
fraud, 51, 77
friendship, xxviii, 98, 227, 234, 348, 365, 369, 370, 371
frigid, 52
frustrations, xxiv, 173

G

gamble, 24
generosity, 77, 144
gossip, 37, 48, 310
Gossip, 34, 37
gossips, 369
government, 114, 409, 410, 411, 412

greed, 8, 77
grudges, 402
guidance, 104, 109, 113, 257
guilt, 52, 81, 82, 142, 144, 165, 195, 214, 259, 297, 302, 305, 308, 397

H

harassment, 245, 361
hard work, 138, 346
hardship, xiii, 34, 56, 166, 232
harm, xxix, 9, 16, 18, 22, 116, 229, 230, 234, 240, 247, 268, 271, 281, 296, 308, 329, 378
healthy, 26, 33, 97, 171, 227, 234, 286, 328, 347, 395, 432
helpless, 7, 22, 50, 54, 61, 84, 91, 134, 135, 144, 198, 246, 257, 350
hermit, 371
hide, 24, 31, 87, 91, 245, 408
homework, 33
homosexuality, 406
honest, 6, 335
hypocritical, 410

I

illness, 30, 70, 123, 280, 283, 300, 302, 315
inaugural, 345
inescapable, 399
inexcusable, 7, 287, 398
Infidelity, 51
infringe, 371
innocent, 54, 77, 79, 80, 81, 115, 133, 166, 181, 190, 192, 241, 248, 254, 289, 327, 343, 361, 383
insecurities, 173
involved, 9, 32, 58, 70, 91, 117, 142, 248, 249, 257, 289, 293, 347, 391, 428
irrational, xxix, 298, 304

J

jealousy, 173, 174, 175
judgment, 144, 304, 341
judicial, 340

K

killing, 47, 160, 161, 172

L

lawyer, 336, 339
leaving, 16, 17, 18, 23, 56, 61, 136, 233, 326, 328, 330, 331, 335, 369, 392
limits, 106, 138, 139, 367, 368, 391

M

maiming, 47, 75, 161, 162
marriage, 30, 35, 114, 142, 145, 225, 294, 304, 388, 390, 391
materialistic, 384
mature, xvii, 114
meddlers, 384
medication, 56, 68, 69, 168, 279, 281, 300, 333, 374
Meditation, 374, 406
meekness, 364
Mentors, 378
money, 24, 50, 86, 92, 150, 168, 233, 261, 262, 269, 289, 331, 333, 344, 346, 367, 373, 375, 384, 389, 409, 412, 415
monopolise, 72, 98, 227, 235, 348
monopolises, 370
mooching, 344, 346
moral, 137, 285, 287
mortgage, 121, 306

N

naivety, 364

INDEX

negativity, 38, 361
Neglect, 56, 65, 127, 168, 262

O

overindulged, 345
Overindulgence, 168, 169, 171
overtime, 359, 360
overweight, 170, 180, 238, 251

P

paparazzi, 39, 299
paranoid, 6, 58, 65, 91, 372
parenting, 118, 126, 127, 377, 407, 443, 444
peace, 47, 69, 254, 390
persistence, xvi, xxi
physical, xxix, 2, 16, 22, 29, 54, 59, 63, 64, 67, 86, 89, 92, 106, 127, 152, 169, 170, 171, 174, 230, 240, 259, 261, 288, 302, 303, 346, 429, 442
Physical, 34, 55, 65, 166, 226, 262, 298
poem, 131, 308, 319, 321
police, 24, 59, 83, 84, 152, 153, 181, 195, 205, 255, 257, 287, 289, 303, 327, 331, 332, 333, 335, 336, 352
possessions, xxvii, 27, 343
post-natal, 95, 113
practical, 3, 329, 362, 384, 407
praise, xx, 33, 169, 173, 177, 248, 258, 259
precarious, 359, 370
predators, 1, 37, 80, 104, 191, 245, 251, 253, 261, 364
pregnant, 50, 68, 115, 226, 361
prevention, 1, 2, 254, 433, 456
prey, 79, 81, 104, 133, 145, 189, 192, 245, 248, 309
prioritise, 387
prisoner, 50, 305
proactive, xxii, 107, 379

professional, xxiv, xxv, 18, 21, 26, 29, 47, 56, 65, 90, 92, 93, 120, 136, 229, 232, 234, 283, 300, 303, 304, 308, 318, 373, 390, 394, 411, 433, 443, 444
professionals, 70, 133, 161, 398, 407, 444
protection, 328
prying, 24, 367
psychologists, 83, 197
punishments, 18, 337, 427

R

Racial, 53
racism, 406
racist, 53
relationship, xxiii, 6, 15, 17, 18, 21, 22, 32, 47, 53, 56, 60, 61, 62, 70, 71, 97, 106, 107, 135, 144, 145, 232, 247, 253, 299, 302, 335, 339, 343, 372, 383, 386, 387, 388, 389, 390, 392, 393, 394, 401, 442, 443
religion, 35, 406
religious, 35, 38, 51, 92, 114, 125, 302, 361, 365
re-parent, 377
repay, 353
report, 8, 84, 205, 251, 269, 285, 287, 288, 289, 440, 444
reputation, 31, 53
resentful, 61, 94, 174, 390
respect, 9, 33, 60, 70, 76, 105, 106, 107, 128, 130, 137, 165, 176, 177, 259, 274, 341, 366, 391
responsibilities, xxix, 346
ridicule, 52, 225
rights, 30, 51, 60, 78, 86, 128, 129, 136, 289, 360
Routine, 13, 17, 18, 26

S

salary, 360
school, 6, 36, 56, 60, 65, 66, 79, 116, 117, 121, 122, 128, 165, 166, 168, 178, 180, 237, 238, 242, 246, 251, 252, 255, 256, 257, 258, 288, 290, 295, 337, 350, 353, 373, 379, 388, 407, 408
self-actuating, 107, 379
self-defence, 162, 241
self-discovery, 5, 377
self-esteem, 106, 133, 135, 139, 149, 229, 238, 248, 298, 354, 364, 391
self-respect, 106, 139, 372
sentimentality, 325
sex, 51, 54, 226, 248, 428
sexual, 29, 63, 64, 68, 81, 82, 83, 86, 89, 196, 226, 249, 264, 288, 361, 427, 433, 438, 442, 444
Sexual, 54
shame, 31, 144, 150, 259
shelter, 328
shyness, 364
silence, 402
sleep, 26, 33, 68, 94, 259, 296, 413
snooping, 367
social, 49, 123, 245, 258, 329, 330, 334, 395
Society, 75, 86, 337
statistics, 63
strengths, 177, 391
suicide, 35, 37, 56, 59, 143, 159, 230, 240, 246, 293, 294, 295, 296, 298, 302, 303, 304, 305, 306, 315, 317, 320, 343, 399, 411, 440, 443
supervise, 254, 266, 349
support, xvi, xxvi, 8, 32, 85, 87, 95, 98, 110, 113, 115, 117, 118, 122, 123, 127, 131, 135, 139, 143, 149, 173, 207, 256, 257, 271, 272, 297, 306, 336, 347, 354, 363, 378, 440, 441, 443
support group, xvi, 347
suspicious, 288, 331, 332
sympathy, xx

T

terrorism, 35, 77
theft, 51, 77
therapist, 120, 136, 233, 257, 283, 318, 394, 433
therapists, 65, 234, 433
thoughtful, 141
traces, 354, 355
tracks, 335, 354, 355, 363
trails, 255, 328, 331, 354
transgender, 31, 54, 361, 406
transgressions, 397
traumatic, 136, 257, 298, 398

U

ugly, 52, 225, 298
unbearable, 160, 246, 302, 399
unending, 399
unfaithful, 145
unforgivable, 398
unpredictable, 15, 16, 341, 401
unsanitary, 57, 277, 359

V

violence, xiii, xxix, 32, 64, 69, 75, 78, 80, 162, 167, 189, 287, 336, 408, 427, 440, 441, 442, 443
violent, 69, 78, 152, 166, 427
violent television programs, 69, 78
Visualisation, 374
vulnerable, xxii, 37, 65, 79, 81, 133, 145, 151, 166, 173, 192, 238, 248, 249, 261, 343, 384, 398

INDEX

W

wages, 360
weakness, 104, 138, 177, 293, 364

Wisdom, xvii
workloads, 359
workplace, 59, 301, 336, 359, 360, 361

"__Together we__ can 'help' break the chain on all forms of abuse!"- A __united__ stance must be taken in order to effect change."

-N J Lutter

"Breaking the Chain on Abuse" is a part of

Series

For a full range of Natalie's books, you can visit her website

www.njlutter.com

About the Author

Natalie Lutter (N J Lutter)

Natalie through her life experience, she writes from her heart to help you, your loved one or friend. She is a voice; now able to help others in need. In Natalie's words, *"I wanted to write a well-rounded book that covered different topics on abuse, in order to give a better understanding of prevention . and awareness . of abuse as it is such a dire situation that just continues to perpetuate down through the ages to our current times. As it is important to alert teachers, parents, caregivers, neighbours that if you see anything suspicious or out of the ordinary; act on it, you 'can' help save a life!"*

Natalie lives on beautiful Macleay Island Qld Australia with her partner. She has watched her daughter her pride and joy, grow and become a successful Ecologist- Environmental Advisor. Natalie is a singer/songwriter and author of self-help books . namely "Conquering Cancer Fears," along with her book "My Body Is Mine Not Yours! Part 2," with *"The 3 E's Educate, Equip and Empower!"*- "Caregivers and Educators Instructional Companion Guide Part 1." and "Absolutely No Excuse For Abuse!" with accompanying "Action

ABOUT THE AUTHOR

Planner Journal" and she has Journals on emotions she is hoping to get out soon. Natalie also keeps busy tending her garden to hold charity high teas. Her interests are philanthropy and she is an advocate of many different charities, particularly humanitarian work.

Natalie's motto is;

"We need to ensure we educate, equip and empower to ensure zero suffering for all. Impart love and goodness wherever we go!"

"Few will have the greatness to bend history itself, but each of us can work to change a small portion of events. It is from numberless diverse acts of courage and belief that human history is shaped. Each time a man stands up for an ideal, or acts to improve the lot of others, or strikes out against injustice, he sends forth a tiny ripple of hope, and crossing each other from a million different centers of energy and daring those ripples build a current which can sweep down the mightiest walls of oppression and resistance."

- Robert F. Kennedy

"Together saving lives!"

Together helping to save emotional and physical suffering of all...

Together...maybe even saving a life from death...

Together making a difference...no matter how small...

Together we can!

www.ingramcontent.com/pod-product-compliance
Lightning Source LLC
Chambersburg PA
CBHW060513230426
43665CB00013B/1494